SOUTHERN RECONSTRUCTION

Also by the Author

Trading with the Enemy: The Covert Economy During the American Civil War

Lee's Lost Dispatch and Other Civil War Controversies

The Confederacy at Flood Tide: The Political and Military Ascension, June to December 1862

SOUTHERN RECONSTRUCTION

PHILIP LEIGH

WESTHOLME
Yardley

First Westholme Paperback 2018

All illustrations are from the Library of Congress unless otherwise indicated.

Westholme Publishing, LLC
904 Edgewood Road
Yardley, Pennsylvania 19067
Visit our Web site at www.westholmepublishing.com

ISBN: 978-1-59416-318-0
Also available in hardback and as an eBook

Printed in the United States of America.

"Papa used to say that the only friends we had down here right after the war were the Irish Democrats in New York. Thad Stevens and the Republican gang would have starved us all out if they could."

—Charles Portis, *True Grit*

"Show me history untouched by memories and you show me lies. Show me lies not based on memories and you show me the worst lies of all."

—Carlos Eire, *Waiting for Snow in Havana*

Contents

Introduction

Partly because of the racial injustices underscored by about four thousand documented lynchings between 1882 and 1951, mostly in the South, modern histories of Southern Reconstruction tend to ignore, or minimize, how developments in one section of the country impacted those of the other, and concentrate almost exclusively on race.

Regarding the first limitation, a valid picture of Reconstruction cannot be drawn without integrating the history of the Gilded Age in the North with that of Reconstruction in the South. Consider the experience of Amos Akerman.[1]

Amos Akerman was one of Republican president Ulysses S. Grant's five attorneys general. He served a little over a year, from November 1870 to December 1871. Born in New Hampshire, at age twenty-one, in 1842, Akerman moved to Georgia, where he first worked as a tutor and later became a lawyer. Despite initially opposing secession, he remained loyal to the South and served as a Confederate quartermaster during the Civil War. He saw combat after Union major general William T. Sherman invaded Georgia in 1864.[2]

Akerman was the most vigorous of Grant's attorneys general in prosecuting the Ku Klux Klan. In order to expedite prosecutions, he expanded the powers of the then newly created federal Justice Department. About six hundred Klan members were convicted. Although most received light sentences, sixty-five were imprisoned for up to five years at a federal penitentiary in Albany, New York.[3]

Grant, however, may have revealed his secondary interest in racial justice when he abruptly asked Akerman to resign in December 1871. Partly at the prompting of Secretary of State Hamilton Fish, Grant had misgivings about Akerman's "obsession" with the Klan. Perhaps more importantly, Akerman also frustrated influential Northern capitalists. He was, for example, critical of the dubious terms under which railroads often qualified for federal subsidies. He may have suspected the long-festering Crédit Mobilier scandal that was a paragon of such corruption and would soon dominate the news. In June 1871, Akerman had denied land and bond grants to the Union Pacific Railroad, which had given Crédit Mobilier lucrative contracts to build the line when the railroad was unprofitable because of the inability of a partially completed line to generate much traffic in a sparsely populated territory. Crédit Mobilier allocated shares of stock—a genteel form of bribery—to influential politicians, including both of Grant's vice presidents as well as a future president, James Garfield, who likely committed perjury when he denied it.[4]

Shortly before resigning, Akerman confronted the previous attorney general, Ebenezer Hoar, when the latter was representing a railroad client's land grant claims. Akerman told Hoar that the client had not completed work required to receive the grants. Nearly simultaneously, Interior Secretary Columbus Delano complained to Grant that Akerman had annoyed railroad moguls Collis Huntington and Jay Gould with rulings unfavorable to their interests. Whether at the urging of Fish, Delano, or Hoar, Grant replaced Akerman with George Williams, who later resigned under bribery accusations, as did Delano.[5]

Grant biographer William McFeely concluded that after Akerman's resignation, "the finest champion of human rights in the Grant administration went home to Cartersville, Georgia, where he practiced law privately for only eight more years. He had given up on his native North and Northerners."

Akerman correctly reasoned that Northerners were too preoccupied with the economic progress and growing wealth of the Gilded Age to be much concerned about racial equality. Following his resignation, he wrote Georgia's carpetbag governor, Benjamin Conley, "Even such atrocities as Ku-Kluxery do not hold their attention . . . the Northern mind being active and full of what is called progress runs away from the past."[6]

Significantly, Akerman was echoing a point that was increasingly obvious to Northerners outside of Washington. Six years earlier, in 1866, the editor of the *Chicago Tribune* wrote US Senator Lyman Trumbull of Illinois:

"You all in Washington must remember that the excitement of the great contest is dying out, and that commercial and industrial enterprises and pursuits are engaging a large share of public attention . . . people are more mindful of themselves than of any philanthropic scheme that looks to making Sambo a voter, juror and office holder."[7]

US Attorney General Amos Akerman. (*Library of Congress*)

The same month that Akerman resigned, the Thirty-Ninth Congress reconvened, after a ten-month recess, under a cloud of suspicion that it was controlled by the railroad industry. One newspaper correspondent famously suggested that notices be nailed to the congressional doors stating, "The business of this establishment will be done hereafter in the offices of the Pennsylvania Railroad." In addition to being the biggest railroad, the Pennsylvania was the country's largest corporation.[8]

Akerman's story also shows how political actions targeted at the South later boomeranged to impact developments in the North. Although urged to destroy the Ku Klux Klan, President Grant had doubts about using stern federal powers to supersede the legal prerogatives of the individual states. He was wary of claims that he wanted to become a military dictator. One bill under congressional consideration that might be subject to such interpretation proposed to give the president the right to use the army to enforce court decisions and suspend the writ of habeas corpus. Nonetheless, reasoning that federal interdiction in local affairs was justified when tax collections and mail transportation were endangered, Grant threw his support behind the 1871 bill, which became known as the Ku Klux Klan Act.[9]

Twenty-three years later, Grant's logic for using federal power to protect the mails during the Ku Klux Klan crisis was applied to striking laborers. During the 1894 Pullman strike, workers disrupted train movements, particularly through Chicago. In response, President Grover Cleveland authorized armed federal troops to run the mail trains. When strikers attacked one regiment, the soldiers opened fire, wounding scores of people and killing about thirty. The strike was broken. Strikers were subjected to arrest and trials without jury. To pleas opposing federal intervention, Cleveland replied, "You may as well ask me to dissolve the government of the United States."[10]

The Fourteenth Amendment is another example of legislation presumably targeted at improving the civil rights of ex-slaves—freedmen—that rebounded to obstruct consumer and progressive interests by guarding the properties of powerful capitalists. The amendment characterized ex-slaves as "persons" and deemed them to be American citizens *and* citizens of the state in which they resided. All states were prohibited from abridging the rights of any "person," which leveraged the Fifth Amendment declaration that no "person" could be "deprived of . . . life, liberty, or property without due process of law." Twenty years after adoption of the Fourteenth Amendment, the Supreme Court ruled in two late 1880s decisions that corporations were also "persons" whose property rights were protected by the Fifth and Fourteenth Amendments. Those two decisions sharply curtailed the powers of states to regulate railroads and other corporations.[11]

Some of the Fourteenth Amendment's authors evidently had such motives from the beginning. When Republican Ohio congressman John Bingham wrote the "due process" clause, he composed it "word for word" to protect property rights as well as civil rights. Later, in 1882, when former US Republican senator Roscoe Conkling of New York represented the Southern Pacific Railroad before the Supreme Court with objections to California taxes, he argued that as an architect of the amendment, he labored to word it in a way to protect both private property rights and black civil rights against the encroachments of state legislatures.[12]

The second limitation of current Reconstruction narratives is the virtually exclusive focus on race. To illustrate, the standard college text and currently most influential academic book about the era is historian Eric Foner's *Reconstruction*, which concludes:

> What remains certain is that Reconstruction failed and that for blacks its failure was a disaster. . . . If racism contributed to the demise of Reconstruction, by the same token Reconstruction's demise . . . greatly facilitated the spread of racism. . . . An enduring consequence of Reconstruction's failure [was that] the [politically Democratic] Solid South helped . . . weaken the prospects not simply of change in racial matters but of progressive legislation in many other realms.[13]

Foner fails to mention any lingering consequences affecting both Southern whites and blacks, even though whites represented 60 percent of the region's population. Nonetheless, the harmful effects of Reconstruction were more substantial, multiracial, and protracted than commonly understood, with poverty being among the most devastating.[14]

Nearly a century after the war, eight of the ten states with the lowest per capita income in 1960 were former Confederate states. Even 150 years later, in 2011, Virginia was the only Southern state to rank among the top ten in per capita adjusted gross income, whereas five of the lowest ten were other Confederate states. The classic example is Mississippi, which ranked number one in 1860 in per capita wealth but was dead last at fiftieth in 2011 per capita income.[15]

Although Southern poverty and cotton culture is commonly associated with blacks, in 1940, whites made up two-thirds of the region's farmers who either rented their lands or were sharecroppers. According to a 1938 presidential economic report, about half of Southern white farmers were sharecroppers "living under economic conditions almost identical to those of Negro sharecroppers." Shortly after the Great Depression began, the president of General Motors (Alfred P. Sloan) voluntarily slashed his annual salary from $500,000 to $340,000. His $160,000 cut was more than all the income taxes paid by the two million residents of Mississippi that year. Widespread Southern poverty led to lower life expectancies, principally because of poor diets and unaffordable medical care. In 1930, sixty-five years after the end of the Civil War, South Carolina was the only state with as much as half of its population under the age of twenty because its residents died earlier.[16]

Memoirist Shirley Abbott, who grew up in Arkansas during the 1930s and '40s, wrote of the period:

> The words of President Roosevelt echoed in our heads—"one third of a nation ill-clothed, ill-fed, and ill-housed," and we certainly knew which third he meant. We knew that we were poor, backward, behind. . . . [As for local politicians] . . . it should be said that most of the post-Reconstruction South was run in [a] more or less . . . [despotic] fashion. In little towns like Hot Springs, the rule of law had not yet outpaced the rule of poverty or the southern code. People, black and white, were mostly poor, trying to survive in an economy that was still largely rural.[17]

Abbott's adulthood illustrates a persistent consequence of Southern poverty. After Arkansas taxpayers funded her public education, Abbott left to become a successful editor and writer in New York and Massachusetts, where she paid taxes to educate the children of those well-endowed states. For at least a century after the Civil War, one of the South's greatest exports included some of its most capable people.

Contrary to Foner's claim that Southerners resisted progressive movements, outside the realm of race relations, Southern Democrats championed some of the most progressive legislation of the late nineteenth and early twentieth centuries. Former Confederate postmaster general John Reagan was an early proponent of federal railroad regulation after he became a US congressman in 1874. After Woodrow Wilson became the first president whose boyhood was in the South following the Civil War, he successfully promoted such measures as a graduated income tax, tariff rate reductions, the Federal Reserve System, the Farm Loan Act, and the Warehouse Act. Finally, the Populist movement originated in the South instead of in the Great Plains as is customarily supposed.[18]

In contrast, Republicans fostered some of the most regressive policies. For forty-five years, between the 1868 election of Grant as president and the inauguration of Democrat Woodrow Wilson in 1913, the Republicans held the White House over 80 percent of the time, the Senate over 90 percent of the time, and the House of Representatives almost two-thirds of the time. During that era, 90 percent of the money collected by the Internal Revenue Service was excise taxes on liquor, beer, wine, and tobacco. There was no income-sensitive tax.[19]

As for external tax revenue, the Republicans consistently favored high protective tariffs, which were essentially a regressive sales tax on consumers. Furthermore, tariffs were the chief federal revenue source during the forty-five-year period and were collected by customs officials, not the Internal Revenue Service. The Republican Party refused to reduce them even when the Treasury reported surpluses every year from 1866 to 1893. Some surpluses were embarrassingly large, particularly toward the end of the era.

Instead of cutting taxes by lowering tariffs, Republicans spent the surplus extravagantly to win political support among favored constituencies. A prime example was the increasingly liberal Union veterans' pensions. Most Southerners preferred lowering the tariff over spending the excess customs duties on Union veterans pensions, which grew to an astounding 40 percent of the federal budget in 1893. Before the surplus was consumed by the growing pensions, however, one sympathetic Northern senator sponsored an education-funding bill to apportion part of the surplus to the states based upon illiteracy rates. It would have particularly aided the South, where such rates were higher, income levels lower, and the school age share of population larger, but the bill never got out of the House of Representatives.[20]

Furthermore, Northern attitudes toward racial equality were more obstructive than is usually assumed. They even provided a precedent that led to the separate-but-equal doctrine of the 1896 Supreme Court decision in *Plessy v. Ferguson*, which legitimized segregation for almost sixty years thereafter. Although the case involved a Louisiana incident, Justice Henry Brown of Michigan cited a Boston precedent upholding segregated schools. Six other justices joined him in the 7–1 decision. The lone dissenter was from Kentucky, while six of the seven justices voting with the majority were from states that were loyal to the Union during the Civil War.[21]

Finally, Republican advocacy of African American civil rights was diluted by a huge dose of self-interest. When the Civil War ended, the Republican Party was barely ten years old. It could be eclipsed, and possibly strangled in its cradle, if the readmittance of Southern states into the Union failed to be managed in a manner that would prevent Southerners from allying with Northern Democrats to regain control of the federal government. With other things the same, the abolition of slavery would increase Southern congressional representation by fifteen members over the antebellum tally because of the obsolescence of the original constitutional provision restricting the counting of slaves to three-fifths of their number for purposes of a state's congressional representation and electoral votes.[22]

The historical facts reveal that Republicans were distressed about the consequences to their party if Southern states were promptly readmitted into the Union without Republican control over the method of readmission. Even before the war ended, a joint congressional resolution in December 1864 proclaimed that Arkansas and Louisiana—temporarily readmitted under a wartime Reconstruction plan by President Abraham Lincoln—were "not entitled to representation in the electoral college." Historian Matthew Josephson concluded:

> The resolution reveals how even in the winter of 1864-65 [before the war was over] the Republican Party leaders were secretly obsessed with once again becoming a minority Party. Even in the twenty-three United States, only 55% of the vote in the presidential election of 1864 had been Republican. The Democratic anti-war vote was thus a big minority. What, then, if eleven unregenerate States returned to constitutional relations with the Union? They assailed

> Lincoln on this ground; they would fall upon his successor, too, should his policies threaten or jeopardize the retention of power by the war party.[23]

If all representatives from the former Confederate states were admitted to the Thirty-Ninth Congress in December 1865, and each added member was a Democrat, the Republican majority in the Senate would have dropped from 43–9 and become 43–31. Similarly, the party's majority in the House would have dropped from 152–40 and become 152–81. In short, the Republicans would have no longer held a veto-proof two-thirds majority in Congress.[24]

Historians William Cooper and Thomas Terrill elaborate in their *American South: A History*:

> Republicans' fears that the Democrats would regain their antebellum political dominance were not fantasies. The dominance of the Republican Party was not assured in 1865, and would not be until the 1890s. Only then were the Republicans able to control the White House and both houses of Congress consistently.[25]

Historian Arthur Schlesinger's analysis of Republican motivations concluded, "The technique of 'waving the bloody shirt'—meaning to advertise for a generation at every post-war presidential election the racial emancipation resulting from the war—enabled the Republicans to long submerge the fact that they were becoming the party of monopoly and wealth."[26] Banker J. P. Morgan, who epitomized Gilded Age wealth, cogently observed, "A man always has two reasons for the things he does—a good one and the real one."[27] Morgan was implying that the good reason is a false, benevolent explanation that conceals the real self-serving one.

If, for example, racial equality was the true objective of nineteenth-century Republican black suffrage advocacy, an explanation for why the party did not promote suffrage for Chinese immigrants is needed. The historical record, however, suggests that there is no good explanation. The inconsistency more likely results from the fact that Chinese exclusion attracted California voters to the Republican Party, whereas the inclusion of black voters transformed the Southern states from a Democratic voting block into a Republican one. Beginning in 1882, the federal government responded to racist pressures from California and other Western states with laws that would help deny the vote to Chinese residents and reduce their numbers. The '82 law was succeeded by additional measures—known collectively as the Chinese Exclusion Acts— that restricted immigration and denied citizenship to the Chinese. California used the acts, which were not repealed until 1943, to deny voting rights to Chinese people. The immigration restrictions effectively cut the number of Chinese in America from 105,000 in 1880 to 62,000 in 1920.[28]

Nonetheless, most contemporary Reconstruction historians are too prone to accept the putative righteous explanations for Republican actions as opposed to the real ones. Conversely, they too readily apply sinister interpretations to the actions of Southern Democrats. Foner, for example, laments that the 1866 Georgia legislature appropriated $200,000 to aid "aged and infirm white persons," including Confederate widows and orphans, while making no allowance for the dependents of deceased Union soldiers or aged and infirm blacks. He failed, however, to disclose four mitigating points.[29]

First, although Georgia didn't aid the survivors of killed Union soldiers, neither did the Northern states aid the widows and orphans in their states who had husbands and fathers in the Confederate army.

Second, the federal government started paying increasingly generous Union veterans' pensions in 1862. The former Confederate states individually paid much smaller pensions to rebel veterans. Moreover, Southern veterans of the Mexican-American War (1846-1848) were not granted pensions until Cleveland became president in 1885. Additionally, Southerners had to pay their share of federal taxes needed to fund the Union pensions. The annual disbursements did not peak until 1921 and trailed off only gradually for years thereafter. Before they became standardized, a study ordered by President Cleveland in 1885 estimated that about one-fourth of the awarded pensions were fraudulent. During the fifty years prior to 1917, the accumulated Union veterans' pensions totaled over $5 billion, which was more than twice the amount spent by the federal and Northern state governments to fight the war.[30]

Third, the 1866 federal Southern Homestead Act gave freedmen temporary preferential homesteading access to 46 million acres of Southern land. The Republican-dominated Congress, however, declined to provide blacks with preferential access to homesteads outside the South.

Finally, even Foner admits that the 1866 Georgia legislature reasoned that aid to blacks should at least temporarily be the responsibility of the federal government through its much better financed Freedmen's Bureau, which was targeted chiefly at African Americans. Emancipation was, after all, a national policy, which justified reliance upon national (i.e., federal) funding sources to pay for the needs of the ex-slaves.[31]

The purpose of this book is to tell the story of Southern Reconstruction by transcending the limitations of a race-centric narrative and to more fully put the account into context with that of the rest of the country. Although racism has been a shameful characteristic and legacy of the era, there is a larger story to be told involving members of all races.

ONE

Foundations of Change

The Civil War transformed our entire country, not merely the South. During the war's first important battle at First Bull Run in July 1861, Union observers saw thousands of slaves doing supportive work for the Confederate army. Since the Union force was defeated at the battle, Northerners concluded that the war would last longer than previously supposed. Consequently, a property confiscation bill targeted at disloyal Southerners was passed by Congress and signed by President Lincoln the following month. It permitted the Union army to confiscate property, including slaves, used in the service of the Confederate government. Generally, court proceedings were required before property could be condemned. In the case of slaves, however, no legal proceedings were necessary.[1]

Before the end of the year, Radical Republicans wanted to strengthen the act so that the private property of disloyal citizens could be seized even if such property was not directly used to support the Confederacy. They also wanted to impose potentially mortal penalties for disloyalty. Democrats and moderate Republicans, including Lincoln, were concerned about the impact of such measures on the loyalties of the border states where slavery was still legal and many families had members serving under Confederate arms. They also questioned the constitutionality of a more liberal seizure policy.[2]

The result was the Second Confiscation Act, which was adopted July 17, 1862, partly in response to Major General George McClellan's reverses on the York-James Peninsula. It essentially declared that any Southerner who served in the Confederate government or military could be convicted of treason, punishable by death. Others who merely aided the rebellion could be imprisoned for up to ten years. Their property, including slaves, was subject to confiscation.[3]

Before signing the bill, however, Lincoln stipulated that confiscation of real property could only be temporary as implied by the Constitution. It could not extend beyond the life of the offender. Thus, the property rights of a Confederate soldier's wife and children would be restored upon the soldier's death. A plantation, for example, would revert to the owner's heirs even if he died years after the end of the war. Congress passed a joint resolution agreeing to Lincoln's limitations.[4]

After the Union won the war, the act might have radically transformed Southern society by creating an opportunity for the general redistribution of land. Since Lincoln nearly vetoed the bill, however, he did little to enforce it. Few Southerners were arrested for treason. Land confiscations were modest, although about a million acres were seized for nonpayment of federal taxes under a different law.

Perhaps most importantly, Article 13 of the Second Confiscation Act permitted the president to exempt Southerners from the consequences of the law by granting them pardon or amnesty. Irrevocable confiscation required court proceedings that might enable a pardoned owner to reclaim his land if it had not yet been sold. As a result, at an unsuccessful peace conference in Hampton Roads, Virginia, in February 1865, Lincoln said he would be generous in restoring Southern property seized under the Confiscation Acts. Equally important, the article would be available to his White House successors.[5]

Modern historians commonly regard the Second Confiscation Act as a precursor to the Emancipation Proclamation and an example of the Northern commitment to racial equality. But the act, together with eventual Northern reaction to it, reveals that those who were against slavery were not necessarily for racial equality. First, Article 12 authorized the president to colonize willing African Americans to Central America. Lincoln told a delegation of blacks that he believed the white and black races should live separately and therefore favored such colonization. Second, even in the North, confiscation was regarded as revolutionary. If permitted in the South, many Northern property owners worried that the concept could take root across the country. Thus, any aggrieved sector of voters might encourage government confiscation against any property owner accused of abusing his or her property rights.[6]

Ultimately, the provisions of Article 13 might determine whether the Second Confiscation Act would be a tool to create a Southern economy populated mostly by yeomen white and black farmers, instead of plantations or tenant and sharecropped farms. Additional bills to augment the power of the federal government to confiscate Southern lands were introduced by Congressman Thaddeus Stevens of Pennsylvania as late as 1867, but they failed to pass even though the Republican Party held near veto-proof control of Congress.[7]

Although the Confiscation Acts might have nudged the president toward emancipation, he wanted it done by executive order so he could maximize his control over the terms and process. Since 90 percent of African Americans in the South were slaves who represented 40 percent of the region's population, it was obvious that the widespread presence of freedmen would be one of three defining characteristics of the postbellum South. The other two would be near-universal poverty and physical destruction.

While ex-slaves would be free to leave their prior homes and work for wages, they would also be responsible for their own livelihoods. Former slave owners, including a small number of blacks, would lose about $3 billion in previously legal property, which exceeded the combined value of all of America's prewar investment in railroads, factories, and banks. At the start of the Civil War, slaves represented more than half of the property values in the Confederacy. Monetarily, persons in bondage were worth more than all of the South's real estate.[8]

Lincoln assumed his authority to issue the Emancipation Proclamation as an extraordinary wartime power as chief executive. He did not believe the presidency held such powers in peacetime, and he did not believe any other government body held the power even in wartime. Lincoln consistently resisted pressure to emancipate slaves until summer 1862. He twice overruled field generals who announced their own slavery-ending policies, once in August 1861 and again in May 1862. However, Lincoln's language in overruling the second general's announcement signified a subtle change, which Lincoln biographer David Donald summarizes:

> "No commanding general shall do such a thing upon my responsibility without consulting me," [Lincoln] told [Treasury Secretary Salmon P.] Chase. But . . . for the first time he made it clear that he

> had no doubt of his constitutional power to order emancipation. Whether he exercised that authority would depend on a decision that abolition had "become a necessity indispensable to the maintenance of the government." . . . He had no reservations about issuing an emancipation proclamation because "as commander-in-chief of the army and navy in time of war, I suppose I have a right to take any measure which may best subdue the enemy."[9]

In short, Lincoln began to consider the question of emancipation as a military necessity. He did not construe his power to enact it to be based upon any moral principle. Although he opposed slavery, as will be explained, he could also foresee potentially immoral consequences arising from suddenly freeing the slaves.

He asserted that his 1861 inaugural pledge of noninterference with a state's right to slavery did not apply to the Confederate states. He argued, "The rebels . . . could not at the same time throw off the Constitution and invoke its aid. Having made war on the Government, they were subject to the incidents and calamities of war." He could not, however, use the same argument with the Union-loyal border states.[10]

In July 1862, Lincoln met with border-state congressional representatives. He told them that the "friction and abrasion" of the war would eradicate slavery in their states. He added that he might soon be forced to proclaim emancipation because of rising antislavery sentiment in the North. He urged his audience to adopt gradual compensated emancipation. They rebuffed his suggestion. Shortly thereafter, Lincoln confided to Secretary of State William Seward and Navy Secretary Gideon Welles that he was considering emancipation. Both men were surprised and asked for time to consider the matter. Lincoln urged them to ponder it seriously because "something must be done."[11]

About a week later, on July 22, the president read the first draft of the proclamation to the entire cabinet. For justification, he cited his presumed wartime powers as well as the authority of the Second Confiscation Act. The emancipation draft also pledged pecuniary aid to any state— including the rebellious ones—that voluntarily abolished slavery.[12]

The meeting adjourned with no decision. However, Senator Charles Sumner of Massachusetts learned of the discussion. He pressed Lincoln on each of the next five days to make the announcement. Finally, Lincoln told the senator, "We mustn't issue it until after a victory," which would come with the Battle of Antietam on September 17, 1862.[13]

A number of important Northerners recognized that emancipation might prompt a slave uprising. In fact, Lincoln was among them. On September 13, a delegation of Chicago abolitionists visited the White House to urge immediate emancipation. Lincoln first clarified that he could "raise no objections" to their proposal based upon an argument that he lacked the legal authority to make such a proclamation. Then he added that he could not "urge objections" to their proposal based upon the possibility that it could lead to a bloody slave uprising in the South. Whatever the moral benefits, or immoral consequences, of emancipation, he considered the matter to be exclusively a war measure:

> Understand, I raise no objections against it [the delegation's suggestion of emancipation] on legal or constitutional grounds, for, as commander-in-chief of the army and navy, in time of war I suppose I have a right to take any measures which may best subdue the enemy; nor do I urge objections of a moral nature, in view of possible consequences of insurrection and massacre at the South. I view this matter as a practical war-measure, to be decided on according to the advantages and disadvantages it may offer to the suppression of the rebellion.[14]

In short, Lincoln was prepared to run the risk of a Southern slave uprising if emancipation would give the Union an important wartime advantage. Nine days after meeting with the Chicago abolitionists, Lincoln publicly announced the Preliminary Emancipation Proclamation. The proclamation is described as preliminary because the formal one would not be effective until January 1, 1863. A question that merits consideration but is seldom analyzed is whether some influential Northerners advocated emancipation as a deliberate attempt to provoke a slave uprising.

Following the September public announcement, many voices condemned the proclamation as an attempt to provoke just such a servile insurrection. Unsurprisingly, that was a common interpretation in the South, where Confederate president Jefferson Davis averred that the document "encouraged [slaves] to a general assassination of their masters." But some Northerners had a similar reaction because the decree included a passage instructing that "[the US] military and naval authority . . . will do no act to repress [slaves], or . . . any efforts [the slaves] may make for their actual freedom." Many critics concluded the statement ordered the military to stand aside in the event of a slave rebellion.[15]

Among those critics was trusted Lincoln adviser Charles A. Dana who immediately urged that the inflammatory phrase by erased or changed. Another critic was former Supreme Court justice Benjamin Curtis of Massachusetts. Although he did not believe Lincoln intended to instigate a slave rebellion, Curtis concluded the proclamation's likely result would be to "incite a part of the inhabitants of the United States to rise in insurrection against valid laws." He foresaw "scenes of bloodshed" and "servile war."[16]

Robert Forbes, a Boston maritime mogul and friend to abolitionist Charles Sumner, concluded that Sumner's followers genuinely wanted the slaves to "be made freed by killing or poisoning their masters and mistresses." Representative Stevens, who was a primary abolitionist leader and later the chief architect of Civil War Reconstruction, validated Forbes's conclusion. Stevens later admitted to hoping the slaves would be "incited to insurrection and give the rebels a taste of real civil war." Finally, Senator Sumner himself said, "I know of no principle . . . by which our [Southern white] rebels should be saved from the natural consequences of their own action. . . . They set the example of insurrection. . . . They cannot complain if their slaves . . . follow it."[17]

Colonel Charles Francis Adams Jr., who was the son of Lincoln's ambassador to Great Britain and the great-grandson and grandson of two US presidents, stated that the prevailing belief in the North at the time of the proclamation was that it would spark an immediate slave uprising to bring the war to a sudden end. Major General George McClellan similarly complained that the president sought to stir up slave rebellions in an attempt to end the war. McClellan cannot be dismissed as an isolated example, because he was Lincoln's opponent in the 1864 wartime presidential election when he received over 1.8 million votes, which was 45 percent of the total.[18]

Initial reaction that the Emancipation Proclamation might provoke slave rebellions was also common in Europe, even though Lincoln anticipated the announcement would gain sympathy for the Union overseas. Moreover, the Europeans worried that it could trigger a race war that would extend beyond American borders into the Caribbean and South America, thereby hurting Atlantic trade.[19]

In time, Lincoln was able to win the moral high ground with contemporary Europeans as well as with posterity. It is impossible to be certain about his full intentions. Nonetheless, there is a subtle but important difference in language between the Emancipation Proclamation of September 22, 1862, and the final one on January 1, 1863. Lincoln added the following paragraph to the last version: "And I hereby enjoin upon the people so declared to be free to abstain from all violence, unless in necessary self-defence; and I recommend to them that, in all cases when allowed, they labor faithfully for reasonable wages."

Traditional opinions of the sixteenth president suggest it is difficult to believe he intended to provoke slave uprisings. Instead, however, he may have been willing to run the risk of their spontaneous combustion in order to win the war.

A little over two years after releasing the proclamation's final version, Lincoln reflected upon four years of warfare in his second inaugural address by saying, "All knew that . . . [slavery] was somehow the cause of the war. . . . Neither [side] anticipated that the cause of the conflict might cease . . . before the conflict itself. . . . Each looked for . . . a result less fundamental and astounding."[20]

Regardless of Lincoln's wartime expectations for the Emancipation Proclamation, his second inaugural suggests that he realized a change so "fundamental and astounding" implied that Reconstruction would evolve into a critical stewardship needing to be implemented "With malice toward none [and] charity for all." Beyond its advice that the freedmen work for fair wages, the proclamation said nothing of the president's future vision for a slave-free and reunited America. To learn how he planned to reunite the country and include the ex-slaves, it is necessary to examine his wartime Reconstruction proposals, which will be taken up in the next chapter.

In combination with the Confiscation Acts, the Emancipation Proclamation left white Southerners in great anxiety about the consequences of having lost the war. The Confiscation Acts, for example, could be used to charge any ex-rebel with treason, which was punishable by death. They also implied that properties might need to be forfeited by large numbers of families who had members in the Confederate army. Although the Emancipation Proclamation had freed the slaves, it did not define their legal status as, for example, citizens or voters. Since few white Southerners had money to pay ex-slaves for labor, they worried that the freedmen might evolve into a gigantic outlaw class in order to obtain food, shelter, and other necessities. Southerners of both races sensed that Northerners had little sympathy for the consequences of such chaos in the South. In truth, during the first nine months of peace, Northerners chiefly sought assurances that Southerners had given up the rebellion for good. Much remained to be worked out.

WHILE THE STATUS of the ex-slaves as a freedmen started to evolve during the war, so did that of America's railroads. The Civil War transformed the railroads much like World War I transformed the airplane. They evolved from multi-gauge lines and wood-burning engines into standard-gauge lines and coal-burning engines. The makeover, however, inaugurated an era of demagoguery, corruption, and state-assisted capital formation that would become alternately known as the Gilded Age or the Great Barbecue, to which only the privileged and politically connected were invited. One of its chief characteristics was private exploitation of public resources, especially land.

Prior to the Civil War, Northerners and Southerners alike wanted a transcontinental railroad. Republicans made construction of such a railroad a plank in their 1856 and 1860 party platforms. Likewise, the 1860 Democratic Party platform endorsed one. But the parties differed on two points.

First, Republicans wanted liberal federal government subsidies to finance the venture, whereas Democrats opposed direct use of federal dollars. Southerners long opposed federal land giveaways, which were often used to finance public works. Instead, they preferred that federal lands be sold as a way to raise a portion of the money required to operate the government, thereby reducing the traditional reliance on tariff revenue. Second, Republicans wanted the railroad's eastern terminus to be in the northern part of the Mississippi Valley. Democrats were divided: Southern Democrats wanted the terminus to be in the lower Mississippi Valley, but one the party's leading presidential candidates and a railroad investor, US senator Stephen Douglas of Illinois, wanted it in the upper part of the valley.[21]

In 1853, Congress authorized surveys of four possible routes. The project fell under the responsibility of War Secretary Jefferson Davis, who hoped the surveys could settle the sectional rivalries by discovering a single superior route. The great equalizer would be the matter of grade (slope).

Locomotives could not climb steep hills. They would simply stagger to a halt if they could not pull their loads up an incline. Thus, steep-graded routes would require expensive tunneling and railroad cuts. The more northerly and high-altitude routes would also be more subject to snowfall disruptions. To later objective observers, the 1855 reports suggest that a path from Fort Smith, Arkansas, to Los Angeles was the most promising. Survey participants, however, usually returned from their missions as strong proponents for their own routes. In the end, their findings merely fanned the flames of sectional rivalry.[22]

After Southern secession left Congress firmly under Republican control, the contest was winnowed to the rival Northern routes. Furthermore, Lincoln had been a persistent supporter of federal subsidies. One congressman reported, "Mr. Lincoln said to us that his experience in the West was that every railroad that had been undertaken there had broken down before it was half completed. . . . He had but one advice for us and that was to ask [for] sufficient aid."[23]

Consequently, Lincoln signed the First Pacific Railroad Act on July 1, 1862. It was the same day the Battle of Malvern Hill ended Union major general George McClellan's failed attempt to take Richmond by advancing up the York-James Peninsula. The act provided subsidies to two railroads, the Central Pacific and the Union Pacific. When the president signed the act, each company was a railroad in name only. Their chief occupation for years to come would be to complete construction.

The Central Pacific had been organized in Sacramento, California. It was responsible for building a line east over the Sierra Nevada Mountains into Nevada. The Union Pacific was to simultaneously build a road from Omaha, Nebraska, west. The two would either connect at an undetermined point in between, or a third railroad would be organized to join them.

Four of California's pioneering leaders, Leland Stanford, Collis Huntington, Charles Crocker, and Mark Hopkins, controlled the Central Pacific. Initially, all four were Sacramento storekeepers, but Stanford was elected governor in 1861. Huntington returned to the East to become the group's chief political lobbyist and representative to Wall Street.

After the 1849 gold rush, talk of an independent California republic gained traction. Many of the residents were Southern sympathizers, and the state's economy suggested it could be self-sufficient. Early Republican sponsorship of a transcontinental railroad shifted the political tide. The thought of returning to the East for business and home visits in a matter of days instead of weeks appealed to many Californians, including the Central Pacific shareholders. They became staunch Republicans because of the party's railroad plank. Slavery and racial justice were immaterial concerns to such men. In speaking of California's growing Chinese population, for example, Stanford said, "I am in favor of free white American citizens. I prefer white citizens to any other class or race."[24]

One indication of the project's expected size was the Union Pacific's initial stock capitalization. It was only the second corporation to have a federal charter. (First was the Bank of the United States, whose charter controversially lapsed in 1837 because of President Andrew Jackson's hostility toward eastern bankers.)

The Union Pacific was authorized to issue a hundred thousand shares with a par value of $1,000 each. Thus, stock capitalization alone (excluding debt) could total as much as $100 million. By comparison, the entire federal budget in fiscal year 1861 was only $80 million. The speculative nature of the venture was underscored by the fact that only forty-five shares were sold in 1861. Furthermore, only the five purchased by Mormon Church leader Brigham Young were paid in full. The other buyers subscribed to the remaining forty shares by initially paying only 10 percent down, with the balance to be paid upon future assessments.[25]

In addition to the Union Pacific's large stock capitalization, the transcontinental railroads were granted generous federal subsidies. Aside from a four-hundred-foot right of way along its route, each railroad was to be given land grants in a checkerboard pattern totaling five square miles (three thousand two hundred acres) for each mile of track completed. Such land might be sold to raise money or developed to encourage settlement. Moreover, each company would receive financial aid in the form of government bonds, which could be resold to investors. Although the railroads were required to repay the loans themselves, the federal government guaranteed interest payments. Finally, the railroads were permitted to charge the federal government for services such as carrying the mail, conveying troops, and transporting military freight.

The amount of government bonds granted would depend upon the miles of track completed in one of three terrain categories. The rate was $16,000 per mile on flat land, $32,000 per mile in the high plains, and $48,000 per mile in the mountains. The sums eventually totaled about $65 million. The railroads were also permitted land for sidings and stations. During construction they were also allowed to use whatever was needed in the way of timber or stone.[26]

Despite its generous appropriations, the '62 act was merely the industry's opening bid for subsidies. Two years later, the Second Pacific Railroad Act increased the largesse. Land grants were doubled to six thousand four hundred acres per mile and included mineral rights, which had previously been excluded. The companies were also given the right to issue first mortgage bonds of their own, which would have superior creditor status over the government bonds. Thus, if either the Union Pacific or Central Pacific went bankrupt, first mortgage bondholders would be paid off before holders of the government-sponsored bonds.

The Pacific railroad acts triggered three lasting unintended consequences.

First, the large subsidies encouraged a culture of bribery and fraud. As the second bill was under consideration, one Union Pacific lobbyist distributed $250,000 in bonds. Twenty thousand dollars in bonds went to Charles Sherman for "professional services." He was the eldest brother of Union major general William T. Sherman and Ohio senator John Sherman. The New York lawyer who wrote the bill also got $20,000 in bonds. One of the Union Pacific's New York investors visited Omaha, charging $4,000 for "expenses and services." Railroads often fraudulently tried to collect subsidies on poorly constructed and unusable track.[27]

Second, the acts prompted an increasing tendency toward government subsidization of politically connected industries. Capitalists outside the railroad sector demanded that they also be invited to the Great Barbecue. While arguing that privately owned lands in the rebellious Southern states should be confiscated, Radical Republican congressman Thaddeus Stevens insisted that the railroad acts require all of the rails and other ironworks of the railroads be "of American manufacture of the best quality"—meaning the highest price. Stevens's motives may have been selfish because he owned a Pennsylvania iron foundry and was a persistent advocate of high tariffs, particularly for iron products.[28]

Third, the entire railroad industry was soon obsessed with getting subsidies from all levels of government. Other transcontinental roads that were hardly beyond the planning stages were granted federal aid to build their lines. Examples include the Northern Pacific, the Santa Fe, and the Southern Pacific. The Northern Pacific alone was granted forty-four million acres, which is about the size of Missouri. By 1917, it had raised an accumulated $136 million from land sales, compared to a cost of $70 million to build the railroad. Although state and local governments had often provided aid before the war, the demands railroads made on such governments escalated after the Pacific acts.[29]

Most roads routinely asked for, and got, grants of state, county, and city bonds. Such awards that started after the Civil War throughout the former Confederacy drove the impoverished state governments toward bankruptcy. They were a prime reason that tax-burdened Southerners opposed carpetbag governments. Ultimately, through a combination of federal and other government grants, the railroads accumulated land grants greater than the size of Texas.[30]

Although the Central Pacific and the Union Pacific would link the eastern and western parts of the country, railroads require traffic to generate revenue. Since most of the region between the Mississippi River and California was lightly populated, the 1862 Homestead Act was passed to promote settlement. The law gave each settler occupying and improving 160 acres of public land the right to assume ownership after five years. Alternately, the settler could buy the 160-acre tract for $200 ($1.25 per acre) after only six months.[31]

Although the Homestead Act was adopted with the best of intentions, its results were dubious. Often by prearrangement, speculators would buy homesteaded land at bargain prices from the homesteader after the latter exercised the six-month option to buy the tract instead of waiting the full five years to get it free. The technique enabled speculators to amass large land holdings.

Most settlers who chose to stay often discovered that a 160-acre farm was not large enough to support a family. Those who sought to buy more land soon discovered that railroads and speculators already owned large tracts that made it hard for the 160-acre farmers to buy adjacent land. The 1889 Oklahoma land rush attracted booming interest partly because the territory was one of the last areas where big, unbroken tracts were still available. Ultimately, less than 20 percent of the land awarded under the Homestead Act from 1860 to 1900 resulted from claims as opposed to purchases. The proportion of such purchases that was represented by speculators is unknown.[32]

In retrospect, after the railroads became self-propelling businesses, the financial aid and land grants seem excessive. Nonetheless, they were not without justification. No railroad operating in the vast expanse between the Missouri River and California could expect to find enough traffic to be profitable until the region became settled. But the land would not be settled unless reliable transportation was available. The land grants and federal bonds provided the money to build such transportation facilities. Since the railroads were only granted alternate land sections, ownership was transformed into a checkerboard of public and railroad land. Yet the value of all sections on the checkerboard increased after the railroad was built. By the turn of the nineteenth century to the twentieth, the railroads had repaid all their government bonds and interest.[33]

Since a transcontinental railroad was unprofitable during the early years of operation until population density increased, informed shareholders arranged matters so that they could profit during the construction phase, as will be explained in chapter 6. Their machinations, however, underscore the culture of low business morals triggered by the Pacific railroad acts. In the end, construction costs of the roads were about three times larger than they should have been because of the greed of the promoters, inadequately offset by federal oversight.[34]

THE CIVIL WAR also initiated a shift in tariff policy that would have long-term consequences generally favorable to the North but unfavorable to the South. Due to the resignations of Southern congressmen two days before Abraham Lincoln's first inauguration, President James Buchanan signed a long-pending protective tariff bill sponsored by Vermont congressman Justin Morrill on March 2, 1861. It increased rates, expanded the list of dutiable items, and was intended to protect select industries, such as Pennsylvania iron manufacturers, New England woolen suppliers, and wool growers in the present-day Midwest. As the war progressed, the so-called Morrill Tariff was twice amended—in 1862 and 1864—to increase average rates and shrink the list of exempted items. Consequently, the average tariff collected on dutiable items increased from 19 percent in fiscal 1861 to 48 percent in fiscal 1865.[35]

When a New York banker attempted to get a loan for the Union from Great Britain during the initial stages of the Civil War, he reminded Lord Palmerston, the British prime minister, of the South's commitment to slavery, which was unpopular in Europe. Palmerston replied, "We do not like slavery, but we want cotton and dislike your Morrill Tariff." Before the year ended, another British statesman observed that his countrymen were "unanimous and fanatical" in support of free trade.[36]

Great Britain adopted its free trade policy in 1846 by repealing the Corn Laws that artificially inflated the price of domestic grain in order to protect aristocratic landowners. It took a near famine, caused partly by a grain shortage, to persuade the government to adopt a free trade policy that had long been urged by commoners. Thereafter, the British concluded that they had seen a great light. Free trade, they finally realized, resulted in the most economical allocation of resources. Benefits from growing manufactured exports and cheaper grain imports more than offset the economic losses caused by an eclipse of domestic grain production.[37]

Tariff policy had long been contentious between the North and the South prior to the Civil War. On the eve of the war, the South's was overwhelmingly an export economy. In 1859, the region produced 80 percent of all US exports. Cotton alone accounted for 68 percent. Conversely, the country's manufacturing was centered in the North. In 1860, there were 110,000 factories in the North that employed 1.3 million workers. The eleven Confederate states had but 18,000 factories employing 110,000 workers. Eighty-five percent of the capital invested in industry was in the North, where fifteen times as much iron was manufactured as in the South. Such differences nearly compelled opposite opinions on tariffs.[38]

The North preferred high tariffs to protect domestic industries from overseas competition, whereas the South favored low tariffs because they artificially inflated the price of the protected goods. Without them, consumers throughout the country could often import foreign-made items at lower prices than the comparable domestically produced versions, particularly for manufactured items. More importantly, the South's export economy was dependent upon foreign buyers. Such buyers could more readily purchase Southern exports by selling their own (typically manufactured) goods into America in order to secure the exchange credits needed to purchase Southern output. There was also the possibility that high domestic tariffs could tempt foreign governments to reciprocate by imposing tariffs on goods exported into their countries from America. Such reciprocity would be harmful to the South by making the region's exports less competitive on the world market. If, for example, British textile mills were required to pay a tariff on Southern cotton, they would be motivated to purchase feedstock from other cotton-producing countries.

Prior to the Civil War, and for many years thereafter, over 90 percent of federal tax revenues were obtained from tariffs. More than two-thirds of the duties were collected in New York, which would continue to be the center of tariff collections into the twentieth century. The city's status also meant that the New York customs collector persisted as a lucrative political appointment controlled by whichever party occupied the White House. Federal revenues from internal taxes were negligible for more than forty years before the Civil War. The virtual complete dependence upon tariffs for the funds needed to operate the federal government made regional differences over tariff policy especially contentious. A compromise was needed if the Union were to remain intact.[39]

By the eve of the Civil War, the conflicting North-South tariff interests had settled on a unified national principle. It is described by Ida Tarbell in her *Tariff in Our Times*, published in 1911, when customs duties represented about 45 percent of the federal budget:[40]

> As a nation we intend to raise money to carry on our business by putting a duty on certain . . . goods brought from foreign countries. If we find we are getting too large a revenue we will cut down the duty, if too small we will raise it. . . . [I]f there is a young industry in the country trying to produce something which is *essential* to war or on which our daily living depends, we will protect it from foreign competition until it is established—*but no longer*.
>
> For ten years the country had been working on this tariff platform, and so satisfied were they with it that when they found in 1857 they were taking in more money than . . . needed for expenses, they . . . [cut] the duties . . . to an average of 20 percent—the lowest . . . since 1816. Nobody, except the Pennsylvanians and a few New Englanders objected. . . .
>
> That was fifty years ago. To-day the average tax on dutiable goods . . . is nearer 50 percent than 20 percent. What has become of the theories and practices of fifty years ago?[41]

AMERICA'S CIVIL WAR also prompted a radical shift in US monetary policy that fostered the adoption of fiat currency and a dubious partnership between national banking and the financing of the federal government. To appreciate the change it is necessary to explain banking theory, beginning with the gold standard.

In English-speaking countries, banking evolved among merchants in the mid-seventeenth century. Shopkeepers normally stored their surplus gold in the king's mint for safekeeping, until Charles I needed money shortly before the English Civil War in 1638. He confiscated much of the merchants' gold, calling it a loan. Although it was eventually repaid, merchants thereafter preferred to deposit their gold with private goldsmiths who issued warehouse receipts to each depositor. Such receipts essentially became paper money and were preferred in many transactions in place of bulky coins.

Soon goldsmiths realized that most of their receipts would remain in circulation and rarely presented for redemption. Therefore, they could lend money in the form of newly issued receipts maintaining a gold inventory equal to only a fraction of the face value of receipts outstanding. Theoretically, once such loans were repaid, the amount of receipts remaining in circulation would equal the gold inventory, and the smith would have earned interest income on the loan. Pragmatically speaking, however, new loans were constantly created as old ones were paid off. As long as the receipts presented for redemption never exceeded the smith's gold inventory, there was no harm. But if ever a holder presented a receipt that could not be redeemed in gold, public confidence in the smith's warehouse receipts would vanish, and the paper would no longer be accepted in transactions, except perhaps at a discount to face value.[42]

At the start of the American Civil War, about one thousand six hundred banks operated in the above manner. There were no federal minimum reserve requirements. Regulations regarding reserve ratios, interest rates, and loan activities were set by the states individually. The federal government was even prohibited from issuing paper currency. While the US Mint coined money, the coins were struck in gold or silver and thereby became specie. Taxes and other funds due the federal government were paid to the Treasury either in specie or Treasury notes, which were short-term Treasury debt securities.[43]

On the eve of the Civil War, the nation's total currency was about $450 million, of which only $250 million was specie. The remaining $200 million was composed of private paper issues. The wheels of commerce required the circulation of specie or banknotes typically of a nearby bank with a reliable reputation.[44]

The enormous Civil War financing needs impelled changes to the monetary system, as federal spending grew from $80 million in fiscal year 1861 to $1.3 billion in 1865. During the war, the federal debt similarly leaped from $65 million to $2.7 billion. As Table 1 indicates, taxes met only 25 percent of the needs, whereas federal borrowings accounted for 57 percent, and a new, federally issued paper currency, commonly known as greenbacks, represented 18 percent.[45]

The first legislated monetary change was the 1862 Legal Tender Act, which authorized greenbacks. Although greenbacks were not redeemable in specie, the federal government tried to mandate their acceptance by declaring the bills to be "legal tender for all debts, public and private," except customs duties and interest on federal debt which had to be paid in specie. About $430 million in greenbacks were issued before the war was over. Treasury Secretary Salmon P. Chase proposed to make the paper money more palatable by adding the "In God We Trust" motto that he had earlier put on coins, but Lincoln suggested wryly, "If you are going to put a legend on the Greenbacks, I would suggest that of Peter and John, 'Silver and gold I have none, but such as I have I give to thee.'"[46]

Overseas merchants who shipped products into the United States normally required that US buyers settle accounts in gold. Thus, early in 1862, the New York Stock Exchange set up a Gold Room to enable holders of greenbacks to buy gold. Although a greenback dollar traded below parity to a gold dollar, the amount of discount fluctuated. At the low point in early summer 1864, when Lieutenant General Ulysses S. Grant was stalled before Petersburg and Major General William T. Sherman did not seem to be making much progress in Georgia, a greenback was only worth about thirty-seven cents in specie. While greenbacks could not be redeemed for gold at face value, they could be used to purchase federal bonds.[47]

Since gold was common on the West Coast, Californians and Oregonians were immediately contemptuous of greenbacks. In November 1862, San Francisco merchants refused to accept greenbacks at anything above the discounted rates quoted in the Gold Room of the New York Stock Exchange. In April of the following year, the California legislature adopted a Specific Contracts Act. It clarified that contracts entered on the basis of specie were enforceable in specie. Finally, the California state government refused to accept greenbacks in payment of taxes.

Oregon quickly followed California. For years, gold had been the exclusive Oregon currency. Shortly after the San Francisco merchants' agreement, those in Salem and Portland followed suit. Portland mer-

Table 1.
Civil War Financing, US Federal Government

Source	Percent of Total
Bond Issues	57%
Taxes	25%
Printing Money ("Greenbacks")	18%
Total	100%

Source: Roger Ransom "The Economics of the Civil War," https://eh.net/encyclopedia/the-economics-of-the-civil-war/.

chants also circulated a black list of residents and businesses that tried to settle bills with greenbacks. Finally, the state's Supreme Court ruled that it was unconstitutional to accept greenbacks for tax payments.[48]

From a national perspective, however, the greater unintended consequence of greenbacks stemmed from a combination of their discount value in relation to gold and their use in purchasing federal bonds at par value. The gold discount created an arbitrage opportunity in the US government bond market.

Suppose an investor had $1,000 in gold when the exchange rate was two greenback dollars for each gold dollar. He could exchange his gold for $2,000 greenbacks and then purchase federal war bonds with an interest rate of, say, 6 percent annually. Since the Treasury was required to pay bond interest in gold, the bondholder would collect $120 of interest annually instead of a mere $60 if he had purchased federal bonds with his gold. Basically, he would double his annual investment yield from 6 percent to 12 percent.

Given a return of peace, however, bondholders discerned an even bigger opportunity. They urged that war bonds be redeemed at par value in gold upon maturity. The principle, which became known as the sound money policy, implied that greenbacks must also be made convertible into gold at face value. Such a policy, sound money advocates argued, was essential if the American dollar was to be accepted at face value in international markets. In our hypothetical example, bonds redeemed at par in gold enabled the investor's $1,000 gold investment to be returned as $2,000 in gold when his bonds matured. Until then he would earn a handsome 12 percent annual interest rate on his original $1,000 gold outlay.

Taxpayers would be the losers in the above scenario, especially those who didn't own bonds, which would include nearly all Southerners. Since most of the federal tax revenues for decades following the war were derived from tariffs, consumers throughout the nation basically paid for the bondholders' windfall gain. It soon became apparent that removing greenbacks from circulation would also tend to cause widespread price deflation, thereby penalizing Midwestern grain farmers as well as Southern cotton growers. Both groups were dependent upon distant world markets where prices were directly impacted by changing currency values, among other factors. Consequently, the greenback discount would become "the largest single financial problem facing the United States after 1865."[49]

While the Civil War was still in progress, few people gave much thought to the matter of bond redemption for gold. However, Congress passed another wartime act that ultimately put bankers on the side of sound money. The 1863 National Bank Act required that one-third of each national bank's equity capital be invested in federal bonds and placed on deposit with the comptroller of the currency. In return, each bank was issued national banknotes equal to 90 percent of the value of the bonds. Since the bonds could be purchased with greenbacks or specie, most buyers paid with greenbacks since they traded at a fluctuating discount to gold.[50]

National bankers could use the banknotes to make interest-bearing commercial loans. Thus, the arrangement enabled the bankers to earn interest income twice from a fixed amount of invested capital. One source was the bank's borrowers, who paid interest on their borrowings. The other source was the federal Treasury, which paid the interest on the bonds. It was a lucrative arrangement for such banks as qualified for a national charter.[51]

In order to motivate state-chartered banks to convert to national charters, the federal government taxed state banknotes. An initial 2 percent tax in 1863 was raised to 10 percent in 1865. As a result, independent banknotes were driven out of the market, and the country's post-Civil War currency was dominated by greenbacks, national banknotes, and specie. Even today our paper money is uniform and colored green, much like the original greenbacks and national banknotes. Since national banknotes were convertible into greenbacks, they also traded at a discount to gold. National banknotes were issued until 1938.[52]

The advantages of a federal charter combined with the penalties on state banknotes increasingly led America's monetary system to gravitate toward national banks. The requirement that such banks buy federal bonds as reserve collateral created a powerful alliance between a wartime government insatiably hungry for money and a banker class that increasingly became a primary holder of federal bonds. Shareholders of national banks, therefore, became among the strongest advocates of government bond redemption in gold. On top of this, the Invalid Pension Act of 1862 ignited explosive and long-term growth in federal spending on pensions for Union, but not Confederate, soldiers. By the early 1890s, the amounts would represent over 40 percent of the federal budget. As late as 2016, one recipient was still collecting a monthly stipend.[53] The resolution of postwar bond and paper currency gold redemption, issues involving the geographic distribution of national bank charters, and veterans pensions will be addressed in chapter 8.

THE LONG-TERM—and often unintended—consequences of the Confiscation Acts, Emancipation Proclamation, Legal Tender Act, national banking acts, Pacific railroad acts, Morrill Tariffs, and Union veterans pension programs had enormous impact on Southern Reconstruction as well as the entire nation for a century or more, and all began as wartime legislation.

TWO

Wartime Reconstruction

Contrary to popular belief, Reconstruction started before the Civil War ended. Although the war began in April 1861 and ended in April 1865, President Lincoln announced a Proclamation of Amnesty and Reconstruction on December 8, 1863, when almost a year and a half of fighting remained. He was prompted by two factors.

First, advancing Union armies occupied key parts of several Southern states—Tennessee, Arkansas, and Louisiana—and had hopes of picking up Florida and Texas. Some sort of local governments needed to be established. As chief executive, the president felt compelled to act. Second, Lincoln also hoped to pick up delegate support at the next presidential nominating convention, scheduled for June 1864. State governments formed under his plan were likely to provide Lincoln-friendly delegates.[1]

The December 1863 proclamation permitted new state governments to be formed once a mere 10 percent of a state's voters in the 1860 elections took a loyalty pledge to the United States. Significantly, the pledge stipulated by Lincoln did not require oath takers to say they never supported or aided the Confederacy. Instead, they were merely required to state that they would "henceforth . . . support . . . the Constitution of the United States, and the union of States thereunder." After meeting the 10 percent threshold, oath takers could vote to form new state governments, although such governments were prohibited from legalizing slavery.

While the great majority of voting-age Southern males were qualified to take Lincoln's oath, there were some exceptions. Among them were Confederate army officers above the rank of colonel and Confederate civil authorities. All oath takers who might have served the Confederacy in other ways, or had been ordinary rebel soldiers, were pardoned. Stricter oaths later imposed by Radical Republicans disqualified many former Confederates from voting.[2]

Lincoln's plan was never tested in Florida and Texas because military reverses kept those states in the Confederacy. Union major general Nathaniel Banks's Red River Expedition, partly aimed at conquering Texas, was turned back at the battle of Mansfield, Louisiana, in April 1864. Similarly, the Union invasion force intended to occupy Florida was repelled at the battle of Olustee in February 1864.

Nonetheless, Union armies occupied enough of Louisiana, Arkansas, and Tennessee to permit elections under the plan. Louisiana and Arkansas held their votes in February and March 1864, respectively. Both sent delegates to the Republican—temporarily renamed National Union—Party convention that nominated Lincoln for president and Andrew Johnson of Tennessee for vice president. Congress, however, later refused to seat the elected representatives of both states.[3]

Tennessee did not get a Union-loyal civilian government until early 1865. When the war started in 1861, Johnson was the only Southern senator refusing to resign. As a reward, when Union forces occupied Nashville in February 1862, Lincoln appointed him as the state's military governor. Before the 10 percent plan was announced, Johnson formulated a more-restrictive loyalty oath for Tennesseans who wanted to vote under a Union-loyal state government. His oath required pledge takers to swear they prayed for Union victory and wanted slavery abolished. Finally, in February 1865, a total of twenty-five thousand Tennesseans satisfied the qualifications and voted to ratify a new constitution outlawing slavery. Since Johnson would be heading to Washington as the new vice president, the state also elected a new governor, William "Parson" Brownlow. Brownlow was from the mountainous eastern part of the state where slavery had been less common.[4]

Prior to announcing his 10 percent plan, however, Lincoln did recognize a state government-in-exile for Virginia in June 1861. The so-called restored Virginia government was used for the purpose of legitimizing the formation of West Virginia as an independent state. Since the US Constitution specified that no state could be carved out of another without the approval of the parent state, the new Virginia government was formed under Governor Francis Pierpont. Although initially located in Wheeling, it moved to the Washington suburb of Alexandria after West Virginia became a state in June 1863. While Pierpont's government served as a pretext for sanctioning West Virginia's birth, its federal representatives were never seated in the House, and its senators were only seated in the Thirty-Eighth Congress, which ended before the war was over.[5]

Congressional Radical Republicans regarded the 10 percent plan as too lenient. Consequently, Ohio senator Benjamin Wade and Maryland representative Henry Winter Davis prepared a Reconstruction bill, which passed Congress on July 2, 1864, only two days before the first session of the Thirty-Eighth Congress expired. The Wade-Davis Bill directed the president to appoint, with the Senate's advice and consent, provisional governors for the rebel states. Only after armed resistance had ceased in all such states could each governor attempt to form a new electorate in his state. Moreover, there would be no plebiscite for a new constitutional convention unless more than half of the number of 1860 voters could swear an oath that they had never supported the Confederacy. If there were enough oath takers, the resultant convention had to prohibit slavery, repudiate Confederate debts, and disallow former legislators or Confederate officers above the rank of colonel from voting or serving as elected officials.

Although the bill did not require the new constitutions to grant voting rights to freedmen, none of the former Confederate states would likely have enough oath-qualified voters to allow convention plebiscites. Consequently, military rule would probably last for years.

Since the Wade-Davis Bill specified that Reconstruction could not begin until the war was over, Lincoln felt it would negate the progress already made in states like Arkansas and Louisiana. It might also lengthen the war by preventing Union-loyal governments from being formed in states that might qualify under his 10 percent plan in the future and thereby hasten the fall of the Confederacy. The differences were an early indication of a conflict between Congress and the presidency that would dominant Reconstruction politics until 1869.

Ordinarily a bill becomes law when the president signs it or fails to return it with a veto within ten days. An exception occurs, however, if a president declines to return it and there are fewer than ten days left in the congressional session. Such a situation is termed a pocket veto. Lincoln used the technique to reject the Wade-Davis Bill. Despite declining to proactively veto the bill, Lincoln announced his reasons for failing to sign it.

First, he argued that Congress did not have the power to pass laws outlawing slavery in the states where it lawfully existed. He believed that emancipation was an executive power that could only be used as a wartime necessity. Given the onset of peace, the president believed, it would be necessary to pass a constitutional amendment to forbid slavery and thereby settle the matter beyond dispute of judicial review or authority disagreements between Congress and the president.

Second, Lincoln argued that it was too early in the war to affix Reconstruction to an inflexible scheme. While he felt the Wade-Davis plan was an acceptable one to any state that might choose to agree to it, he wanted the option to offer less restrictive plans, particularly if they might accelerate the demise of the Confederacy.[6]

The president's pocket veto enraged Wade and Davis. Together they secretly prepared a written objection that would become known as the Wade-Davis Manifesto. In early August 1864, Wade asked Horace Greeley of the influential *New York Tribune* to publish it. Greeley complied on August 5. The manifesto accused Lincoln of usurping Congress's power to manage Reconstruction. The president, it argued, "must confine himself to his executive duties—to obey and execute, not make the laws—to suppress . . . the rebellion . . . and to leave political reorganization to Congress." It further accused Lincoln of designing the 10 percent plan to provide electoral votes for his "personal [presidential] ambition."

James Gordon Bennett, who published the equally influential *New York Herald,* was startled by the venomous Wade-Davis attack. Not even Lincoln's sharpest Northern Democratic critics, which Republicans derisively termed Copperheads, ever made such condemning allegations. That Republicans would do so convinced Bennett that Lincoln could not win the November presidential election. Consequently, he suggested that the president voluntarily step aside so a winning candidate could be put forth. He suggested Lieutenant General Ulysses Grant. Even Thurlow Weed, who was a political wheel in New York's Republican Party and a confidant to Lincoln and Secretary of State Seward, concluded, "Lincoln is gone."[7]

Soon, however, Lincoln gained support. Henry Raymond, who published the *New York Times* and was chairman of the Republican National Committee, warned that the manifesto might elect a Democrat to the White House in November. Wade and Davis, he argued, were traitors to the cause. Less influential but far more numerous, Midwestern newspapers also sided with Lincoln. They seemed to more accurately reflect public sentiment. In the end, Wade and Davis were unsuccessful in wresting control of Reconstruction away from the president, at least while Lincoln lived.

Although the president was concerned that the manifesto might damage his reelection prospects, his objections to the Wade-Davis Bill were authentic. Lincoln wanted the flexibility to offer Reconstruction programs that might differ from state to state and situation to situation. As he often did during stressful periods, he tried to relax the tension by expressing himself to a trusted journalist in a parable involving a mythical Greek giant named Procrustes. The giant placed his victims in an iron bed. If they were too short, he forcibly stretched them. If they were too long, he cut their legs to fit the size of the bed. The Wade-Davis Bill, he joked, was a Procrustean bed.[8]

Lincoln's desire for flexibility remained evident until his assassination nine months later, in April 1865. One example was an early February 1865 peace conference he attended aboard a Union transport near Hampton Roads, Virginia. It was a serious opportunity, as evidenced by Lincoln's personal attendance as well as the presence of the Confederate vice president, Alexander Stephens, with whom Lincoln had served in Congress eighteen years earlier.

The meeting lasted about four hours, and it was the first time a US president met with opposing emissaries to negotiate peace. Lincoln had only two nonnegotiable conditions, while he was flexible on a third. The first two required that the rebel states disband their military force and agree to rejoin the Union. On the third matter, emancipation, Lincoln suggested conciliatory qualifications.[9]

During the meeting, Seward, who had accompanied Lincoln, announced that the Thirteenth Amendment ending slavery had passed Congress a few days earlier and had been sent to the states for ratification. To Seward's surprise, the president added that he was willing to consider compensating Southerners for their loss of slaves and suggested $400 million as a fair amount. When Seward objected, Lincoln rebuked him by replying that both North and South were culpable for slavery. "If it was wrong in the South to hold slaves, it was wrong in the North to carry on the slave trade and sell them to the South."[10]

In Stephens's account, Lincoln added that it might not be necessary that freedom be immediate. He suggested that Stephens return to his home state of Georgia, where he could urge the legislature to recall the state's rebel soldiers, elect representatives to the US Congress, and prospectively ratify the Thirteenth Amendment freeing the slaves "so as to take effect—say in five years [thereby enabling Georgia to] avoid the evils of immediate emancipation. Such a ratification would be valid in [Lincoln's] opinion."

While some students doubt Stephens's record, Lincoln expert David Donald explains:

> Stephens's record would be highly suspect were it not confirmed by other, more contemporary, evidence. . . . [Earlier Lincoln] told . . . [General James W.] Singleton 'that he did not mean to make abolition of slavery a condition' of peace. . . . The day before Christmas Lincoln repeated these views to [Illinois Senator Orville Browning] . . . "that he never entertained the purpose of making the abolition of slavery a condition precedent to the termination of the war."[11]

On collateral issues, Lincoln assured the Southerners that executive policy would be lenient. As president, he explained, he held the powers of pardon and property restoration, which he intended to use "with the utmost liberality."[12]

Upon returning to Washington, Lincoln drafted a proposal in the form of a joint congressional resolution offering $400 million in US government bonds to the slaveholding states, including the border states. They were to be distributed in proportion to each state's 1860 slave population. Half the bonds were to be distributed by April 1 if the Confederate states had laid down their arms. The other half would be allocated on July 1, assuming the Thirteenth Amendment had been ratified. The proposal was presented to his cabinet two days after the peace conference. Since the cabinet members were unanimously opposed, the president reluctantly dropped the plan.

Thus, contrary to popular impression, even late in the war, Lincoln did not consider unconditional and immediate freedom of slaves to be a necessary condition for peace. Most modern historians who acknowledge the iconoclastic point speculate that Lincoln was more concerned with ending the war promptly than with shaping America's postwar society. On two official occasions during the last month or so of his life, Lincoln provided additional hints about his Reconstruction plans. One was his second inaugural address, on March 4, 1865, and the other was his last public speech, on April 11, four days before he died.[13]

Although less famous than his Gettysburg Address, the mere 703 words of Lincoln's second inaugural compose perhaps his most compelling speech. It is elegantly written in common language with 90 percent of the words being two syllables or fewer. After four years of reflection upon his first administration, he concluded:

1. Both sides tried to avoid the war. Neither side expected the catastrophe it became.

2. Slavery "somehow" caused the war even though it ironically had ceased before the war itself had ended.

3. Although both sides prayed for God's approval it "may seem strange" that Southerners sought his approval while supporting slavery. Nonetheless, Northerners should not "judge" themselves to be morally superior to Southerners. The prayers of both could not be answered, and those of neither were fully answered. Perhaps God gave the war to both the North and South as a just consequence.

4. As for the future, the war must be completed and a lasting peace established "with malice toward none and charity for all."[14]

In short, while Lincoln held Southerners responsible for the war, as at Hampton Roads, he implied that Northerners were not faultless. Also consistent with his Hampton Roads remarks, the inaugural's famous last sentence underscored his intent to avoid a punitive Reconstruction and perhaps even provide generous aid for the defeated.

Since Lincoln's last speech on April 11 was only two days after General Robert E. Lee's surrender at Appomattox, the audience expected a rousing victory address when news of Lee's defeat reached Washington. To be sure, the president did not fail to provide a few words of congratulations and thanks to the army. Most of the address, however, was a defense of his 10 percent Reconstruction plan, with the Louisiana state government as the focal point. He concluded:

1. The plan was not the only one Lincoln would consider acceptable. All his cabinet members, however, approved of it, which by implication included the Republican Louisiana state government installed in 1864.

2. He acknowledged that only Congress had the authority to decide whether representatives of any Reconstructed state might be seated.

3. While acknowledging his earlier promise to sustain the Louisiana state government, he admitted that he would break his promise if Louisiana's future actions proved it to be unworthy of his support. He announced, however, that Louisiana's conduct to date had not yet suggested he should break his promise.

4. Questions about whether the Southern states were technically members or nonmembers of the United States during the war are worse than useless. They are "pernicious abstractions" because they retard progress. His prime objective was to promptly establish civil governments in the South as part of the United States.

5. While he would have preferred that a larger percentage of 1860 voters were presently included in the Louisiana electorate, he implied that it would be wiser to take the state government as it is rather than start over again. Louisianans had already abolished slavery, ratified the Thirteenth Amendment, offered public education to blacks and whites, and authorized the legislature—at its own choosing—to provide for African American suffrage.

6. Lincoln admitted that the Louisiana government was not all that he ultimately wanted. For example, he preferred that "highly intelligent" blacks and those among the race who had served in the Union military be granted voting privileges rather than leave them for uncertain adoption by the legislature.

7. Cryptically, Lincoln concluded by saying it may soon be necessary for him to make an "announcement to the people of the South."[15]

While it is impossible to know what the proposed announcement might have contained, a couple of points seem obvious. First, together with his recent approval of the Freedmen's Bureau Act, the president was interested in the welfare of ex-slaves. Additionally, he wanted to "confer" a limited form of African American voting rights. He stopped short, however, of suggesting universal black suffrage. Second, he preferred to build upon the foundations already laid by the 10 percent plan instead of starting over. He was apprehensive about the consequences of delay and uncertainty that might result from congressional interference.

During the last few weeks of his life, Lincoln also participated in at least two private meetings where he voiced Reconstruction opinions. One was with top military commanders in the field and the other was his last cabinet meeting on the very day he was assassinated.

On March 28, he met with three key military leaders near General Grant's Virginia headquarters. In addition to Grant, General Sherman was summoned from North Carolina, and Admiral David Porter also attended. One of the president's biggest concerns was that surrender terms for all Confederate armies should be expressed in a manner to discourage the Rebels from continuing to fight as guerrillas. After they surrender,

"Let them all go, officers and all. I want submission and no more bloodshed. . . . I want no one punished: treat them liberally all around."[16]

Lincoln hoped to remain in Virginia until Lee's surrender and lingered until April 8. In the meantime, he was joined by his wife, who brought along a visiting young French aristocrat who was a descendent of the Marquis de Lafayette but out of favor with the present monarch, Louis-Napoléon (Napoleon III). During the visit, the Frenchman lamented that Napoleon III forbade the playing of "La Marseillaise" in his home country. When the group finally left to return to Washington, Lincoln requested that a nearby military band play the revolutionary tune for his guest. Next, he asked the band to play "Dixie." He wanted "to show the rebels that [even] with us in power they will be free to hear it again."

Lincoln's last cabinet meeting was on April 14. A temporarily bedridden Seward substituted his son, Fred. General Grant also attended. Afterward, Fred Seward wrote that everyone voiced "kindly feelings toward the vanquished, and [a] hearty desire to restore peace and safety at the South, with as little harm as possible to the feelings or the property of inhabitants." Lincoln firmly stated there should be no attempt to manage the Southern state governments from Washington. They must be permitted to govern themselves, even if they may initially "do it badly."

Secretary of War Edwin Stanton suggested a plan for temporary military governors, specifying, for example, that Virginia and North Carolina have a single such governor. Lincoln asked him to revise the plan so that Virginia and North Carolina could be treated separately. Recognizing that some Radical Republican congressmen thought the tone of his April 11 public address was too lenient, Lincoln commented that it was fortunate that Congress would not again be in session until December. He intended to use the intervening eight months to "reanimate the [Southern] States and get their governments in successful operation . . . before Congress [reconvened]." When Grant replied to a question about his conversation with Lee at the surrender, Lincoln radiated satisfaction when Grant said, "I told [Lee that his soldiers were] to go back to their homes and families, and they would not be molested, if they did nothing more."[17]

Aside from Lincoln's recorded statements, perhaps nobody had better knowledge of his intentions than his two private secretaries, John Nicolay and John Hay. They authored a ten-volume study of the president after the war. In remarking upon the reaction of Radical Republicans to Lincoln's assassination they wrote:

> There was one exception to the general grief too remarkable to be passed over in silence. Among the extreme Radicals in Congress, Mr.

> Lincoln's determined clemency and liberality towards the Southern people had made an impression so unfavorable that . . . they did not, among themselves, conceal their gratification that he was no longer in the way. In a political caucus held a few hours after the President's death, "the thought was nearly universal . . . that the accession of Johnson to the Presidency would prove a godsend to the country."[18]

Lincoln's actions and statements suggest that he had a least two objectives: reunification of the states and an end to slavery. There is not, however, convincing evidence that he sought full racial equality. At best he expressed a preference for limited equality.

Four years before the war, he remarked that whites had "a natural disgust . . . to the idea of indiscriminate [race] amalgamation." But any blacks who earned their way, he conceded, were equal to any whites as to their rights for the rewards of their labor. A year later, in 1858, when debating Stephen Douglas for a Senate seat, he said,

> I am not . . . in favor of bringing about . . . the social and political equality of the white and black races. I am not . . . in favor of making voters or jurors of Negroes, nor of qualifying them to hold office. . . . [The] physical difference between the two . . . will probably forever forbid their living together . . . [in] . . . perfect equality and . . . [if] . . . there must be a difference, I . . . am in favor of . . . [whites] . . . having the superior position.[19]

During his presidency, and for decades before it, he urged that blacks leave the United States to colonize other countries. In June 1862, Congress appropriated $500,000 to facilitate such emigration, and the following month a House emancipation committee recommended that the amount be raised to $20 million. In August 1862, Lincoln met a group of black leaders at the White House to discuss the matter. "You and we," he said, "are of different races. We have between us a broader difference than exists between almost any other two races." He told his guests that they were responsible for the Civil War but also admitted that they were not treated as equals anywhere in the country. He concluded, "It is better for us both, therefore, to be separated." Since the early days of his administration, Lincoln had been working on plans to colonize a part of present-day Panama with black volunteers. According to historian Sebastian Page, he never gave up on the idea, if not in Panama, then somewhere else with a climate "congenial" to African Americans.[20]

While it is not possible to know how Lincoln's Reconstruction plans might have evolved, there is good reason to believe that one of Lincoln's primary aims was to attract Southern whites into the Republican Party. He realized that Republicans were vulnerable to defeat at the polls if their party only appealed to Northerners.

Since the divisive issue of slavery had been settled, Lincoln perceived that the former Whigs of both sections had enough in common to unite as Republicans. Southern planters and Northern industrialists, for example, were both capitalists. Moreover, each supported large ecosystems including merchants, bankers, financial factors, insurance companies, lawyers, and newspapermen. Lincoln was himself a Whig before he was a Republican. Confederate vice president Stephens, who had initially opposed secession, was also a former Whig. Lincoln and Stephens had exchanged a series of friendly letters trying to settle the sectional crisis while the former was president-elect.

If the postwar political environment in the South would enable former Whigs to emerge as the region's leaders, the Northern Republican Party might be transformed into a national one. Thus, Lincoln wanted to encourage an alliance with native white Southerners. When Louisiana's civil government was elected under his 10 percent plan, he specified that the candidates must be "respectable citizens of Louisiana" instead of "a parcel of Northern men . . . elected . . . at the point of the bayonet." He sent a similar message to Andrew Johnson during Tennessee's wartime election.[21]

As will be explained, however, Radical Republicans also perceived the political necessity of spreading the party's power nationally. Their approach—to be enforced by the bayonet—was to extend the vote to ex-slaves while simultaneously disfranchising many Southern whites.

THREE

Ruination

Although many Northerners were angered by the reluctance of Southerners to follow Northern dictates for the South's recovery, a postwar review of the respective regions suggests that it might have been too much to expect given America's widespread racism and the South's impoverishment. Racial adjustment was bound to be different in the South, where blacks composed 40 percent of the population, compared to the North, where they made up only 1 percent. Moreover, much of all the Southern states except Texas and Florida were overrun by opposing armies that drained most of their resources. As Union armies grew steadily more confident of victory and the South's inability to retaliate, they increasingly destroyed whatever assets might sustain the South's civilian economy. Wartime emotions and propaganda convinced many Union soldiers that Southerners were a wicked people responsible for starting the war who had no rights that need be honored. After the war, Sherman wrote that he had fought "the holiest fight ever fought on God's earth." To Yankees, the Civil War was an echo of the presumably righteous biblical wars.[1]

A month after Appomattox, Grant wrote his wife, "The suffering that must exist in the South the next year . . . will be beyond conception. People who talk of further retaliation and punishment . . . do not conceive of the suffering endured already, or they are heartless." Another Northern observer wrote, "Never was there greater nakedness and destitution in a civilized community." The mayor of Columbia, South Carolina, said hundreds of people lived on loose grain picked up where army horses were fed. One federal official wrote, "It is common . . . [to see] women and children, most of whom were formerly in good circumstances, begging for bread from door to door. . . . They must have immediate help or perish. . . . Some are without homes of any description."[2]

The war had destroyed two-thirds of Southern railroads, and two-thirds of the region's livestock was gone. One railroad that had owned about 50 locomotives, 40 passenger cars, and 550 freight cars before the war had only 1 locomotive, 2 passenger cars, and 4 freight cars after Appomattox. Steamboats had nearly disappeared from the rivers. One hundred million dollars in insurance investments and twice that amount in bank assets had vanished. Approximately 300,000 Southern white males in the prime of adulthood died during the war, and perhaps 200,000 more were incapacitated, which translated to about 18 percent of the region's approximately 2.75 million white males in all age groups in 1860. It was about 36 percent of those over age nineteen.[3]

During the war, Southern farms drifted back to nature. Since their protective levees had been destroyed, thousands of square miles of Mississippi delta cotton lands were overrun with briers and cane thickets. Returning Confederate soldiers often found their families existing in conditions of near, if not actual, starvation. The governor of the Union-loyal Arkansas state government, established in 1864 under Lincoln's plan, reported many people living in the woods and begging for food. Within thirty miles of Atlanta, an estimated thirty-five thousand were destitute and near starvation. In December 1865, an estimated half-million whites in three gulf states were without life's necessities, and some had starved to death.[4]

In her *Memorials of a Southern Planter,* Susan Smedes wrote that when her seventy-year-old father returned from the Confederate army to their ruined Mississippi plantation, he promptly planted a vegetable garden to feed his family and sell his surplus in New Orleans. Thousands more like him rebuilt their burned homes and wrecked farms. Historian David L. Cohn adds:

> When there was a shortage of work stock, the few surviving animals were passed from neighbor to neighbor. [When] there was no

Destroyed Richmond & Petersburg locomotive photographed in April 1865. (*Library of Congress*)

> work stock [the men] hitched themselves to the plow. By ingenuity, backbreaking toil, and cruel self-denial thousands of Southern farmers survived reconstruction. . . . They received no aid from any source, nor any sympathy outside the region.[5]

By 1870, Southern bank capital totaled only $17 million, compared to $61 million in 1860. Over the same period, the region's currency in circulation dropped from $51 million to $15 million. At the end of the war, Southern property values (excluding slaves) were less than half of the 1860 figure. Five years later they had increased to only 63 percent, whereas wealth in the Northern states increased by 150 percent over the same five years. In 1880, fifteen years after the war, the value of Southern farms was only two-thirds of the antebellum figure. Not until 1879 did cotton production return to prewar levels, despite a 47 percent population increase. So great was the devastation and anemic the rebound that by 1900, the South had barely recovered to the level of economic activity prior to the Civil War.[6]

When Lee surrendered to Grant at Appomattox, more than two million fungible cotton bales were scattered across the South. Given an average price of 43 cents per pound, each 400-pound bale was worth about $172. That put the value of the entire inventory at nearly $345 million, which was gigantic compared to the tiny amount of US currency then circulating in the South. The cotton might have been an invaluable resource to prime the pump of Southern recovery but instead it was plundered.[7]

Union soldiers, US Treasury officials, and Northern businessmen stole most of it under the pretext of legitimate confiscation—such as the seizure of cotton owned by the Confederate government—or often no pretext at all. A dismayed Treasury Secretary Hugh McCulloch remarked, "I am sure that I sent some honest cotton agents South, but it sometimes seems very doubtful that any of them remained honest very long."[8]

Cotton was not all that was looted. Anything that could be sold for cash was targeted. McCulloch reported to Congress that there was "general plunder [involving] every species of intrigue . . . speculation and theft." Whitelaw Reid, who was then traveling through the South for the *New York Tribune* and would later serve under Presidents Benjamin Harrison and Theodore Roosevelt as ambassador to Britain and France, respectively, observed a "general practice of regarding everything left in the country as the legitimate prize of the first officer who discovers it."[9]

Real estate values dropped precipitously. Land that previously sold for $50 or more per acre now brought no more than $3 to $5. Less desirable lands could not be sold at any price. There was an acute shortage of tools, seed, and labor to work the farmlands, which held real estate prices down.

Southern lands were confiscated for nonpayment of federal taxes. Soon after the war began, the federal government imposed a direct tax on the private properties in each state with the object of raising $20 million to fight the war. Residents of Confederate states naturally ignored the tax, but after invading Union armies occupied portions of those states, US Treasury agents selectively enforced it by seizing properties and selling them. Sometimes the agents bought the best properties themselves for the price of the unpaid taxes and quickly resold them at much higher market prices. After 1866, the federal government ceased trying to collect the tax, and in 1872 it permitted the previous owners to reclaim such properties still held by the government; but those that had been sold to private buyers remained the property of the new owners.[10]

The worst of the immediate aftermath was lawlessness. Beyond the confines of garrisoned towns, outlaws did as they pleased. There were no civil authorities to stop them. Theft and battery were common, while murder was not far behind. Long-festering disagreements between families were settled with violence. Blacks and whites were victims. Such conduct fostered insecurity that particularly demoralized the aged. "Many simply sat down and died, succumbing to bereavement, hardships and heartbreak. They felt their country was dead." Some were dismayed by the social revolution implied by emancipation, but nearly all were poverty stricken regardless of their prewar circumstances.[11]

Two years after the war ended, no less an authority than General Sherman, who had earlier led his army on a destructive March to the Sea from Atlanta to Savannah, wrote:

> Look to the South and you who went with me through that land can best say if they too have not been fearfully punished. Mourning in every household, desolation written in broad characters across the whole face of their country, cities in ashes and fields laid waste their commerce gone, their system of labor annihilated and destroyed. Ruin, poverty, and distress everywhere, and now pestilence.[12]

Massachusetts journalist Sidney Andrews toured Georgia and the Carolinas for three months in fall 1865. Of Columbia, South Carolina, he said, "You can only get in through one of the roads built by Ruin. . . . You can only get out over the roads walled by Desolation." He described Charleston as "a city of ruins, of desolation, of vacant houses, of widowed women, of rotting wharves, of deserted warehouses, of weed wild gardens, of miles of grass grown streets, of acres of pitiful bareness." Even five years after the war, a British traveler in the Tennessee River valley wrote that the region "consists for the most part of plantations in a state of semi-ruin. . . . The trail of war is visible throughout the valley in burnt-up gin houses, ruined bridges, mills and factories . . . and of large tracts of once-cultivated land stripped of every vestige of fencing."[13]

Confederate lieutenant general John Bell Hood had lost a leg and the use of an arm during the war but refused to accept charity. Nonetheless, the *Albany (NY) Evening Journal* wrote sarcastically, "It is the first instance we have ever seen recorded of a 'Southern gentleman' too proud . . . to accept filthy lucre, come from what source it may." When the people of Texas presented Lieutenant General John Magruder a purse with which to buy a plantation, he refused it, saying, "No, gentlemen, when I espoused the cause of the South, I embraced poverty and willingly accepted it."[14]

Brigadier General William Pendleton, who once commanded General Lee's artillery and was an Episcopal priest, plowed his own farm while his wife fed meals to returning soldiers who chanced along their road. Since no livestock survived on his family farm, an armless Georgia veteran had his wife harness him to a plow while she drove from behind. In North Carolina, a white mother pulled the plow while her ten-year-old son drove and a younger child dropped seeds, received from Northern charity, into the furrows. Upon returning home, one colonel concluded that he and his wife had to earn a living by selling apple pies to nearby Yankee soldiers. He gathered the apples and she baked the pies. Wounded rebel brigadier general Stephen Elliot returned to discover that his plantation had been sold for nonpayment of property taxes. He moved to Charleston, where he earned a living catching fish and oysters with his own hands but died a year later of his wounds.[15]

Early in 1865, when Lincoln was asked how ex-slaves should feed themselves, he answered with one of his numerous parables. An Illinois farmer with a large herd of hogs decided he would feed the herd by turning it loose on a field of potatoes. That would save him the labor of digging up the potatoes himself. But an alert neighbor who was listening to the story asked how the hogs would get the potatoes after the ground froze in November or December. "Well," answered the farmer, "it may come pretty hard on the snouts, but I don't see how it can be anything but root, hog, or die."[16]

Lincoln's "root, hog, or die" admonishment to ex-slaves also applied to Southern whites regardless of their antebellum status. Under such circumstances, Southerners had no time or reason to plot Reconstruction schemes for the empty purpose of angering the Yankee victors.

FOUR

"Joshua" Johnson

Several Judeo-Christian narratives suggest parallels to the story of African American emancipation. Like the crowds welcoming Jesus to Jerusalem on the original Palm Sunday, grateful ex-slaves triumphantly greeted Lincoln as he toured Richmond on the first Palm Sunday following Robert E. Lee's surrender. Both Jesus and the president were executed on Good Friday. Finally, the parallel between Lincoln's African American emancipation and the Israeli exodus from Egypt under Moses is obvious. Death prevented both leaders from joining their followers to a promising land of just reconstruction.

Such parallels were evident among contemporary abolitionists almost immediately. One example was journalist Jane Swisshelm, who was dissatisfied with Lincoln's apparent postwar leniency toward Southern whites. When she learned of the new president's hatred of Southern aristocracy, she metaphorically pronounced Andrew Johnson to be the "American Joshua," succeeding Lincoln as the "American Moses." She presumed God had tested Southerners with Lincoln's mercy, which she falsely accused them of rejecting with assassination. In her analysis, Johnson would mete out their just punishment.[1]

Other Radical Republicans initially shared Swisshelm's opinion and expected that Johnson would be harder on the Rebels than Lincoln. Among them were Zachariah Chandler, Benjamin Butler, George Julian, and Benjamin Wade.

Chandler was a senator from Michigan, chairman of the Commerce Committee, and a sharp critic of Lincoln's leniency. After the president was killed, Chandler wrote his wife, "I believe the Almighty continued Mr. Lincoln in office as long as he was useful and then substituted a better man to finish the work." He pronounced Booth's bullet a "godsend." Although Indiana congressman George Julian was less inclined to speak disrespectfully of the martyred president, he felt that Lincoln's "weakness" had been swept aside, thereby enabling Johnson to conclude "the righteous ends of the war."[2]

The day after Lincoln died, Senator Wade—of the anti-Lincoln Wade-Davis Bill—led a delegation of Radical Republicans to see the new president. Among the group was Butler, who would become the chief prosecutor of Johnson during the president's 1868 impeachment trial.

Wade announced, "Johnson we have faith in you. By the gods there will be no trouble running the government now." Before returning to his home state of Massachusetts in summer 1865, Senator Sumner met with Johnson at least twice to say the president should leave Reconstruction to Congress. Since Sumner had always been more prone to lecture than to listen, he left Washington telling his friends that Johnson shared his viewpoints.[3]

To understand how Radicals like Wade—who once suggested that slaves should "rise up in insurrection to slay one half the Southern whites"—would reason that Johnson would share their perspective, it is necessary to examine Johnson's background.[4]

Andrew Johnson was born into poverty in North Carolina in 1808. At age fourteen, he was apprenticed to a tailor in Raleigh. Many of the clients were aristocrats who treated white workers like Johnson as second-class citizens, or so Johnson inferred. Two years later, sixteen-year-old Andrew ran away from his mentor because of mistreatment. In 1826, he returned home and took his mother and stepfather to Greenville, Tennessee, where the eighteen-year-old set up a tailor's shop. He also met Eliza McCardle in the town and married her the following year. Since Eliza was educated at a nearby girl's academy, she taught Andrew how to read and write. She was the only teacher he ever had.

As he matured, Johnson joined a debating society at a local college. He ran for alderman and won but drew the opposition of Greenville's aristocrats, such as they were. In 1835, he was elected a representative

President Andrew Johnson. *(Library of Congress)*

to Tennessee's legislature. Andrew Jackson was president at the time, and Johnson fell under his influence. Next Johnson went to the Tennessee Senate, and in 1842, at age thirty-four, he was elected to the US House of Representatives. It was the first time a slave state sent a tradesman to Congress. In a debate with the aristocratic Representative Jefferson Davis of Mississippi who questioned the ability of commoners to design and build fortifications, Johnson snarled, "I am a mechanic and when a blow is struck on that class I will resent it. . . . Sir, I vindicate the mechanical profession . . . the man who earns his living by the work of his hands."[5]

At forty-five he was elected Tennessee's governor, and four years later, in 1857, he graduated to the US Senate. There he was more concerned with the interests of consumers and the working classes than with the sectional differences over slavery. He authored the Homestead Act, opposed protective tariffs as well as the sale of timber and mineral lands in the public domain to private corporations, considered national banking to be a dangerous monopoly, and voted against increasing federal spending. "The public domain," he said, "is a national trust . . . held for the general welfare . . . and not to be bestowed as a special privilege upon a favored class." As for monopolistic privileges, he said, "Wherever monopoly attains a foothold, it is sure to be a source of danger, discord and trouble."[6]

Although he owned two household slaves and their children at the time he became a senator, he reasoned that the Constitution required all states to remain in the Union. But he also maintained that the nation's sectional differences could only be settled by adherence to the Constitution, which he regarded as sacred. His personal forty-year-old and marked-over copy of the Constitution pillowed his head at his burial. Johnson's respect for the document became the root cause of his disagreements with Radical Republicans.[7]

In June 1861, Tennessee held a plebiscite to determine whether the state should secede. Johnson returned to stump in favor of staying in the Union. At least once he was violently threatened, and he felt compelled to brandish a revolver in self-defense. Although Tennessee voted to secede, Johnson remained in the US Senate. He joined the influential Joint Senate-House Committee on the Conduct of the War as the only Democrat.

After Union forces captured Nashville in February 1862, Lincoln asked Johnson to return to Tennessee as the state's military governor with the rank of brigadier general. During his administration, Johnson ordered that uncooperative residents be escorted to the city's southern limits and told to continue in that direction. He required that preachers take strict loyalty oaths to the Union and threw them in jail if they refused. For months, however, Nashville was a federal island surrounded by Confederate sympathizers. Unlike Northern Radicals in Congress, Johnson's presence in Nashville put his very life in peril. Confederates might execute him if he was ever captured.[8]

The Republican Party split during the 1864 presidential elections. The Radical wing deserted Lincoln and nominated John C. Frémont. By organizing a temporary fusion party, Lincoln-loyal Republicans sought to attract support from the wing of the Democratic Party that supported the war. The result was the National Union Party, which convened its nominating convention in June. Although Lincoln officially expressed no running-mate preference, most party leaders understood that he wanted to balance the ticket politically and geographically. The incumbent vice president, Hannibal Hamlin, was from Maine and philosophically allied with the Radicals. In contrast, Andrew Johnson was a staunch war Democrat from a Southern state. By 1864, Johnson realized the war was not merely a matter of preserving the Union. He foresaw that slavery would end and accepted emancipation "first because it is right in itself, and second . . . [through it] we break down an odious and dangerous aristocracy." Lincoln got his man.[9]

Immediately after Lincoln's death, Johnson's disdain for Southern aristocracy provoked him to comments that implied that his Reconstruction policies would be consistent with the harsh wishes of the Radical Republicans. For example, he wrote Governor Oliver Morton of Indiana, "Treason must be made odious . . . traitors must be punished . . . [and] their social power destroyed. I say as to the [Southern] leaders, punishment. I say leniency . . . and amnesty to the thousands they have misled." The day after Lincoln died, Johnson told Senator Chandler, "Treason must be made infamous and traitors must be impoverished."[10]

Since Johnson once identified Lincoln as "the greatest American that has ever lived," he came to regard it as his duty to be the trustee of the martyred president's legacy. Johnson resolved that his Reconstruction policies would follow in the great man's footsteps, or try to. Among the clearest signals from his predecessor was that Reconstruction should proceed promptly and under the authority of the federal executive branch. There should be no delay to wait for Congress to reconvene. Johnson quickly settled on such a plan and discussed it thoroughly with his Lincoln-inherited cabinet. None of the members voiced "[any] doubt of the power of the executive branch . . . to reorganize [the former Confederate] state governments without the aid of Congress."[11]

On May 29, 1865, Johnson released a proclamation of pardon and amnesty to the Rebels. He also appointed W. W. Holden as North Carolina's provisional governor with instructions concerning how the state could qualify for readmittance into the Union. Pardon and amnesty required that each applicant take an oath to "henceforth faithfully support . . . the Constitution . . . and abide by . . . all laws . . . made during the . . . rebellion with reference to the emancipation of slaves." Significantly, it did not require applicants to say that they had never rebelled against the Union. There were some exceptions, which were similar to those specified by Lincoln's 10 percent plan, such as elected officials of the Confederacy. Johnson's limitations, however, were stricter than Lincoln's. For example, Johnson's policy required that any rebel owning more than $20,000 in property must apply directly to him for pardon and amnesty. Such applications would be judged on a case-by-case basis. Nonetheless, all those granted pardon were simultaneously restored their rights to private property, except for slaves.[12]

Johnson directed that Governor Holden organize a convention to write a new state constitution and set future voter requirements. Only Union-loyal men and former Confederates who had been granted pardon were permitted to vote for delegates or be delegate candidates. Identical proclamations were soon released for each of the remaining former Confederate states that did not have Lincoln (10 percent plan) governments. Johnson essentially set three conditions for the new state constitutions. First, they must outlaw slavery. Second, they must renounce secession. Third, they must repudiate all Confederates debts.

The conventions were also authorized to set dates to elect state officers and congressional representatives. Once the legislatures were chosen, the Southern states also supplied the incremental votes required to ratify the Thirteenth Amendment abolishing slavery. According to historians J. G. Randall and David Donald, martial law ruled during the transition process "without any of the attributes of terrorism, violence or menace to the tranquility of the people."[13]

Johnson felt that pardoned Confederates should be permitted to participate as voters in the formation of the new state governments. Like Lincoln, he wanted the Southern states to become functioning parts of the federal Union as soon as possible. Congress, however, held a trump card because no state representatives could be seated in either the House or Senate without approval of those bodies. They would use their seating authority to claim the exclusive right to set terms for Reconstruction while conceding to the executive branch nothing more than the responsibility to enforce those terms.[14]

When Congress reconvened in December 1865, the Southern representatives asked to be seated. Their request was denied for three reasons. First, some of them were former high-level members of the Confederate military or government who had not yet been pardoned or were otherwise disqualified under Johnson's terms. Second, many Northerners were angered by the Black Code provisions in some of the Southern state constitutions. These codes itemized discriminatory rights of conduct for freedmen. They were, however, also adopted ostensibly to impel the many ex-slaves who had mistaken freedom for vagrancy to seek employment. Third, none of the Southern states extended voting privileges to ex-slaves.

Radical Republican objections to such matters no doubt seem uncontroversial to the modern reader, until contextual circumstances as well as dubious party motivations are considered. First, nearly all the Democrats and some of the Republicans were willing to seat the Southern representatives. But their seats were denied through parliamentary trickery orchestrated by Thaddeus Stevens. When the minority objected to the tactics, Stevens successfully introduced a resolution to form a Joint Congressional Committee on Reconstruction—alternately known as the Committee of Fifteen—for the purpose of evaluating the qualifications of the Southern representatives and other matters related to Reconstruction. The committee's findings were a foregone conclusion.[15]

Second, most Northerners failed to credit Southerners with trying to choose their best leaders. Yet Southerners often purposely selected representatives who had initially opposed secession, which was more common among those who were previously Whig Party members. Former Whigs won eight governorships, eleven Senate seats, two-thirds of the House seats, and composed even larger majorities of the state constitutional conventions. One example was Alexander Stephens, who was elected to represent Georgia in the Senate. Southern voters appeared to be following Lincoln's Reconstruction playbook explained in chapter 1.[16]

But the Radical Republicans construed the slate of Southern representatives to be an act of defiance. They did not consider that Southerners who were surrounded by economic and social chaos had little time to plot defiance. Similarly, during their day-to-day struggle to avoid starvation, Southerners had little chance to understand the perspectives of Northerners who lived contrastingly amid peace and prosperity.

As for the Black Codes, it should be understood that while the Thirteenth Amendment ended slavery, it did not transform blacks into citizens. In fact, the Supreme Court's 1857 Dred Scott decision said African Americans could not be US citizens even if they were not slaves. It was, therefore, necessary for the states to individually define the rights and obligations of the freedmen. The consequent restrictions were not unique to the American South. None of the other nations that abolished slavery in the nineteenth century granted former slaves rights equal to those of whites.[17]

Many freedmen equated freedom with not working and wandering. Some traveled widely to find lost family members. Others moved about simply because, for the first time, they could. According to historians Francis Simkins and Charles Roland, "Everywhere Negroes traveled in crowds like packs of gypsies, not knowing how they would exist when they came to their journey's end. A Northern observer in the summer of 1865 was convinced that, 'the race is, on a large scale, ignorantly sacrificing its own good for the husks of vagabondage.' Many died for want of food, shelter, or medical attention."[18]

As the war was ending the federal government responded by organizing the Freedmen's Bureau in March 1865 to assist Southern blacks in their transition from slaves to free workers. It distributed food and medical services, established schools and hospitals, and found employment for the ex-slaves. But the bureau exercised considerable authority over blacks *and* whites. It could arbitrarily fix wages and employment terms for anyone hiring ex-slaves. Its special courts had wide jurisdiction in matters involving freedmen and could override the rulings of state courts. Unfortunately, many bureau officers were corrupt, exceeding their authority and pocketing funds. After blacks gained the right to vote through the 1867 Reconstruction Acts, the bureau became a tool for black voter registration and election turnout drives that propagated Republican control of the Southern states.[19]

After the Confederacy's surrender, the Southern state governments organized under Johnson's plan appreciated that Southerners of all races needed to earn a living. The 40 percent of the labor force that was black could not remain idle if the region was to recover economically, even if only to a subsistence level. Accordingly, some of the former rebel states enacted Black Codes based partly upon the vagrancy laws of Northern and Southern states, and upon the regulations of the Freedmen's Bureau, as well as the statutes in the West Indies governing free blacks. Although often overly restrictive, the codes were also consistent with Lincoln's wartime proposal of emancipation-through-apprenticeship.[20]

A week after issuing the Emancipation Proclamation, on January 8, 1863, Lincoln wrote Union major general John McClernand suggesting that the rebel states could still have their rights restored in the Union by adopting "systems of apprenticeship for the colored people, conforming substantially to the most approved plans of gradual emancipation." Six months later, he told his Arkansas military commander that apprenticeship could be an acceptable form of emancipation to qualify the state for readmission.[21]

Although the Black Codes relegated former slaves to a lower caste, by focusing on the worst examples in Mississippi and South Carolina, where over half the population was black, Northerners erroneously interpreted them as a pervasive attempt to revive slavery and deny Union victory. Code restrictions were, however, less harsh in North Carolina, Alabama, and Georgia, while Tennessee and Arkansas initially had none. In any event, the occupation armies and the Freedmen's Bureau overruled the codes before they could take effect.[22]

Finally, the failure of the Johnson-plan state governments to grant voting rights to blacks reflected three points.

First was racial prejudice. But racism was prevalent throughout America and not merely isolated to the South. While most Northerners were against slavery, they were not for racial equality in their own states. For example, Horace Greeley's prominent opposition to slavery did not include support for racial integration. His *New York Tribune* advocated that occupied Southern lands be given to ex-slaves in order to avoid mass black migration to the North. Also, during the war, Union adjutant general Lorenzo Thomas who was sent South to manage black refugees wrote, "It will not do to send [black refugees] . . . into the free states, for the prejudices of the people of those states are against such a measure and some . . . have enacted laws against the reception of free negroes."[23]

The second reason the Johnson state governments declined to grant voting rights to freedmen was that ex-slaves had little experience or knowledge of democratic government. Indeed, few had even an opportunity for elementary education. Many whites felt that suddenly granting the vote to a poorly educated and inexperienced group composing four-tenths of the region's population was to invite even more social and economic chaos than already existed.

Third, the Southern states shared the prevailing viewpoint throughout the United States that suffrage was constitutionally a state's right at a time when only six of the twenty-two Civil War Union-loyal states let blacks vote (most required property and education tests), even though they were only a tiny percentage of the Northern population. Although

Johnson personally favored the gradual adoption of black voting rights, he did not feel he had the authority to demand it of any state. When Mississippi became the first former Confederate state to convene a constitutional convention, however, Johnson urged the state's provisional governor to set an example by granting voting rights to blacks who could read and write and owned at least $250 in property. In October 1865, he commented to a former abolitionist leader that if he were still governor in Tennessee, he would "try to introduce [black] suffrage gradually," first to military veterans and then to the literate and taxpayers. His stance was much like the only one Lincoln ever voiced.[24]

When all the smoke is cleared, however, the most likely reason the Republican-controlled Congress failed to seat the Southern representatives was because the party wanted to retain political power. When the Civil War ended, the Republican Party was barely a dozen years old. Its leaders worried that it might be strangled in its cradle if readmittance of Southern states into the Union failed to be managed in a manner that would prevent Southerners from allying with Northern Democrats to regain control of the federal government.

If representatives from all former Confederate states were seated in the Thirty-Ninth Congress in December 1865 and each added member was a Democrat, the Republican majority in the Senate would have dropped from 43–9 and become 43–31. Similarly, the Republican majority in the House would have dropped from 152–40 and become 152–81. Southern representation in the House would be greater than in 1860 because the former Confederate states would gain fifteen additional representatives by virtue of the negation of the three-fifths clause limiting slave counts to three-fifths of their number for purposes of representation.[25]

The infant GOP reasoned it must ensure that most of the new Southern senators and congressmen be readmitted as Republicans. One way would be to establish vassal governments in the Southern states. Since there were few white Republicans in the region, the party concluded it needed to create a new constituency. It spurned, or was unaware of, the opportunities to join forces with Southerners who were formerly Whigs, although it would hunger for such an alliance after 1876.

Nonetheless, in 1866, Republicans settled on two objectives. First was mandatory African American suffrage in all former Confederate states. They expected that such a mostly illiterate and inexperienced electorate could be manipulated to consistently support Republican interests out of gratitude for emancipation and voter suffrage. Second was to disfranchise the Southern white classes most likely to oppose the Republicans.[26]

As the Committee of Fifteen, which was composed of three Democrats and twelve Republicans under the leadership of Thaddeus Stevens, held hearings to craft its Reconstruction plan, a new version of the Freedmen's Bureau Act passed Congress in February 1866. It considerably extended the bureau's power over economic and civil affairs and authorized federal and military enforcement. It also extended the bureau's activities into the previous Union-loyal slave states where it could be used to enlarge Republican influence.

President Johnson vetoed the bill. He chiefly objected to its passage at a time when none of the most affected states were represented in Congress. It was, he reasoned, an unconstitutional continuation of war powers during peacetime and a usurpation of states' rights. He predicted that the funding and the other powers the bill gave to the bureau would lead it to become a source of "fraud, corruption, and oppression." Congress attempted to override the veto but fell two votes short of the necessary two-thirds majority when the Senate voted 30–18.[27]

Shortly thereafter, Congress passed a civil rights bill that declared blacks to be US citizens with most of the rights and obligations of whites. (Native Americans, however, were not deemed to be citizens unless they paid taxes.) It was to be enforced by federal officers, including those of the Freedmen's Bureau. Such officers were paid generous fees to prosecute and arrest offenders, whether genuine or doubtful. The fee arrangement was based upon the 1850 Fugitive Slave Act, which abolitionists roundly condemned earlier as providing financial incentives to prosecute innocent victims. Although officially represented as a bill to promote racial equality, it was also intended to ensure that Southern blacks had enough freedoms to remain in the South instead of moving North in order to obtain such freedoms.[28]

President Johnson vetoed the civil rights bill as well. Again he objected that eleven of the thirty-six states were not represented in Congress when it passed and that it was a usurpation of states' rights. He also argued that the fee schedule "might convert any law . . . into an instrument of persecution and fraud" and that it would create a bureaucracy with a vested interest in perpetuating racial discord. His message concluded by proclaiming a willingness to work with Congress "in any measure [for] the civil rights protection of the freedmen . . . that may be constitutional." This time the Republicans overrode the veto but again resorted to parliamentary trickery by temporarily removing a New Jersey senator known to support the president's veto. Shortly thereafter, Congress overrode Johnson's veto of a second Freedmen's Bureau bill.[29]

Despite overriding Johnson's veto of the civil rights bill, some congressmen perceived the merits of his constitutional objection. Deliberations by the Committee of Fifteen led to a consensus that a new amendment must be adopted. The putative purpose was to protect the civil rights of ex-slaves, but Republicans also wanted the amendment's terms to enable the formation of Republican-controlled puppet regimes in the South in order to avoid losing control of Congress to the Democrats. Republicans also hoped to win the White House in the 1868 elections and wanted Southern states to provide reliable electoral votes. The result was the convoluted Fourteenth Amendment.[30]

The amendment has four key provisions. First, almost anyone born in America, including former slaves but excluding untaxed Indians, was held to be a citizen and guaranteed civil rights. Second, states refusing suffrage to male citizens of any qualified race would have their congressional representation cut by subtracting the number of members in the excluded race from the applicable state's population for purposes of calculating its House representation and electoral votes. Because of the tiny black populations of Northern states, the provision was inconsequential for them. Third, many former Confederates were to be denied office-holding privileges, and all states were compelled to repudiate Confederate debts. Fourth, despite the fact that Congress considered their governments unlawful, all Southern states would be required to ratify the amendment before they could be readmitted into the Union.[31]

The contradictory requirement that former Confederate states ratify the amendment before being allowed to rejoin the Union merits comment. First, Congress had no objections less than a year earlier when the Southern state governments were used to ratify the Thirteenth Amendment freeing the slaves. Even though Congress refused to seat their elected representatives after the former rebel states approved the Thirteenth Amendment, each one had been permitted to vote either thumbs up or thumbs down. Except for Mississippi, which had abolished slavery in its own state constitution, all approved the amendment.[32]

Second, congressional terms applicable to the Fourteenth Amendment were different. They did not give the Southern states a right to freely vote either yea or nay. In order to rejoin the Union they could only vote yea *and* form new state governments to specifications set in Washington. Historians J. G. Randall and David Donald conclude the process was unconstitutional:

> In reality Congress . . . was not merely submitting an amendment to the states. It was creating fabricated governments in the South. . . .

> As a matter of constitutional law the *method* of amending the constitution does not lie within . . . Congress. It is prescribed in Article V of the Constitution [and requires either a national convention or state ratification of a congressional submission]. . . . It is for Congress to choose between [the two alternatives] . . . but not to create new . . . conditions as part of the amending process.[33]

After the Fourteenth Amendment was submitted to the states for ratification in June, Johnson realized he was in a fight to the finish with Congress for control of Reconstruction. The next month, three of his cabinet members resigned because they declined to support his plan over the one emerging from Congress. Secretary of War Edwin Stanton felt the same way but remained in the cabinet as a spy for the Republican Radicals and as their tool to implement congressional Reconstruction policies through the force of arms.[34]

Consequently, Johnson decided to make his case to the public. Although not a common practice at the time, the president set out on a trip to visit every Northern state outside of New England. He pleaded his case in public speeches during August and September, before the autumn elections. Secretary of State William Seward, Navy Secretary Gideon Welles, and General of the Army Ulysses S. Grant accompanied him.

It began with enthusiastic greetings in Baltimore, Philadelphia, and New York, but by the time the four-car train reached Cleveland, audiences were hostile and mostly interested in seeing Grant. In response, the president began denouncing the congressional plan and attacking its leaders, Representative Thaddeus Stevens and Senator Charles Sumner. The receptions got more ugly as the procession went farther west. When the tour reached southern Illinois, Grant left to visit his father in Cincinnati. Despite an obvious preference among the public for the general, Grant had not enjoyed the trip. He had been drinking and left the caravan in a drunken state.

Receptions on the return trip through Indiana, Ohio, and Pennsylvania went from bad to worse. One man was killed in a disorderly Indianapolis gathering. Johnson was shouted off the stage in Ohio, and a Pittsburgh crowd would not let him speak as it repeatedly called for the no-longer-present Grant. After a hundred speeches and nineteen days of travel, the president returned to Washington on September 15.[35]

His trip might have been more productive had he emphasized other differences with Congress aside from Reconstruction: Congress, for example, had voted itself a pay raise and granted federal lands and other subsidies to the railroads. Additionally, Republican advocacy of high tariffs, opposed by Johnson, was unpopular in the Midwest. The Republicans had a 45–8 majority in the Senate and a 143–45 majority in the House when the Fortieth Congress convened the following March, in 1867.[36]

Meanwhile, only twenty of thirty-eight states had endorsed the Fourteenth Amendment, which was nine short of the twenty-nine required for ratification. Except for Tennessee, none of the former Confederate states had ratified the amendment. Congress, however, was determined to compel ratification by adopting three Reconstruction Acts passed over Johnson's vetoes.

The first act, which passed on the first day of the Fortieth Congress, declared that no lawful state governments existed in the former Confederacy except Tennessee. The rest of the South was to be ruled by martial law and divided into five military districts.

A second act passed three weeks later. It required each military occupation commander to compile a roster of voters based upon eligibility standards within the act. Although the act provided for universal suffrage among black adult males, it has been estimated that the registration procedures disfranchised about 150,000 former Confederates. Upon completion, about 1.3 million men were declared legal voters. Blacks outnumbered whites by 703,000 to 627,000 (53 to 47 percent), although they represented only about 40 percent of the region's population. Blacks were the majority of voters in Mississippi, South Carolina, Louisiana, Florida, and Alabama.[37]

Voters thus declared legal were to elect delegates to constitutional conventions in each state. Such constitutions had to provide for universal black suffrage but might disfranchise former Confederates. The resulting constitutions were to be submitted to a statewide voter referendum. Once passed in such referendums, the constitutions were to be presented to Congress, where they might be accepted or rejected. Following acceptance of its constitution by Congress, each Southern state had to ratify the Fourteenth Amendment. Its representatives could not join Congress until the Fourteenth Amendment had been ratified *and* the applicable state also endorsed ratification.

The third act, passed in July 1867, provided for liberal interpretation of the first two acts.[38]

In addition to the two Reconstruction Acts passed in March, Congress enacted two bills that same month over Johnson's vetoes to limit the president's powers. First was the Command of the Army Act. It required that all of the president's orders to military officers be delivered through the general in chief, who, at the time, was Ulysses S. Grant. Furthermore, the general in chief could not be ordered away from Washington without his consent. The act made it illegal for any other military officer to accept orders directly from the president.

Second was the Tenure of Office Act. It required that civil officers appointed by the president with the consent of the Senate could not be dismissed without the Senate's consent. The chief purpose of the Tenure Act was to prevent Johnson from removing War Secretary Stanton, who, as noted, had become an ally of the congressional Republicans in their battle against presidential Reconstruction. It might also block Johnson from replacing lesser federal officers in the South who were implementing congressional Reconstruction.[39]

In combination, the two acts were designed to increase the power of Congress over the military and correspondingly render the military less responsive to the president. Congress was overly apprehensive that Johnson might abuse his normal powers over the military to enforce his own Reconstruction policies. In reality, however, Congress was abusively making the military subservient to its whims.

Johnson argued that Radical Reconstruction demonstrated the Southern states had been correct in supposing that the 1860 presidential election would result in the loss of constitutional liberties and guarantees. It was contradictory to fight the war on the presumption that no state could leave the Union only to conclude at the end of the war that eleven Southern states were no longer Union members. If they could not leave the Union, he reasoned, they could not constitutionally be transformed into military districts. His veto message on the first Reconstruction Act stated:

> Those [Rebels] who advocated the right of secession alleged in their own justification that we had no regard for law and that the rights of property, life, and liberty would not be safe under the Constitution as administered by us. If we now verify their assertion, we prove that they were in truth fighting for their liberty and instead of branding their leaders as traitors against a righteous and legal government, we elevate them in history to the rank of self-sacrificing patriots.[40]

Although Johnson should have asked for Stanton's resignation months earlier, he was finally prompted to act in August 1867, after learning that Stanton had withheld a clemency recommendation pertinent to the trial of Lincoln's assassins two years earlier. Specifically, the secretary failed to inform the president that the military court judging the conspirators recommended that the only female accomplice, Mary Surratt, be exempted from execution. As a result, Johnson failed to intervene, and she was hanged.[41]

If Congress was not in session, the Tenure Act permitted the president to temporarily suspend the officeholder until such time as the Senate reconvened to vote on the matter. Consequently, Stanton temporarily yielded the office after Johnson appointed Grant as War Secretary *ad interim* in August. When the Senate reconvened the following January, it voted 35–16 to reject Stanton's removal.

Johnson would ever after claim that he and Grant had an understanding that would enable the president to challenge the Tenure Act in court. Specifically, Grant would either (1) hold the office while the matter was litigated or (2) permit Johnson to replace him so that the case could be contested under a different department head. Grant later denied there was such an understanding, but the balance of evidence is with Johnson. Grant, for example, did not tell the president at a January 13 White House evening reception that the general had already written his resignation earlier in the day. In any event, the next morning Grant resigned and turned the office keys over to Stanton before Johnson could appoint a Grant replacement. The stage was finally set for a showdown with Congress on February 21, 1868, when Johnson appointed Adjutant General Lorenzo Thomas to replace Grant, but Stanton refused to yield the office.[42]

The showdown did not take long. The House voted on February 24 to impeach Johnson. A week later, it formally presented eleven impeachment articles to the Senate for trial. Alleged violation of the Tenure Act was central to the bulk of them.

The prosecution was hyperbolic and vicious. Its lead prosecutor was Representative Benjamin Butler of Massachusetts. He authored the tenth article that accused Johnson of making speeches that were disrespectful of Congress even though it is difficult to conclude that such a charge could qualify as an impeachable offense. Such offenses are supposed to be limited to treason, bribery, and high crimes or misdemeanors. When the president's lawyers requested forty days to prepare a defense, Butler sarcastically objected, remarking that forty days was as long as God needed to destroy the world by flood. Instead, a ten-day delay was granted. Butler also paid spies to search the trash baskets of defense counsel William Evarts's hotel room. Out of the courtroom, he denounced Johnson as the soul of corruption, assassination, cowardice, and murder, thereby falsely implying that Johnson was involved in Lincoln's killing.[43]

Since conviction required a two-thirds majority, the Radicals guarded every presumed yea vote and attempted to seize others. The president pro tempore of the Senate, Republican Benjamin Wade of Ohio, would replace Johnson upon a conviction because there was no vice president.

Consequently, Senator Thomas Hendricks of Indiana suggested that Wade abstain from voting since a sitting vice president would have been legally prohibited from voting except in the case of a tie, which would be irrelevant in an impeachment trial.

But Hendricks was quickly persuaded to withdraw his objection and leave the matter to Wade's conscience, which led the Ohioan to vote for conviction. Additionally, Wade told Butler that Butler would be his secretary of state should Johnson be convicted. Wade also attempted to add two likely conviction votes before the trial by a surprise move to admit Colorado as a state, but he was unable to gather the required two-thirds majority needed to override Johnson's likely veto. Even after the trial was under way, prosecution leader Thaddeus Stevens made a similar failed effort to admit the newly formed Republican regime in Arkansas.[44]

The president had good legal counsel. Johnson paid five lawyers out of his own pocket. Perhaps most notable was New York Republican William Evarts, who otherwise opposed the president's policies. (Maxwell Perkins, who was the Scribner's Publishing editor for Ernest Hemingway, Scott Fitzgerald, and Thomas Wolfe, was one of Evarts's grandsons.) In response to the tenth charge that Johnson spoke disrespectfully of Congress, Evarts pointed out that senators and congressmen also publicly disparaged the president and made reckless accusations against him. For example, Radical leader Charles Sumner had previously announced from the Senate floor that Johnson was an "enemy to his country." When Sumner was called to order, other Republican senators, like John Sherman of Ohio and Henry Anthony of Rhode Island, averred that Sumner's accusations were permissible in debate. Evarts argued against the hypocrisy of denying the president similar latitude.[45]

Chief Justice Salmon P. Chase presided over the trial. Before his 1864 Supreme Court appointment, Chase was well known as a Radical Republican. He made an unexpected ruling when the defense called Navy Secretary Welles to testify about the president's intent in appointing a successor to War Secretary Stanton. Defense counsel wanted to show that it was a deliberate attempt to test the Tenure Act's constitutionality. When the prosecution objected, Chase ruled that Welles should be permitted to testify. A Radical senator then moved for a vote to overrule Chase's decision. Much to Chase's chagrin, the motion carried.[46]

On May 16, Johnson was acquitted on a vote for the eleventh article of 35–19 because the yeas were one vote short of a two-thirds majority. Radicals manipulatively adjourned the Senate for ten days in hopes of persuading at least one of the acquittal votes to switch sides when other articles would be held to a vote on May 26. During the interval, Butler put through a resolution to investigate allegations that "improper or corrupt means" were used to influence the May 16 vote. Butler's resolution, and other pressures, failed to change the outcome. Johnson survived the last impeachment attempt on May 26, again by a single vote.[47]

Chief counsel William Evarts. (*Library of Congress*)

Twenty years later, when President Grover Cleveland questioned the Tenure Act's legitimacy, it was repealed. If the Tenure Act had prevailed, the presidency could not have remained as an independent branch of government. Those voting for acquittal realized that Congress was running amok, intimidating the executive, and increasingly, the judicial government branches. Some senators voting for conviction, including John Sherman and even Charles Sumner, later admitted they were wrong.[48]

In 1926, almost sixty years after the Tenure Act was passed over Johnson's veto, the Supreme Court ruled in a test case involving Woodrow Wilson's removal of his postmaster general that a president had the right to remove cabinet members. Nine years later, it also ruled that Congress could limit a president's power to remove other officers. The court never addressed the Tenure Act specifically.[49]

After his prosecutorial failure, Butler proceeded with hearings to learn whether bribery was used to secure acquittal votes. In the end, no charges were filed and nobody was convicted or censured. In fact, the hearings even disclosed evidence that one senator who voted for conviction offered to sell his vote. Kansas senator Samuel Pomeroy wrote Johnson's postmaster general offering his vote, together with three or four others in his caucus, in exchange for $40,000.[50]

Failing to remove Johnson from office, Republicans became increasingly anxious that the Fourteenth Amendment be ratified because a new president would be elected in the fall. Since the 1867 Reconstruction Acts effectively mandated universal African American suffrage in the South (but not the North) and the disfranchisement of many former Confederates, they reasoned that the Southern states admitted to the Union after passage of the Fourteenth Amendment would be reliable sources of Republican electoral votes.

The Republicans reasoned correctly. Their presidential candidate, Ulysses S. Grant, picked up forty-one electoral votes from former Confederate states, compared to only sixteen for his Democratic opponent,

Horatio Seymour. Although Grant won a lopsided Electoral College victory, the national popular vote was much closer, with 3 million for Grant and 2.7 million for Seymour. Since it's estimated that Grant won 450,000 black votes, compared to only 50,000 for Seymour, Grant's popular vote margin would have vanished without African American votes, which were overwhelmingly from the South.[51]

When impeachment proceedings started in late February 1868, the Fourteenth Amendment still needed ratification in at least six more states in order to become law. By process of elimination, at least several would have to be former slave states. All the former Confederate states, except Tennessee, had yet to ratify it. They basically concluded they would prefer to remain under martial law than be members of the Union if they had to submit to its terms. Undoubtedly, universal black suffrage and significant white voter disfranchisement were the biggest objections, but a resolution of Florida's House of Representatives explained others:

> Beyond the postal service our people derive no benefit from our existence as a State of the Union. We are denied representation even when we elect a man who . . . never . . . sympathized with [the Confederacy's armed rebellion]. . . . We are at the same time subject to the most onerous taxation; [and our] civil law . . . is enforced . . . only when it meets the approval of the local [military] commanders.[52]

When Alabamans discovered a way to avoid ratification by declining to vote, Congress changed the rules. The state's constitution required that ratification be approved by a majority of all registered voters as opposed to a majority of votes cast. Thus, many white Alabamans registered without voting. Consequently, even though a majority of the votes cast were for ratification, the total failed to exceed half of the voters registered. In response, on March 11, Congress passed a supplemental Reconstruction Bill over Johnson's veto stipulating that a majority of votes cast was sufficient.

On April 3, Arkansas became the first Southern state to ratify the Fourteenth Amendment under the bill. Six more, including Florida and Alabama, followed over the next four months. As a result, the Fourteenth Amendment was ratified in July. Eight of the eleven former Confederate states were readmitted to the Union as Republican-controlled vassal states. They were commonly known as carpetbag regimes because many of the Union-loyal leaders arrived from the North with their possessions packed in cheap carpetbag luggage.[53]

Although most Confederate veterans had already been pardoned, on Christmas Day 1868, Johnson excused the remaining three hundred. Pardons enabled former Confederates to conduct ordinary business functions, such as title transfers, that might otherwise have been legally challenged. While the pardons did not restore voting rights to whites disfranchised by means of the 1867 Reconstruction Acts, they did restore property rights. Consequently, the action blocked any potential federal efforts to confiscate privately owned Southern lands and redistribute them to freedmen. Thereafter, such efforts would need to be led by the state governments individually.

But carpetbaggers typically forced confiscation indirectly by increasing property taxes beyond the ability of the impoverished owners to pay. As a result, well-financed speculators who could buy the tax-defaulted properties at bargain prices were the chief beneficiaries instead of the ex-slaves. Many such well-financed speculators were transplanted Northerners. At the peak, as noted, about one-fifth of Mississippi's land was for sale due to delinquent taxes, and an Arkansas newspaper required sixteen pages to list the delinquent properties in that state.[54]

Although Johnson was sometimes charged with trying to block Radical Reconstruction chiefly because of his racism, his three essential differences with the Radicals did not reflect hostility toward blacks. First, he was suspicious of Republican motives. Their demand for universal black suffrage in the South, while retaining it as a state's right in the North, was an obvious attempt to perpetuate Republican Party control by establishing Southern puppet regimes. Second, he interpreted the Constitution strictly. Therefore, he believed the Reconstruction Acts that enfranchised ex-slaves and disfranchised many former Confederates were unconstitutional because voting privileges were a state's right. Third, he believed it was unfair, and perhaps unconstitutional, for Congress to enact Reconstruction laws while excluding the eleven states most affected.

FIVE

Carpetbagged

The carpetbag governments of the Southern states trace their roots to the First Reconstruction Act, passed in March 1867 over President Johnson's veto. At the time, Congress recognized only Tennessee among the former rebel states as having a legitimate government. The Volunteer State was excepted because Radical Republicans already controlled it. That happened shortly before Governor Andrew Johnson left to become Lincoln's vice president and a tightly controlled electorate of Union-loyal voters picked his replacement. The other ten states were divided into five military districts, each governed by an officer with the rank of brigadier general or higher. Their occupation forces totaled about twenty thousand soldiers distributed among 134 posts providing an average of 150 men per post. Many of the soldiers were blacks who had been slaves prior to the war.

The generals removed the Johnson-era governors of Georgia, Louisiana, Texas, Mississippi, and Virginia for alleged reluctance to cooperate in congressional Reconstruction. Before their tenure was over, military commanders also removed thousands of local officials and replaced them with Southerners who had never supported the Confederacy, recently arrived Northerners, or Union army officers. During the occupation period, army orders were the law, and military commanders levied and collected taxes.[1]

The chief objective of the military occupation was to organize new state governments in conformity with the congressional Reconstruction plan. As a result, universal manhood suffrage for all races except Native Americans was mandatory in the election of delegates to the state constitutional conventions. As noted earlier, however, there was an important exception that excluded many former rebel soldiers and office holders because Republicans regarded them as political enemies.

The history of the carpetbag era underscores the ancient wisdom that people should be judged by what they do as opposed to what they say. The state constitutions formed under Radical Reconstruction were generally more progressive than the antebellum ones they replaced. Aside from mandatory black suffrage, they typically reduced voter discrimination between the regions controlled by former planters and those populated by yeomen farmers. Provisions were made for poor homes, insane asylums, and other services. Public education, to which Southern aristocrats were previously indifferent, was also emphasized. Some eliminated property requirements for elected officials and provided for popular vote elections of senators. Local governments and the court systems were also reformed.[2]

Once the states approved the new constitutions and ratified the Fourteenth Amendment, each could apply to Congress for permission to seat its senators and representatives. By the November 1868 presidential election, all but three had complied, and Republican-controlled governments ruled the other eight. Only Mississippi, Texas, and Virginia had not yet approved the amendment, and all would do so within fourteen months, thereby also becoming Reconstructed states. The three laggards, however, were able to adopt constitutions that avoided disfranchising former Confederates while some of the earlier states duplicated, or exceeded, the ex-Confederate disfranchising effects of the 1867 Reconstruction Acts.

Political officials in the Reconstructed states were composed of three groups: white Northerner opportunists who typically arrived in the South hoping to capitalize on the pending political reorganization, known as carpetbaggers; native white Southerners who claimed to have been Union-loyal during the Civil War, called scalawags; and African Americans, including ex-slaves as well as blacks that had earlier been free.

When ratified early in 1870, the Fifteenth Amendment required African American suffrage for the entire country. Since Southern state constitutions already included black suffrage, the amendment's practical effect was in the Northern and former border states, where blacks composed less than 5 percent of the population. The amendment did, however, ensure that no Southern state could avoid black suffrage in the future by repealing such terms in its own constitution.[3]

For the seven states that were readmitted in 1868, thirty of forty-nine senators and representatives were carpetbaggers who came down after the war, as were four of the seven governors. In 1870, twenty of the twenty-two senators from former rebel states were Republicans, as were forty-four of the fifty-eight representatives. The South had been transformed into a Republican stronghold. From 1868 to 1870, two Southern blacks served as senators and a dozen others as congressmen. There were no blacks representing Northern states in either chamber. Several Southern blacks became lieutenant governors, and large numbers served in state legislatures, although they composed a majority only in South Carolina from 1868 to 1874, and even more briefly in Louisiana.[4]

Even though their constitutions said the right things, the carpetbag governments often failed to do the right things. High taxes, corruption, large indebtedness, and wasteful spending were prevalent.

Although progressive by comparison to the antebellum constitutions, the incremental services were costly. They necessitated high taxes for the part of the country that was least able to afford them. While the Thirteenth Amendment that freed the slaves was an act of national policy, it burdened the impoverished South with the requirement to educate 90 percent of the country's blacks, with only seven years of help from the Freedmen's Bureau. The war-devastated South endured some of the highest property taxes in relation to wealth in the history of the United States. Even though 1870 property values in the eleven former rebel states were less than half the value in 1860, the amount of property taxes paid was four times greater. The relative burden, therefore, increased eight-fold.[5]

Whites correctly suspected that a major objective of the higher taxes was to force landowners to forfeit their properties through bankruptcy. In 1866, eighty-one Mississippi plantations were put up for sale. Within five years, 1.4 million acres in seven of Mississippi's most productive cotton counties along the delta were sold for nonpayment of taxes. Planters in the region surrounding Natchez, which had been the crown jewel of Mississippi's cotton empire, lost 150 plantations by 1875, at least partly because of tax deficiencies. One Republican state senator in South Carolina named William Beverly Nash, an ex-slave, was unsympathetic:[6]

> [White Democrats] complain of taxes being too high. I tell you they are not high enough. I want them taxed until they put these

> lands back where they belong, into the hands of those who worked for them. You [ex-slaves] worked for them, you labored for them, and were sold to pay for them, and you ought to have them.[7]

(He would resign his position in 1877 in the face of bribery charges and misuse of his office.)

Legitimate state services, such as education, were only one reason for the sharp tax increases. Another was corruption. For example, a single session of Louisiana's carpetbag legislature cost ten times that of any of the state's antebellum legislatures. The money "was squandered in paying extra mileage and per diem of the members for services never rendered; for an enormous corps of useless clerks and pages, for publishing the journals of each house in fifteen obscure parish newspapers, some of which never existed . . . in paying extra committees authorized to sit during vacations . . . and in an elegant stationary bill which included ham and Champagne" among other luxuries.[8]

Enterprises to build infrastructure, especially railroads, were granted liberal state and local subsidies that were often abused. At the end of the Civil War, the South had only ten thousand miles of track, much of which needed to be repaired. An additional two thousand to three thousand miles were laid during carpetbag Reconstruction. Nonetheless, such growth was below the national average and accomplished at scandalously high costs. Subsidies were granted even before construction began, and some lines benefitted without ever laying a mile of track. When loans were the subsidy form, even the roads that were finished were often worth less than the debt incurred, thereby leaving the applicable governments as the losers when the underlying railroads failed. Aside from loans, the states also supplied land grants; Texas led the way with donations totaling over 32 million acres. All Southern state governments were thus exploited except Mississippi, whose constitution forbade railroad subsidies.

Since such investments could not be funded even by the high taxes of the carpetbag era, both the Johnson-era and carpetbag governments borrowed heavily. By 1874, the ten Reconstructed states were almost $300 million in debt, which was at least as large as the combined debts of the remaining twenty-seven states of the Union that year. In fact, the 1874 Southern indebtedness was bigger than the assessed value of all property in the former Confederate states at the end of the war. Put another way, Southern states could not have paid off their debt even if they had sold every acre of land at the 1865 tax-assessed valuations.[9]

The railroad industry was sufficiently powerful to play a central role in the Reconstruction history of Alabama and Virginia. As Alabama's iron industry began to realize its potential after the Civil War, railroad access to the emerging city of Birmingham became the chief prize for two principal rivals. One was the Louisville & Nashville Railroad, which was owned by August Belmont, a New York Democrat. (The popular Belmont Stakes thoroughbred horse race bears his name.) Belmont's rival was Philadelphia's Jay Cooke, a Republican. Both attempted to secure favored Birmingham access through unscrupulous arrangements with Alabama politicians of the Johnson and carpetbag periods. Belmont eventually prevailed because of Cooke's 1873 financial failure. When the two were at peace, Alabama Reconstruction proceeded calmly, but when they were at war, contrived race riots broke out.

Virginia's Reconstruction story was shaped by a rivalry between the Baltimore & Ohio Railroad owned by John Garrett and the Southside Line headed by former Confederate general William Mahone. Garrett wanted to funnel Virginia traffic through Baltimore, whereas Mahone favored Norfolk, Virginia. To capture traffic from states southwest of Virginia, both sides needed to gain control of the Virginia and Tennessee line that linked the Old Dominion to Chattanooga, which was a gateway to the rest of the South. Neither Mahone nor Garrett could gain control without the approval of the state of Virginia. The two men, therefore, decided to compete for control of the state government.

Despite being a former Confederate, Mahone supported the 1868 white Republican gubernatorial candidate. When that governor failed to back Mahone's interests, the latter skillfully undermined his reelection by successfully promoting a black as his running mate. Mahone realized that many white Virginians who voted for the governor in 1868 would abandon the candidate in 1870 because of his running mate's race. Mahone next persuaded the Democratic candidate that he could win with Mahone's backing. Everything worked to the general's satisfaction. The Democrats gained control of the governor's mansion in the election, thereby ending Republican Reconstruction. As a reward, the legislature promptly approved Mahone's railroad proposal.[10]

Mahone continued to build his railroad empire for several more years, but Jay Cooke's failure also led to the demise of the general's railroad. In 1881, a Philadelphia investment firm bought it and soon consolidated it under the Norfolk & Western name, which is presently part of the Norfolk Southern.

While Virginia escaped Radical Reconstruction within a couple of years, after an early misstep, Georgia was also restored to home rule fairly quickly. Georgia ratified the Fourteenth Amendment and was readmitted by Congress in July 1868. In September, however, the state's legislature removed black members because the congressionally approved state constitution only extended the right to vote to blacks and did not give them the right to hold legislative office. Despite its mistake in approving the constitution, the Republican Congress responded predictably by expelling Georgia and put the state back under military rule. The military commander then reinstalled the dismissed blacks in the legislature, and Georgia was once again admitted to the Union as a Radical state government in summer 1871.

Meanwhile, Georgia's autumn 1870 elections put conservatives back in control of the legislature. In October 1871, the Radical governor resigned rather than face impeachment charges for authorizing dubious state bonds. The following month, a conservative Democrat was elected to replace him because the Republicans had no candidate. In short, Georgia endured only two years of Radical rule, but the state's debt climbed from $1 million to $18 million during that period. In one example of the excesses, the carpetbag manager of the state-owned railroad explained that he was able to bank $30,000 a year for himself out of a $3,000 annual salary by exercising "the most rigid economy."[11]

Tennessee and Texas each endured about three years of carpetbag state government, although their Radical congressional representatives lingered for a few more years. When the Republican governor left for the US Senate in 1869, Tennessee was saddled with $21 million in debt, which was even more than Georgia, although the two states had comparable populations. Although the Texas Republican governor was honest, his legislature was not. The governor was ousted in an 1873 election, leaving the state with $4.5 million in debt and high taxes.

Shortly after Lincoln's death, President Johnson appointed W. W. Holden as North Carolina's governor. Holden evolved into a vindictive Radical Republican. Despite Holden's personal honesty, crooks surrounded him. Even though he used the state militia to intimidate opposition voters in two heavily Democratic counties during an 1870 election, he lost control of the legislature, which impeached him for using the militia to suppress votes. During Holden's tenure, North Carolina's indebtedness increased by $20 million, which was more than in either Georgia or Tennessee despite the Tar Heel State's smaller population.[12]

Arkansas's first Radical governor, Powell Clayton, also subdued opposition with a militia. Corruption was rampant. The state had the second smallest population in the former Confederacy, but its debt reached amounts comparable to larger states, rising from $3.5 million in 1868 to $15 million in 1875. To that amount should be added $5 million in local government indebtedness. By 1875, Arkansas's per capita debt exceeded $115, but it had almost nothing to show for such borrowings.

Clayton departed Little Rock for the US Senate in 1871 and left the governorship in the hands of a caretaker appointee. In an increasingly familiar pattern, a falling out among thieves led Arkansas's Republican Party to split in the 1872 general elections. Democrats were so demoralized by the fraudulent elections of the preceding four years that they did not even offer a candidate.

Both Republican candidates, Elisha Baxter and Joseph Brooks, claimed victory. As a result, a brief civil war erupted with militia fighting on both sides. About two hundred militia and citizens were killed. President Grant finally arbitrated on the side of Baxter. He threatened to use the US Army against Brooks's supporters if violence continued. Nonetheless, the split weakened the state's Republican Party, and Arkansas escaped Radical rule in the 1874 elections.[13]

Mississippi attempted to comply with the congressional plan by establishing a state Republican Party composed of conservative whites and newly freed blacks. It came as close as any state to fulfilling Lincoln's hope that erstwhile Whigs could become Republican Party leaders in the former Confederacy. The state's first elected Republican governor, James Alcorn, fit the bill.

Although Alcorn owned a twelve-thousand-acre plantation before the war, he opposed secession. While he served in the Confederate army for about a year, he conflicted with Jefferson Davis. Alcorn explained to his army superior that he (Alcorn) should resign if Richmond lacked confidence in him. The resignation was accepted. Upon returning home, he secretly sold cotton from his plantation to Northern buyers. In one letter to his wife about a cotton-selling expedition, he wrote that numerous other prominent Mississippians participated in the trade.

After Congress blocked Andrew Johnson's presidential Reconstruction, Alcorn believed that Mississippi could succeed under congressional terms if former Whigs united with freedmen to form a conservative Republican Party. He reasoned that the congressional mandates for universal black suffrage in the South and disfranchisement of many former Confederates would require Mississippi whites to ally with ex-slaves if the state was to have a responsible government. Further, he concluded, it would be necessary to grant blacks lawful equality in order to achieve such an alliance. He became governor in a landslide 1869 election victory.

Alcorn moved to the US Senate in 1871 to replace a black ally who had resigned to become president of Alcorn A&M College (founded by

Alcorn). In the Senate, he drew fire from the other Mississippi senator, Adelbert Ames, who was a Maine carpetbagger. At the time, Ames was not even a Mississippi citizen and had never paid taxes in the state.

But Ames had powerful political allies. Among them was his father-in-law, Benjamin F. Butler. Like Alcorn, during the Civil War Butler illegally traded commercially with the enemy while he commanded the Union occupation armies in New Orleans and Norfolk, Virginia. He quickly became famous as the first general to permit escaped slaves to remain free behind federal lines as "contraband of war."As noted in chapter 3, he was also the lead prosecutor in President Johnson's impeachment trial.

The Ames-Alcorn showdown came in 1873, when both ran for governor. When Ames won by a large majority, Alcorn took his followers into the Democratic Party. Ames had successfully disrupted Alcorn's white and freedmen alliance, and appointed many blacks to government offices, but otherwise his was a high-handed and rapacious administration. Whatever the progress of blacks, overall conditions in Mississippi were bad. The state government's operating costs soared by 1,400 percent and indebtedness multiplied. Finally, Ames did not like living in Mississippi, partly because his wife refused to join him there.

When Ames organized two regiments of black militia and requested federal troops from President Grant to prevent Mississippi whites from interfering with black voters, a race riot erupted in Vicksburg in December 1874. Under the threat of federal intervention, Mississippi Democrats compromised with Ames. If Ames would disband the state's militia, the Democrats promised the 1875 legislative elections would proceed without interference. A decisive Democratic victory led Ames to resign about six months later rather than face impeachment for various charges, most having to do with the incitement of race riots. Although it was generally quiet on the day of the election, the Democrats had not honored their promise, and prior threats and violence were sufficient to keep many blacks away from the polls. Consequently, Mississippi's carpetbaggers were overthrown.[14]

By the 1876 presidential election, only three Southern states, Florida, Louisiana, and South Carolina, remained under congressional Reconstruction rule. The story of how they ended carpetbag rule is told in chapter 7.

SIX

Railroaded

No single factor shaped America's economy during the fifty years between the Civil War and World War I more than the railroad industry. Ultimately it railroaded (in the slang meaning of the term) both the freedmen and the ordinary white Southerner.[1] Historians Samuel Eliot Morison and Henry Steele Commager wrote, "Twenty years after the attack on Fort Sumter the railroads alone represented a greater investment and concentration of power than had ever the slave interest, and their influence in politics and in the economic activities of free men were scarcely less far-reaching."[2]

When the war ended, the country had thirty-five thousand miles of track, but by 1900, the total was one hundred ninety-two thousand, which translated to a compound annual growth rate of 7.5 percent. In 1900, America's tracks accounted for about 40 percent of the world's total mileage. Railroad expansion stimulated growth in other backbone industries as well, such as iron and steel. It enabled cattle ranchers and farmers to tap into distant markets. It transformed Chicago into a metropolis, while towns bypassed by railroads withered. The telegraph and nascent telephone industries depended upon railroad right-of-ways to provide pathways for their wires. Although sporadic depressions made for uneven progress, by 1900, America had the world's mightiest economy. Finally, railroads eclipsed river traffic, which had dominated the earlier eras and favored the South.[3]

While the Republican Party schemed to retain political dominance through control of Reconstruction, the typical American outside the South was preoccupied with the economic opportunities of the emerging Gilded Age. Despite wretched and stubborn poverty in the South, historians of the Gilded Age simply overlook the region and describe the period as a halcyon era. For example, Matthew Josephson wrote, "The decade after the Civil War was on the whole an ingenious and lighthearted one." In writing of the industry moguls, he added, "The newly rich who had so quickly won to supreme power in the economic order enjoyed almost universal esteem for at least twenty years after the Civil War. Their glory was at its zenith; during this whole period they literally sunned themselves in the affection of popular opinion."[4]

There was not much room for the concerns of blacks and white Southerners. Racial equality, for example, was immaterial to iron and steel producers. They wanted protection against foreign competition. The Republicans obliged. From 1870 to the end of the century, the tariff duty on rails at times approached 100 percent. Consequently, railroads using British-produced rails would sometimes have to pay twice as much for the imports. Foreign producers discovered they were basically cut off from the American market. Therefore, US iron and steel output grew from 20 percent of Britain's 1870 production to a level that exceeded the combined production of Britain and Germany in 1910. Although California's black population was tiny, because of prejudice against Asian-Americans who immigrated to help build the railroads, it refused to ratify the Fourteenth Amendment until 1959.[5]

Californians were as much obsessed with railroads as anyone. Once the Central Pacific and Union Pacific connected in Utah, travel between their state and the population centers east of the Missouri River was a matter of days instead of weeks, or even months. As explained in the introduction, however, it would take years for the Union Pacific and Central Pacific to be profitable because of the low population density of the lands between the eastern and western terminals. Meanwhile, they would earn land grants and federal bonds for each mile of track laid. The Union Pacific was given twenty million acres, while the Central Pacific and its successors were given twenty-four million acres.[6]

Consequently, the leading shareholders of each railroad set up construction companies to build the tracks. If the railroads could not be immediately profitable the construction contractors could because they were empowered to charge their affiliated railroads whatever fees were required to turn a profit. The roads would pay with funds obtained through a combination of the applicable railroad's shareholder capital and government subsidies. The winners were the shareholders of the construction companies. Financial paybacks for the taxpayers and investors in the operating railroads were delayed.

Charles Crocker, Mark Hopkins, Leland Stanford, and Collis Huntington (the Big Four) were the sole owners of the Central Pacific's construction arm, the Contract & Finance Company. The railroad paid about $79 million in cash, bonds, and stock to Contract & Finance. Experts estimate that reasonable construction costs should have totaled about $40 million, thereby implying that the excess $39 million lined the pockets of the Big Four. When an 1873 congressional investigating committee asked to see the Contract & Finance Company records, Huntington explained that Hopkins had destroyed them because the railroad's construction had been completed four years previously.[7]

The Union Pacific's construction arm became infamous. George Train was a Union Pacific shareholder who had been assigned the duty of persuading potential investors to buy stock. He was largely unsuccessful but soon stumbled upon the construction company concept. The Boston-based Train had earlier founded a clipper ship line, which yielded overseas business acquaintances. He learned of two French brothers who had been successful in similar circumstances with construction companies named Crédit Mobilier and Crédit Foncier.

In order to attract investors into a Union Pacific construction company, Train realized the affiliate must provide limited liability. He located such a corporation in Pennsylvania that was comparatively inactive and bought it for a moderate sum. He changed the name to Crédit Mobilier of America. Its charter was perpetual and permitted the company to engage in most any kind of business. Like the Central Pacific's Contract & Finance Company, Crédit Mobilier was certain to be immediately profitable. Gifts of the shares were essentially donations of a stream of reliable dividends over the period of years that the Union Pacific remained under construction. Consequently, it was not long before shares of Crédit Mobilier were given to key politicians. The distributor was Massachusetts congressman Oakes Ames (no relation to Adelbert Ames).

Ames and his older brother, Oliver, earned a fortune supplying shovels and similar instruments during the California Gold Rush and the Civil War. They also furnished shovels for railroad construction, which led them to become involved with the Union Pacific. Oakes Ames started distributing shares of Crédit Mobilier to influential politicians in 1867 because, "We want more friends in this Congress. There is no difficulty getting men to look after their own property."

Railroad magnate Collis Huntington. (*Library of Congress*)

Five years later, his cover was blown during President Grant's 1872 reelection campaign. An anti-Grant newspaper discovered a partial list of recipients disclosed in testimony involving a Crédit Mobilier lawsuit. The list included Grant's previous vice president, Schuyler Colfax, and his current running mate, Henry Wilson. Other names on the list, or that were soon disclosed, included James Brooks, George Boutwell, William "Pig Iron" Kelley, John Bingham, James Patterson, and William Allison, as well as a future president, James Garfield. All but Brooks were Republicans and none were Southerners.[8]

Garfield and Kelley accepted dividends from shares that were bought with prior dividends, but the two were spared official reprimand. Wilson said he lost money on his transaction. Bingham was permitted to buy his stock at a bargain price without rebuke. Colfax and Patterson were seriously compromised but not officially reproved. In the end, only Brooks and Ames were censured, and both soon died. The public was appalled by the whitewashed investigations. Of his censure for gifting the shares, Ames correctly commented to a reporter, "It is just like the man in Massachusetts who committed adultery and the jury brought in a verdict that he was as guilty as the devil but that the woman was as innocent as an angel. [The non-censured recipients] are like that woman."[9]

More importantly, however, Crédit Mobilier was an early public indication of the shameless corruption and abuse of power that accompanied the railroad industry's growth. The industry compelled entire states to make land grants similar to those provided by the federal government. Texas, Minnesota, Wisconsin, and Illinois granted about fifty million acres. Cities and towns were routinely blackmailed to provide taxpayer funding if they did not wish to be bypassed by railroads under construction, or merely planned. One example was Los Angeles.[10]

After the Big Four connected the Central Pacific to the Union Pacific in Utah, they acquired the charter for the Southern Pacific, which was to connect San Francisco to Los Angeles and San Diego and proceed thence to the Mississippi River along a southern route. When the Big Four pondered bypassing Los Angeles in 1872, they asked the town of five thousand seven hundred people for $860,000 in financial aid, equal to about $150 per person. The request was granted. No doubt Angelenos were more concerned about the debt they had placed on themselves than in the civil rights of ex-slaves in a distant land they would likely never visit.[11]

Yet it was not just far-off Californians who were coerced or corrupted by railroads. If anything, railroad-induced venality was even more prevalent in the East, including the august state of New York. In 1868, two trunk lines connected New York with Chicago, the Erie and the New York Central. Cornelius "Commodore" Vanderbilt controlled the Central and wanted to own the Erie in order to secure a monopoly between the two cities. He began by buying stock on the open market. But as he kept buying, more shares mysteriously appeared for sale.

The shares were coming from the Erie itself. Jay Gould and Jim Fisk, who were both in their early thirties, ran the company. But they were financial speculators, not operating managers. They simply printed new stock certificates every time they chose to offer more shares on the market. Their legal authority for such action was dubious. Vanderbilt pressed his case in the courts, and Justice George Bernard of the state supreme court ordered Fisk and Gould to stop. (Bernard would later be convicted of accepting bribes.) In response, Fisk and Gould moved the Erie's headquarters to Jersey City, New Jersey, across the Hudson River from New York City.

More legal wrangling ensued over the next few weeks until Gould suddenly arrived in Albany with $500,000 in cash. Shortly thereafter, he came to a secret understanding with the legislators, which he later charged to Erie's books as a $1 million legal expense.

The two sides eventually settled their private war. Fisk and Gould had to reimburse Vanderbilt a portion of his losses, and Vanderbilt agreed to let the Erie remain independent. Since Fisk and Gould were speculators with little interest in the day-to-day operations of a business, the Erie remained a weak competitor to the Central.

Because Northern lawmakers could easily profit from railroad corruption, like the Angelenos they had little reason to be concerned about the civil rights of Southern freedmen beyond the electoral votes the blacks could provide. Increasingly, Northerners began to treat the South economically as an internal colony. It was consigned to be a source of raw materials and a secondary market for Northern manufactured goods.[12]

The meatpacking business provides an example. During the Civil War, Chicago packers like Armour, Swift, and Morris prospered by selling pork to the Union armies. Morris soon began sending frozen meat during the winter to markets as far away as Boston. Meanwhile, millions of beeves grazed aimlessly in Texas about one thousand miles from the nearest economical railhead at Abilene, Kansas. In 1867, cowboys drove the first thirty-five thousand cattle to Abilene over the Chisholm Trail. The trail's traffic grew rapidly over the next five years because of the slower rate at which the impoverished state of Texas could build railroads. It would be 1880—fifteen years after the war—before a Texas railroad connected to the national grid extended as far south as San Antonio.

Railroad magnate Jay Gould. (*Library of Congress*)

Texas supplied the cattle on the hoof, while Chicago dominated the greater value added associated with the slaughtering and packing business. In 1874, Swift introduced refrigeration cars, thereby enabling the processors to ship fresh beef instead of only smoked or frozen meat. Suddenly, distant markets were available perennially.[13]

When the Central Pacific and Union Pacific met in 1869, they created the first transcontinental railroad by connecting Omaha with Sacramento. As explained in chapter 1, however, it was not the best route. Because of Southern poverty, the better routes farther south remained a low priority during Reconstruction. The western reaches of the better route mapped in the 1850s out of Fort Smith, however, would later be used by the Santa Fe Railroad.[14]

Nonetheless, lines competitive to the Omaha-Sacramento route were planned. Tom Scott, who managed the Pennsylvania Railroad, backed the Texas & Pacific, which was to connect Texas with Southern California. It was also to have numerous feeder lines in the South for which Scott and the region hoped to obtain federal subsidies. Similarly, the leading financial underwriter of the nation's bond sales during the Civil War—Jay Cooke & Company—backed the Northern Pacific, which was even farther north than the Omaha-Sacramento route. It was to connect Lake Superior with Puget Sound. Although both companies were scarcely out of the planning stages, Cooke's superior ability to attract investors suggested that the Northern Pacific was the more serious contender.

Originally chartered by Congress in 1864, the Northern Pacific had not built a mile of track by 1870, when Cooke reasoned that he could buy the company at a bargain price if he could get Congress to extend the life of its charter and provide him other concessions. After paying consulting fees to one of President Grant's personal secretaries, Horace

Porter, he learned that Grant was "solid as a rock" on an 1870 bill tailor-made to his needs. Cooke decided to raise $100 million directly from investors by selling new issues of Northern Pacific securities in the United States and Europe. In order to stimulate demand among public investors, he persuaded prominent men to become shareholders. Examples included Horace Greeley, Henry Ward Beecher, a future president, Rutherford Hayes, and then-Vice President Schuyler Colfax.

The 1870 act gave the company more time to complete construction without losing rights to its land subsidies, which were unusually generous. It also permitted Cooke to collect a $200 fee in stock for each $1,000 bond sold as well as a 12 percent cash commission. As the railroad stretched west from Minnesota, rumors of corruption filtered back east. Civic leaders in the towns along the route competed to have their sites included on the line, and contractors seemed to be inflating construction costs. Still, Cooke was selling about a million dollars in bonds every month. Overseas investors arrived on junkets to ride the rails to the ever-lengthening end of the line. By late summer 1873, it had reached Bismarck in present-day North Dakota.

But the railroad was generating little revenue. Nearly all its operations and construction were funded by debt. Anything that prevented Cooke from selling more bonds and stock would cause the Northern Pacific to coast to a halt. The Crédit Mobilier scandal was just such a factor. The public perceived it as an indictment of widespread immorality within the railroad industry and the federal government.[15]

About six months after Congress concluded its Crédit Mobilier investigations, Jay Cooke & Company closed its doors. There could hardly have been a bigger surprise to the public confidence. One Philadelphia newspaper reported, "No one could have been more surprised if snow had fallen during a summer noon." Without new sales of Northern Pacific securities, Cooke & Company soon ran out of cash. The collapse came on September 18, 1873, when hinterland banks tried to remove their deposits with Cooke in order to pay farmers for their harvests. The night before it shut down, President Grant was a Cooke houseguest. The two had breakfast the morning of the debacle.[16]

Cooke's failure triggered a panic and then a depression. Massive blocks of railroad securities were quickly put on the market, but there were few buyers. Price declines of 50 percent were common among the leading rail stocks. Brokers called customers for more securities margin, but too many did not have enough cash or liquid collateral to meet the calls. Their brokers failed. The New York Stock Exchange closed for ten days, thereby amplifying the panic. Business failures in 1873 climbed to five thousand from four thousand in 1872 and three thousand in 1871. Cooke's failure was a tocsin for five ensuing years of depression.

Railroads had overbuilt. There was not enough traffic to support the available capacity. In 1860, America had about one thousand residents for each mile of track, but in 1873, density had dropped to about six hundred per mile. About half of the nation's railroads were bankrupted during the resulting depression. No geographical region was untouched. Municipal and state government bonds issued to build the roads remained taxpayer obligations even if the applicable railroad was never built. Towns that gave bonds or cash to roads that failed typically lost all they gave. By the end of 1876, the industry had defaulted on more than $800 million in debt. By comparison, the total federal debt that year was $2.2 billion. Railroad operating revenues dropped by a third.

Track construction also declined by a third in 1874, causing five hundred thousand layoffs within the railroad ecosystem, including the iron and steel industry. Prices fell. Philadelphia pig iron dropped from $56 a ton in 1872 to $17 five years later. Wages fell between 40 and 60 percent from 1873 to 1877. When the poverty income line was a dollar a day, ten thousand Massachusetts textile workers and sixty thousand Pennsylvania miners fell under the threshold. The country seemed to be overrun with hoboes and vagrants.[17]

Nonetheless, the situation was even worse in the South, where per capita income was about half the depressed national average. Under the stress of a depression, however, voters outside the region were little concerned with the South's economic conditions, or the status of ex-slaves.[18]

Initially, railroads responded by cutting rates to compete for the shrinking traffic. Since that merely intensified bottom-line financial pressure, they colluded to allocate the available traffic at common rates in traffic-sharing pools. Toward the end of the 1870s, four trunk lines—New York Central, Erie, Pennsylvania, and Baltimore & Ohio—connected Chicago with the East. In 1877, they organized a pool to divide up the traffic. Next, they raised rates and cut wages.[19]

In response, the workers went on strike. The Great Railroad Strike of 1877 was the first to affect large parts of the country. It started in Martinsburg, West Virginia, and spread quickly to Baltimore, Pittsburgh, Buffalo, Chicago, and St. Louis. It even reached Galveston, Texas, where black and white workers stood united, but it was concentrated in the North.

State militias were deployed to break the strikes in West Virginia, Maryland, New York, Ohio, Illinois, and Pennsylvania. The industry also requested federal troops, which were provided in Pittsburgh, Chicago,

St. Louis, and elsewhere. Since organized labor was incipient in 1877, the work stoppage lasted only about a month. The workers gained nothing. Railroads in bankruptcy used the courts to invoke conspiracy charges against strike leaders, while the profitable railroads blacklisted others. Historian Sean Cashman wrote that the strike "seemed to the upper and middle classes like a slave uprising."[20]

The Cooke-triggered depression led President Grant to set the future direction of the Republican Party. Congress gave him an opportunity to choose between an inflationary or deflationary monetary policy. Workers, farmers, and heavily indebted businessmen wanted an inflationary policy, whereas well-financed businesses and bankers wanted a deflationary one. Grant made his choice on the side of the wealthy. Specifically, he vetoed a bill that would have increased the circulation of legal tender in the form of paper currency that was not backed by specie. As a result, according to biographer William McFeely, "Grant's veto made the stand of the Republican party official. From this date [April 22, 1874] it was the party not of the working class but of those who were or aspired to be the capitalists."[21]

Although the overbuilt railroad capacity led to rate competition, the benefits to shippers were not evenly distributed. Rates were determined by competition as opposed to cost of service. Shippers that were served by more than one line got the best rates since competing carriers fought for traffic. But the railroads with tracks in sparsely populated farming areas could charge much higher rates because shippers on isolated lines generally had no alternative way of sending their products to market. Because of their limited capacity, horse drawn wagons were much more expensive and water routes were limited. Not until the advent of national paved highways and large capacity trucks did the railroads face effective competition.

Thus, at harvest time, nearly all farmers were at the mercy of the local railroad, which usually monopolized access to major markets. The agrarians retaliated by joining the nascent Patrons of Husbandry, commonly known as the Grange, and other organizations such as the Southern Alliance, Northern Alliance, and [Southern] Colored Farmers Alliance. The Grange began as a social union that evolved into a buyer's collective that enabled members to purchase items in bulk at lower prices. It gradually became more political and by 1874 had 1.5 million members in the West and South. Grange chapters lobbied their states for railroad rate regulations, either by law or by regulatory commissions.[22]

State railroad commissions began in New England in 1839, where they mostly protected the industry against farmers. In 1873, Illinois became the first state to form a commission with rate-making authority. Over the next fifteen years, about half the states created similar commissions. But like the New England commissions, they often reflected the interests of the railroads as much as, or more than, the shippers. Consequently, the Grange soon turned against the concept of commissions, preferring statutory prohibitions. As early as 1877, the chief attorney for the New York Central concluded that regulatory protection was as important for the industry as it was for the shippers. From the industry's viewpoint, the Cooke-induced depression had unleashed ruinous rate competition that could only be checked by mandatory regulation.[23]

US representative from Texas John H. Reagan. (*Library of Congress*)

In 1872, Congress passed an amnesty act that restored voting privileges to all but about five hundred former Confederates. One result was the election of the Confederacy's previous postmaster general, John H. Reagan, to the US House from Texas in 1874. In 1877, he introduced a railroad regulation bill that outlawed discriminatory rates, rebates, drawbacks, and traffic-sharing pools. Unlike earlier proposals, his bill did not include a commission, because of his concern that railroad interests might dominate it. Instead, enforcement would be through the courts, which would enable shippers to win judgments on the merits of their case. The bill passed the House in a 139–104 vote, with support concentrated in the South and present-day Midwest.

The Senate, however, refused to consider the bill. It passed the House again in 1885, and this time the Senate set up a study committee. The public demanded protection from rate gouging, and the industry was fearful of nationalization, which had been happening in other countries such as Belgium, France, Austria, Prussia, and even Canada. Meanwhile, the Supreme Court's 1886 *Wabash v. Illinois* decision ruled that state commissions could not regulate traffic that crossed state lines, thereby rendering 90 percent of rail traffic free of state regulation.

The result was the 1887 Interstate Commerce Act, which outlawed certain discriminatory practices and established the Interstate Commerce Commission (ICC). The commission's punitive and rate-making authority was promptly challenged by the railroad industry. During the ICC's first eighteen years, railroads challenged it in sixteen appeals to the Supreme Court and won fifteen of them, including a ruling that prevented the ICC from setting maximum rates. During the ICC's first decade, aggrieved shippers were victorious in only 5 of 225 cases.

Following the formation of the ICC, investment bankers J. P. Morgan, Brown Brothers, Barings, and Kidder Peabody informally agreed to avoid financing new lines parallel to the railroads already operating. In return, the existing roads unofficially agreed to avoid aggressive rate competition. The financiers exercised control through a network of interlocking directorships. The effect was that of a traffic-sharing pool encompassing twelve of the largest railroads that stretched across the country.[24]

Republican US senator Nelson Aldrich of Rhode Island, a champion of Northern industry, privately called the act a "delusion and a sham. . . . An empty menace to the great, made to answer the clamor of the ignorant and unreasoning." Grover Cleveland's attorney general, Richard Olney of Massachusetts, told one railroad executive that the ICC "satisfies the popular clamor for a government supervision of railroads at the same time that the supervision was entirely nominal. Further, the older such a Commission gets to be, the more inclined it will be to take the business and railroad view of things. It thus becomes a . . . barrier between the railroad corporations and a . . . protection against . . . legislation hostile to railroad interests." Liberal Supreme Court justice John Harlan of Kentucky considered the ICC "a useless body for all practical purposes." Northerners had pulled the teeth out of the Reagan bill. Agrarian interests, particularly those in the South, where the average farm size was smaller, got little benefit from the ICC for decades.[25]

Nonetheless, the commission gradually gained more control over the railroads. The 1903 Elkins Act prohibited freight rebates to large shippers. The 1906 Hepburn Act permitted the ICC to set maximum rates. Railroads counterattacked with the 1910 Mann-Elkins Act that established an independent Commerce Court—analogous to the present-day Tax Court—to more promptly contest ICC rulings. It was abolished in less than five years partly because the railroads won most disputes. After America entered World War I, the industry was temporarily nationalized because of gridlock along the Eastern Seaboard as supplies and troops were shipped to Europe. During nationalization, railroad rates increased nearly 30 percent, providing a favorable rate legacy when private companies resumed control of the industry in 1920.[26]

DESPITE ENORMOUS financial subsidies during the carpetbag era, the South's share of America's track mileage dropped by 20 percent in the 1870s. Most of the region's new lines went into bankruptcy after the failure of Cooke & Company in 1873. All the lines that went into receivership were purchased at bargain prices by Northern investors such as Collis Huntington, thereby "fixing the regional economy even more firmly in a colonial mold," according to historian Eric Foner.[27]

A genuine railroad construction boom did not begin in the South until 1879, when new track mileage was double the amount of any previous year. Over the next two years, Southern railroads attracted more than $150 million of outside capital. But the 1893 economic panic and ensuing depression once again forced many of the lines to sell. Northern investors such as J. P. Morgan and the Belmont "Pennsylvania Group" were the chief buyers. By 1900, only two major Southern railroads were not controlled by Northern interests.[28]

After World War I, America's railroads were returned to their private operators. The ICC, however, was given a new mission in the 1920 Transportation Act. Its policy shifted from one of protecting the public from rate abuses to one of ensuring the health of the railroad industry. Railroads were not permitted to freely compete. The ICC issued certificates of convenience and necessity that defined the route structure of each railroad. It also established minimum rates, which prevented any railroad from gaining market share by offering rates below the minimum. The revised policy remained in place until 1975.[29]

The new agenda led to a clash with Southern governors in the late 1930s when it was obvious that their region was the most economically deprived part of the country. Alabama governor Bibb Graves declared, "This freight rate business is at the heart of the whole Southern problem." Georgia governor Ellis Arnall, who became the leading regional spokesman, agreed that rates in the South were artificially inflated. He accused the North of keeping the South in a colonial status in which it served as the "economic doormat of the United States as Ireland was to the United Kingdom." He complained that the ICC permitted over 90 percent of new railroad rate filings to be implemented without objection even though the commission was supposed to ensure that rates were fair and reasonable. At last, a White House occupant—Franklin Roosevelt—was sympathetic.

Almost from the beginning, the ICC sanctioned discriminatory regional railroad rates. Even before it was formed, Southern railroads, most operating under Northern control, charged more per mile than did Northern ones. The disparities were officially acknowledged at the beginning of the twentieth century but were excused on the basis of higher Southern operating cost due to lower population density and seasonal shipment patterns. No careful study was made until 1939, when rates for the same service in the South were found to be 39 percent higher than in the North while those in the Southwestern region (Arkansas, Louisiana, Oklahoma, Texas, and part of New Mexico) were 75 percent higher. The differentials were so discriminatory, for example, that remote Northern manufacturers could ship finished goods to the South at lower cost than Southern makers of the same items could distribute them within their own region.

Due to a shortage of capital in the South for many years after the Civil War, Northern railroads steadily increased their ownership of Southern operators. They quickly began using the rate differentials to block Southern competition to principal Northern shippers such as steel producers and the makers of other manufactured goods. When asked in 1890 why shipping rates into the North for Southern iron products were higher, one Pennsylvania Railroad agent replied, "It was done at the request of the Pennsylvania iron men." Yet because of the region's wealth and population concentration, all manufacturers needed access to Northern markets if they were to compete on a national scale. Without such access they could not achieve the high production volumes needed for low-unit-cost selling prices. As a means of impeding competition from Southern and Western manufacturers, the discriminatory rates were as effective as protective tariffs, which were constitutionally prohibited between states.[30]

As late as 1938, the National Emergency Council's *Report on Economic Conditions in the South* for President Roosevelt explained:

> In effect, this difference in freight rates creates a manmade . . . barrier. [S]outhern manufacturers are hampered because attractive markets are restricted by . . . a barrier that is now completely artificial. The southern producer . . . finds his goods barred from the . . . nation's most populous area [north of the Ohio and Potomac Rivers.]
>
> Two chief reasons for higher freight rates have disappeared. One was the greater expense of railroading in the South, due to physical difficulties, [which] has been minimized by modern engineering. Another was the comparative lack of traffic. . . . This no longer is the case. . . . The operating costs of southern lines today are lower than those in the . . . territory . . . [north of the Ohio and Potomac Rivers.]
>
> The artificial rate structure handicaps the South in its efforts to expand and diversify its industry. For example . . . it is cheaper to concentrate and ship [southern] zinc ore to the North, where it is made into metallic zinc, used to coat northern steel, and shipped back to the South for its tin roofs . . . than it is to convert this zinc ore in the South without the economic loss of cross hauling.[31]

In 1889, when Andrew Carnegie toured the emerging Southern steel industry centered in Birmingham, he declared, "the South is Pennsylvania's most formidable industrial enemy." About ten years later, Carnegie's mills were merged into—and became the largest component of—Pittsburgh-based U. S. Steel. Six years later, U. S. Steel purchased the biggest Southern steel mills and imposed discriminatory pricing on Southern production. Thereafter, steel from the company's Alabama mills included an incremental markup, termed the "Birmingham Differential," of $3 per ton over the Pittsburgh quote.

To further penalize Alabama production, buyers of Birmingham steel were required to pay freight from Birmingham plus a phantom charge as if the shipments originated in Pittsburgh.

After Woodrow Wilson became president, the Federal Trade Commission (FTC) investigated the matter and concluded that Birmingham's steel production costs were the lowest in the country and 26 percent below those of Pittsburgh. Yet U.S. Steel continued to require a $3 per ton Birmingham Differential on Alabama steel, which was raised to $5 after 1920. Six months after the differential was finally abolished in 1939, shipbuilding plants in Pascagoula, Mississippi, and Mobile, Alabama, announced major expansions.[32]

The chief exceptions to higher Southern freight charges were commodity rates for raw materials. Cotton, sugar, iron ore, coal, and petroleum were shipped out of the South at lower rates, but the prime beneficiaries were the Northern manufacturers that transformed the raw materials into finished goods. (Based in New York, American Sugar controlled 98 percent of the refined market and sold under the still-familiar Domino brand.) They perpetuated the South's dependence upon imports, or Northern tariff-protected manufacturers, for finished goods. While cotton and cottonseed oil moved out of the South at low rates, those rates increased sharply in proportion to the fineness of the textiles or finished food products made from the raw materials. The effect was to suppress Southern industrial development.[33]

Finally, in the late 1930s, Southern governors banded together and filed a complaint involving the rates applicable to fourteen items manufactured in the South. After two years of hearings, the ICC handed down a 5–4 decision in favor of the Southern governors. In November 1939, it ordered rate reductions on ten of the fourteen items. The decision reversed the commission's long-standing position that a presumed higher cost of service in the South justified higher rates.

The Transportation Act of 1940 required the ICC to investigate and eliminate geographically discriminatory rates on all freight classes. In

January 1944, Roosevelt told Georgia governor Arnall that the president wanted discriminatory regional rates to end. In May 1944, Georgia filed an antitrust lawsuit against twenty-three railroads for conspiring on rates and named the ICC as a co-conspirator. In June 1944, the ICC completed its investigation. In a 7–2 decision it ruled that rates in the North be increased by 10 percent and that those in the South and West be reduced by 10 percent.[34]

It took eighty years for the South to start getting some relief from regional railroad rate discrimination.

SEVEN

Corrupted

Perhaps nothing could have better promoted just and effective Southern Reconstruction than ethical leadership in Washington. The federal example would have radiated across the country as a role model for state and local governments everywhere. Unpunished bribery in Congress was nearly certain to affect the morals of political leaders in the hinterlands. None would be more likely to follow Washington's lead than the Republican regimes in the South that were the children of Radical Reconstruction.

Unfortunately, congressional Republicans started setting a poor example during the Johnson administration, almost immediately after the war ended. It culminated with the shameful and failed effort to impeach Johnson that would have enfeebled the executive branch and given Congress tyrannical power for decades thereafter. Regrettably, ethics declined even lower during the eight years of Ulysses S. Grant's presidency, this time in both the congressional and executive branches. The Crédit Mobilier incident discussed earlier was only the tip of the iceberg. At least ten other scandals rocked the Grant administration, often touching family members. According to historians Louis Hacker and Benjamin

Kendrick, who were not influenced by current attempts to rehabilitate Grant, the mutation point in Grant's evolution from military leader to political opportunist was his break with Johnson. Thereafter, Grant was transformed from a "first-rate soldier into a time-serving, third-rate politician."[1]

Grant got off to a bad start in the selection of his personal aides and cabinet.

He entered the White House in March 1869 with three former army assistants, John Rawlins, Horace Porter, and Orville Babcock. Each would be touched by scandal. Rawlins advocated war with Spain in order to liberate Cuba. When he died six months after Grant's inauguration, his estate included $28,000 in Cuban bonds that would be valueless without the defeat of Spain but worth full value upon a successful Cuban revolution. Porter was implicated, but not convicted, in improprieties involving an attempted gold market corner, customs house profiteering in New York, and influence peddling to secure favorable legislation for Jay Cooke's Northern Pacific Railroad. Babcock was even more strongly implicated, but also not convicted, in misconduct involving tax evasion in the distilled spirits industry and attempts to profit from a failed effort to annex Santo Domingo as well as the attempted gold market corner.[2]

Grant did not consult with Republican leaders about his cabinet appointments. His choice of Alexander Stewart as Treasury secretary underscored his infatuation with the wealthy. Stewart owned a retailing empire that made him one of America's richest men. The appointment, however, violated an eighteenth century law that prohibited business owners from holding the post. When informed of the problem, Grant unsuccessfully asked Congress to grant a waiver. When forced to choose a successor, he selected George S. Boutwell who insisted that federal war bonds be redeemed in specie (gold or silver coins) even though they were often purchased with discounted paper currency. Earlier, as a failed Missouri farmer, Grant was personally familiar with the hardships that such a stern monetary policy would impose on nonbondholders. Nonetheless, his sympathies shifted to the wealthy classes after he became accustomed to gifts such as donations of residential and vacation homes from men like Jay Cooke. His selection for secretary of state, Elihu Washburne, was an Illinois political crony who helped promote Grant's interests during the Civil War and who held the state post only a matter of days before being reassigned as ambassador to France. Washburne may merely have wanted to burnish his resumé.[3]

The president's scandal-ridden tenure began with nepotism. One Grant cousin was appointed minister to Guatemala, and a brother-in-law was named counsel to Leipzig. Another brother-in-law, James Casey, was a customs collector in New Orleans, where he profited by skimming fees. Grant's wife's brother, Frederick Dent, was employed by the White House and profited from selling insider information. A total of forty relatives were estimated to have benefitted financially, directly or indirectly, while Grant was president.[4]

The first scandal, and one of the biggest, began only a few months after Grant took office and culminated in the collapse of the gold market in September 1869. Financiers Jay Gould and Jim Fisk hatched a scheme to drive the price of gold up and corner the market. Since the underlying gold contracts could be used as collateral for loans to buy those very contracts, immense profits could be realized on the smallest of out-of-pocket margin payments. The key was to ensure that the US Treasury did not sell gold on the exchange and thereby drive the price down.

In order to keep the Treasury out of the market, Gould arranged to gift gold purchase contracts to influential Republicans, Grant family members, and White House insiders. Among them was former Civil War general Daniel Butterfield, who, as an assistant US treasurer, was well situated to provide advance warning of pending Treasury gold sales. Another was Abel Corbin, who was the husband of one of Grant's sisters. Also implicated, as noted, were White House aides Porter and Babcock. Jim Fisk believed that the president's wife was involved. Adams Express Company records reveal that she received an ambiguously disclosed amount of money delivered to her at the White House, which some congressmen speculated was for the profit received on gold purchase contracts gifted to her. She wrote a personal letter to her sister-in-law Mrs. Corbin shortly before Treasury sales buckled the market that led Grant biographer McFeely to conclude:

> She knew little of the ways of the New York financial world, but she knew everything about being deprived of money. She believed fervently that her Ulysses—and she—deserved well of the Republic, and she lived in a world that, in large part, saw rewards in terms of money. They had been able to accept gratefully . . . houses with closets full of fine linen, financed by [gifted] subscription; why could there not be a small loan permitting her to make a perfectly legal investment?[5]

While the gold corner episode was forming, Grant launched a failed effort to annex Santo Domingo, the island containing present-day Haiti and the Dominican Republic. It was done without regard for the wishes of the residents and became another example of attempted profiteering by Oliver Babcock and others. Grant wanted to transform Santo Domingo into a largely black territory by emigrating freedmen from the South. Migration was, after all, a traditional American method of bettering one's prospects. The Santo Domingo idea, however, was as impracticable as Lincoln's wartime proposal for blacks to move to Nicaragua. Ex-slaves simply didn't want to go.

When the effort stalled in the Senate, where treaty ratification was necessary, in January 1870 Grant called upon Senator Charles Sumner, who headed the chamber's Foreign Relations Committee. The president hoped to appeal to the senator's well-known sympathy for freedmen. Upon leaving the meeting Grant believed he had secured Sumner's agreement, but he was either mistaken or Sumner reneged. To complicate matters, Grant's own secretary of state, Hamilton Fish, privately opposed annexation.

The Senate held hearings to investigate rumored corruption involving treaty negotiations. Interrogation suggested that Babcock had been given land on the island that would increase greatly in value upon annexation. The investigations also revealed that Babcock used the US Navy to sustain the rule of one of the island's political leaders who favored annexation. Since Grant stuck doggedly by Babcock and annexation in the face of such disclosures, the public came to doubt his putative motivations, and annexation failed.[6]

Grant struck back by removing John Motley, a Sumner protégé, as ambassador to Great Britain despite the fact that it was a critical time of negotiations between the two countries. Diplomats were trying to reach a financial settlement to compensate the United States for Great Britain's interference with US maritime commerce by providing the Confederacy with warships to raid Northern cargo ships during the Civil War. Motley's replacement, former congressman Robert Schenck, was a bad choice. Already a paid influence peddler for Jay Cooke's Northern Pacific, he quickly embarrassed America in London by selling worthless Utah mining securities to British aristocrats.[7]

Shortly before Grant's re-election in 1872, it was discovered that at least two presidential appointees at the New York Customs House were profiting by abusing their influence. At the time, customs duties were the principal source of federal tax revenue, and New York was the major collection point. Appointees Moses Grinnell and Thomas Murphy stored imports in private warehouses and charged shippers excessive storage fees. Grant's friend, George Leek, was allegedly also involved.[8]

Another scandal involved the post office. In the early 1870s, independent contractors delivered mail in sparsely populated regions of the country. They normally used a horse and buggy, whereas railroads and steamships sent the mail between towns and cities where postal employees distributed the letters locally, but not in the countryside, where the independent contractors had the job. Since the rural contract routes were notated on post office ledgers by three asterisks, they were informally known as Star Routes.

Bidders won lucrative Star Route awards through bribery and confined the selected contractors to a closed group of participants by straw bidding. Bribe participants included delivery contractors, postal employees, and intermediary brokers. Newcomers were kept out of the ring when participating members deliberately submitted artificially low bids, which they were later permitted to renegotiate at more lucrative rates through bribery. Grant's first postmaster general, John Creswell, was officially exonerated by an 1872 congressional investigation, although the committee's minority report censured him. The practice survived until President Chester A. Arthur shut it down in 1882, when one of the leading culprits was the chairman of the Republican Party.[9]

Shortly after the whitewashed Crédit Mobilier investigations were concluded, Congress had the insensitivity to secretly vote a salary increase for its members and other high government officials in March 1873. President Grant was given a raise from $25,000 to $50,000 yearly. House members and senators gave themselves raises from $5,000 to $7,500 annually and provided themselves a bonus of $5,000 for the previous two years. After newspapers disclosed the developments and the failure of Jay Cooke & Company started an economic depression, public pressure forced Congress to repeal the law in January 1874. Congressmen also reimbursed the Treasury for the bonuses distributed earlier. President Grant, however, was permitted to keep his raise, as were the Supreme Court justices.[10]

After his re-election in 1872, Grant appointed a new Treasury secretary, William A. Richardson, whose term of office would be cut short. Soon after he was appointed, it was discovered that Richardson had been involved in questionable activities when he was an assistant to the prior Treasury secretary. Urged by Senator Benjamin Butler of Massachusetts, Richardson had appointed John D. Sanborn to identify and collect delinquent taxes in the Bay State. Sanborn earned a 50 percent commission on the collections. He simply went to the Boston internal revenue office and secured a copy of an already-compiled list of delinquents. The collections required no effort whatsoever. While the procedure was legal, it was egregiously abusive. Sanborn was paid $213,000 for collecting $420,000 in taxes.

A later congressional investigation revealed that Sanborn split $156,000 of his fee with unnamed persons, which he charged off as "expenses." Richardson and Butler were suspected of being the unidentified beneficiaries, but there was no proof. Sanborn refused to identify the recipients of the $156,000.[11]

As noted in the introduction, in 1871, Grant's removal of Attorney General Amos Akerman, who had been a vigorous defender of freedmen, was partly triggered by railroad lobbyists who objected to Akerman's less-than-generous attitude toward the industry's federal subsidies.

Grant's failure to correct his eldest son's racial prejudice provides another reason to doubt the president's sincerity for the interests of African Americans beyond their role as a voting bloc in the South to provide congressional and electoral votes for the Republican Party.

In 1870, the first black cadet, James Smith, was admitted to West Point but was harassed out of the corps in about a year. Grant's eldest son, Fred, was also a cadet at the time and scheduled to graduate in 1871. Although Fred could have been a great help to Smith, he was likely on the side of Smith's harassers. While Fred denied organizing a conspiracy against Smith, he never denied being a member. After the persecution started, Smith's sponsor met with the president while Fred was in the room. Fred volunteered, "[N]o damn nigger will ever graduate from West Point." Despite his unprecedented influence with the military, Grant was silent and did nothing to promote racial integration at the academy by helping Smith.[12]

After Richardson was forced out of the Treasury by the Sanborn scandal, Grant selected Benjamin Bristow as the new Treasury secretary. Bristow discovered the biggest fraud of the Grant era, which involved the evasion of the whiskey tax. Although import duties were the largest source of federal revenue at the time, there were also a number of internal excise taxes, and those on distilled spirits were the biggest. Distillers and distributors routinely evaded the tax by bribing federal collectors to supply stamps in amounts greater than the actual taxes paid. Then, as today, stamps were affixed to unopened bottles. After 1870, an estimated ten million to fifteen million gallons of distilled spirits escaped taxes. The shortage was generally known, but it was Bristow who discovered the culprit.

A St. Louis newspaper reporter found the first traces of the criminal's trail in 1875. Bristow obtained a $125,000 congressional appropriation to investigate. The St. Louis collector, General John McDonald, was implicated. Over the objections of both Missouri senators, Grant had appointed the disreputable McDonald, from whom the president had received gifts, including a fine pair of horses. After McDonald was caught, investigators claimed he promised to collect all the taxes owed if he would be granted immunity from prosecution. Initially the president seemed to encourage the investigation, even though McDonald was a close friend. Grant's attitude changed, however, when the evidence trail led to Orville Babcock and the White House.

Eventually Bristow recovered over $3 million in whiskey taxes. He launched almost 250 civil and criminal lawsuits, and about 350 men were arrested. Despite such successes, Grant dismissed him after two years, although it was officially termed a resignation. Even though Bristow was convinced that presidential aides Babcock and Porter were complicit, Bristow refused to testify against Grant by invoking executive privilege after Grant left office.

Evidently, Grant did not believe Porter was guilty, and he protected Babcock all he could. When Babcock learned Bristow had enough evidence to indict him, he asked for a military court of inquiry based on his status as an army officer. The cabinet reluctantly agreed, and Grant selected loyal tribunal members. The judge advocate general (i.e., prosecutor) had previously done legal work for Babcock. Although Babcock was officially cleared, he left the White House under a cloud of suspicion when Grant appointed him to the lonely sinecure of a lighthouse inspector. About eight years later, Babcock drowned on a Florida inspection trip.[13]

Grant biographer McFeely ponders:

> There is no getting round the evidence tying [Babcock] to McDonald . . . [who] went to jail. While there, McDonald wrote a fascinating book . . . in which he made no bones about the fact that Babcock ought to have been there with him. And surprisingly, Babcock carefully preserved material . . . that fully corroborates his guilt. Why . . . ? [One] possibility . . . is that Ulysses or Julia Grant too [were] banking the proceeds of some of the frauds and Babcock could prove it. McDonald came right out and said that the president was doing just that. However, he did not offer any concrete evidence.[14]

EARLY IN GRANT'S second term, another scandal erupted in the Interior Department, where land grants to homesteaders, railroads, and industrialists were administered. Interior Secretary Columbus Delano took bribes in awarding some grants and in ruling upon the authorized uses of such grants. Additionally, he hired his son, John, and President Grant's brother, Orvil, to execute lucrative cartographical contracts. Neither was qualified nor had ever previously performed such work. Columbus Delano resigned in October 1875, and his successor discovered that some patent clerks employed by Delano were fictitious and others never performed any work.[15]

A few months before George Armstrong Custer and 263 members of the 7th Cavalry were killed at the Battle of the Little Bighorn in June 1876, misconduct involving bribery for awards of Indian trading posts by War Secretary William Belknap and his wife became public. Custer was among those who disclosed it. Furthermore, he suffered Grant's wrath for accusing the president's brother, Orvil, of being involved.

Since every trading post was a monopoly, the shops enjoyed high profit margins despite the fact that Native Americans were poor. The *New York Times* estimated that a $15,000 investment in a post would return $40,000. Belknap's first wife originated the plan to award posts in exchange for a share of profits at each one. After she died unexpectedly, Belknap married her sister, who urged the secretary to continue the practice. As is often the case with corruption, once started it inevitably grew until the culprits were exposed.

As the situation began to unravel, Grant realized that the trail might once again lead to the White House and family members. Orville Babcock's brother had one post that he "rented" at a good profit. Julia's brother, John Dent, also had a post that he specifically requested in a letter nine years earlier. Orvil Grant admitted having a partial interest in two posts.

In March 1876, Belknap went to the White House and, in tears, confessed his guilt to Grant. The secretary realized he was likely to soon be impeached and asked Grant to accept a one-sentence resignation letter because Belknap reasoned that if he was no longer secretary of war he could not be impeached. Grant promptly obliged, accepting the resignation "with great regret." An enraged investigating House committee soon got the word but presented the Senate with an impeachment anyway. Belknap was acquitted because the conviction votes fell short of the necessary two-thirds majority. Nonetheless, twenty-three senators who thought him guilty voted for acquittal chiefly because they assumed the technicality of his resignation prevented an impeachment since he no longer held office.[16]

When Grant first became president in 1869, most observers were puzzled by his selection of Adolph Borie as secretary of the navy. Few business or political leaders had heard of the modestly accomplished

Philadelphia businessman. Shortly after Borie took office, the Philadelphia grain merchants of Cattell & Company began receiving sizable contracts. Borie resigned after serving only three months, but Cattell continued to execute the contracts under Borie's successor, George M. Robeson. About seven years later, Robeson released his bankbook to a congressional investigating committee. It showed that he made deposits of $320,000 during the time he was navy secretary on a salary of $8,000 a year. Robeson was also accused of accepting a vacation home in Long Branch, New Jersey, from the Cattell family. Nonetheless, upon investigation, the financial records of Cattell & Company were in such disorder that Robeson could not be convicted of bribe taking despite the powerful circumstantial evidence.[17]

Grant's second term ended in 1876. Although he was interested in running for a third term, the twin burdens of his scandal-ridden administration and the economic depression triggered by Jay Cooke's failure dashed his hopes. At the June Republican convention in Cincinnati, the two leading contenders were former House Speaker James G. Blaine of Maine and Senator Roscoe Conkling of New York. Both, however, were out of step with a rising public cry for honest government.

Blaine had regularly used his influence to benefit railroad interests and was implicated in dubious financial dealings. In one episode, he earned generous commissions when selling bonds to prominent Maine constituents of an Arkansas railroad that he had helped legislatively. When the railroad failed, Blaine repurchased the bonds to protect his investors from loss. To avoid absorbing the loss himself, however, he sold the worthless bonds to the Union Pacific Railroad. Since the Union Pacific had benefitted from Blaine's legislative activities for years, it paid Blaine an inflated price for the securities and put them in a company investment account. As for Roscoe Conkling, he was a strong proponent of the political spoils system, which the public increasingly regarded as a prime source of corruption. Eventually, Republicans settled on a compromise candidate, Ohio governor Rutherford B. Hayes. He promised reforms.

Later in June, the Democrats met in St. Louis and quickly nominated New York governor Samuel Tilden. He earned his credentials by exposing and destroying New York City's notorious Tammany Hall political machine. Even though Tammany's Boss Tweed was also a Democrat, Tilden's prosecution put him behind bars after Tweed first fled the country, and was captured in Spain.

Shortly after his nomination, Tilden wrote a 4,400-word letter explaining his positions. Similar to Hayes, when addressing the racial and regional divides, he urged "the moral influence of every good citizen to establish a cordial fraternity . . . among citizens, whatever their race or color" and pledged to enforce the laws to "protect every political and personal right" of all citizens. But he also denounced the "insupportable [carpetbag] misgovernments imposed on the South" and called for the removal of "every obstacle to a . . . reconciliation between kindred populations once unnaturally estranged." Aside from his vague stance on Reconstruction, Southerners had misgivings about his traditional association with the railroad industry as well as his advocacy for hard money policies that were burdensome to farmers, especially those with heavy mortgages.[18]

Tilden was the apparent winner of the November 7 election. He had a 51 percent to 48 percent popular vote majority amounting to a 250,000-vote margin. Of the 185 electoral votes required to win, most tallies gave Tilden 184 uncontested votes compared to 166 for Hayes. carpetbag regimes were still clinging to power in Florida, Louisiana, and South Carolina, which had a total of 19 electoral votes. Republican politicos decided to challenge the apparent Tilden victories in those three states. Additionally, one Hayes elector in Oregon who was a postmaster was disputed because his status as a federal officeholder disqualified him from being an elector. Tilden needed to win only one of the doubtful contests to become president, whereas Hayes needed all four. On November 8, Tilden believed he was president-elect, as did candidate Hayes, President Grant, and nearly everyone else.

The carpetbag-controlled election return boards in the three contested Southern states predictably ruled that the Democratic majorities in their respective states resulted from instances of fraud or intimidation. They threw out enough Tilden votes to put Hayes in the winning column in each state. During the process, however, some board members hinted that they would accept bribes to certify a Democratic victory in their state, thereby making Tilden president.

One Republican politico from New York arrived in Florida's capital with $10,000 in cash. Two poll inspectors in Gainesville later admitted accepting bribes to certify Republican-favorable erroneous returns. Another postelection observer from New York, former general Francis Barlow who was a founder of the American Bar Association and a man of impeccable reputation for honesty, was appalled by the Gainesville case. When he became convinced of the Republican fraud, he returned to New York in disgust. Two Democratic observers claimed they were offered a favorable result from Florida's election board in return for a bribe of $50,000 to $200,000. The offer apparently originated with board chairman Samuel McLin, but was never accepted. McLin later admitted that the correct returns from Baker County near Jacksonville, which would have put the state in Tilden's column, were not reported.[19]

There were also unproven, but suspicious, reports of attempted bribery in Louisiana. One account involved postelection observer and Ohio Republican senator John Sherman, who was a brother of General of the Army William T. Sherman. One parish election supervisor, James Anderson, who was also a state senator, later testified that Sherman told him that Anderson would be "taken care of" after Hayes took office. Sherman denied it. Nonetheless, after Hayes's inauguration, the new president offered Anderson three jobs, including one that Anderson took with a Republican Philadelphia newspaper. A Tilden observer reported he was approached by a Louisiana state senator—presumably Anderson—who claimed to be able to deliver the state's electoral votes for a bribe of $1 million, later reduced to $200,000. Tilden's campaign manager in New York turned it down.[20]

The Republicans in South Carolina demanded that the election board decertify selected results in order to keep the party's seven-vote majority in the legislature. Surprisingly, however, a Democratic appeal to the state's all-Republican Supreme Court was sustained. South Carolina Democrats, therefore, got what they most wanted: the governor's office would go to former Confederate lieutenant general Wade Hampton. In the presidential count, however, the board defied the state Supreme Court and certified returns giving South Carolina to Hayes.[21]

Eventually, each affected state sent at least two sets of returns to Washington for the official count. The Constitution does not provide indisputable instructions about how a situation involving contested returns should be resolved. Consequently, the Republican-controlled Senate and the Democratic-controlled House agreed that a fifteen-member Electoral Commission should be temporarily organized for the purpose. Either through machinations or unpredictable developments—depending upon one's political viewpoint—the commission ended up with eight Republicans and seven Democrats.

It selected the Hayes-majority returns for each Southern state and refused to consider how the returns were compiled. The Republican-majority commission members argued that attempts to evaluate how the returns were assembled were too complex and were unlikely to be completed in time for the new president's inauguration. In the case of Oregon, however, Republican members argued that the commission could investigate how the returns were determined in order to select the correct one. Predictably, they decided that Oregon's Democratic governor did not have the authority to replace the disputed elector. Instead, the commission accepted the return signed by Oregon's secretary of state, which gave all three votes to Hayes. In Florida, they had done just the opposite by accepting the governor's tally instead of the secretary of state's. All disagreements were settled by 8–7 votes in favor of Republican returns. Hayes became president.

Democrats might have blocked completion of the roll call of electoral votes with a filibuster to last beyond the inauguration date. Any attempt would need to begin before the roll call reached Wyoming, which was the last state to be tallied. Southerners, however, eventually decided against supporting a filibuster.

Hayes reportedly made promises to support federal public works projects in the South and remove US occupation troops if Southern Democrats declined to join their Northern colleagues in a filibuster. After his inauguration, Hayes moved cautiously, but deliberately, to remove federal troops from Florida, Louisiana, and South Carolina, which were the last three states under occupation. Shortly thereafter, the carpetbag regimes in those states collapsed. Little in the way of federal public works, however, ever materialized. Southerners were told the economic depression that began in 1873 also shut down the "Great Barbecue." From ratification of the US Constitution in 1789 to the 1873 economic collapse, the federal government invested $105 million in transportation facilities such as railroads, canals, and ordinary roads, but less than $5 million was deployed in the South. Over $80 million had been invested in the Northern transcontinental railroads during the preceding fifteen years.[22]

Democratic governors soon replaced carpetbag Republicans in the three disputed Southern states, but Hayes arranged appointments of their former GOP governors and other state officials who helped him win the election. Louisiana's 1876 gubernatorial candidate became the US counsel to Liverpool, and the outgoing governor who signed the returns sent to Washington in favor of Hayes was moved to the US Senate in a deal arranged by Senator John Sherman. The four members of Louisiana's election board were given federal posts, including one who was appointed the chief customs collector in New Orleans. In total, sixty-nine men involved in the Republican-winning Louisiana count got federal appointments. In all, some fifty relatives and friends of the Louisiana Returning Board got positions at the New Orleans customs house.[23]

Florida's Republican governor became a federal commissioner in the health-spa town of Hot Springs, Arkansas. Samuel McLin of Florida's canvassing board was appointed to the Supreme Court in New Mexico

Territory. South Carolina's carpetbag governor, Daniel Chamberlain, resigned his office in disgust and condemned President Hayes. Consequently, the president withdrew his offer of a sinecure. Eventually, however, the Massachusetts-born Chamberlain, who had also been an officer in a Civil War black regiment, reversed his opinion about the merits of Reconstruction. He later denounced it as a "frightful experiment" that attempted to "lift a backward or inferior race" only to produce "shocking and unbearable misgovernment."[24]

Twenty-four years after leaving office, Chamberlain summarized his analysis of Reconstruction in an article for *Atlantic Monthly* in 1901 titled "Reconstruction in South Carolina."[25] He began by partly blaming the "Black Codes" for pushing Congress toward Radical Reconstruction. As Congress debated how to respond, the voices calling for Southern black suffrage gained strength:

> [Republicans considered] the black South . . . equal to all the needs of the hour; ignorant, to be sure, but loyal. . . . Hardly anywhere else in recorded debates can be found so surprising a revelation of the blindness of partisan zeal as these [congressional debates] disclose. . . . [U]nderneath all the avowed motives . . . lay a deeper cause . . . the will and determination to secure party ascendency and control at the South and in the nation through the negro vote. If this is hard saying, let anyone now ask himself . . . if it is possibly credible that the [1867] reconstruction acts would have passed if the negro vote had been believed to be Democratic. Sentiment carried the day, sentiment of a lower kind—hate, revenge, greed, [and] lust of power.

Although some congressmen could foresee problems with Radical Reconstruction, leaders such as Thaddeus Stevens pushed them along. They drove the reluctant, crushed and ostracized the doubtful, and brutally rode down anyone who dared to oppose them. "Not one of these leaders had seen the South, or studied it at first-hand. Not one of them professed or cared to know more. They had made up their minds. . . . The one overshadowing item of their policy was . . . negro suffrage."

Chamberlain explains that South Carolina's most influential men were its war heroes like Wade Hampton who had urged cooperation with black suffrage as early as 1868. Chamberlain admits, however, "nothing would have been more unwelcome in Washington than the knowledge that the whites in South Carolina were gaining influence over the blacks." Having been a carpetbag governor of the state, he reminds the reader, "The writer knows his ground here."

He affirmed that no well-informed political leaders should have expected Radical Reconstruction to succeed: "In the mass of . . . colored voters in South Carolina in 1867, what forces could have existed that made for good government? Ought it not to have been clear . . . that good government . . . could not be had from such an aggregation of ignorance, inexperience and incapacity?"

If an inexperienced electorate was not a big enough challenge, the carpetbaggers who arrived from the North only aggravated the situation. Such freebooters, Chamberlain writes, "had almost as little experience . . . as the negroes" to whom "they [the carpetbaggers] were not morally the[ir] equals." Yet the blacks deferred to the carpetbaggers with "docility." The results were toxic state governments.

Prior to the Civil War, the cost of a South Carolina legislative session was never more that $20,000, whereas in 1871 it was over $600,000. The state had less that $1 million in debt at the start of Reconstruction but $17.5 million five years later. Despite all the borrowing and spending, "the state," Chamberlain noted, "had not a single public improvement of any sort to show." All was wasted on plunder. "Public offices were objects of . . . bargain and sale. Justice . . . in the courts was bought and sold."

Incompetence and corruption was routine, particularly in the lower offices. One county educational commissioner could neither read nor write his own name. Others signed documents for him with his *X* mark. Since whites felt powerless to remove him at the polls, he was murdered. While Chamberlain was appalled by the violence, he was not surprised.

> Such incidents . . . will lead . . . to deeds of violence. The . . . infamous KKK of 1870 was an organized attempt . . . to drive from office Republican state officers, and especially negroes. It was brutal and murderous to the last degree, being . . . in the hands almost exclusively of the lower stratum of the white population. Yet it was symptomatic of . . . the gangrene, dishonesty and corruption in public office. No excuse can be framed for its outrages, but its causes were plain. . . . It flourished where corruption . . . had climbed into power and withered where the reverse was the case. What is certain is that a people of force, pride, and intelligence [when] driven to choose between [temporary] violence and lawlessness and [permanent] misrule will infallibly choose the former.

Chamberlain ultimately concludes that Radical Reconstruction was born of sinister motives, cruelly exploited Southern blacks, and was destined to die of its own inadequacies. In retrospect, he was certain "there was no possibility of securing good government in South Carolina through Republican influences. . . . The vast preponderance of ignorance . . . in that party, aside from downright dishonesty, made it impossible." The blacks, he felt, were egregiously abused. "Race was used as the tool of heartless partisan leaders." Blacks were "mercilessly exploited for the benefit of a political party, and heartlessly abandoned when the scheme had failed."

The cathartic 1876 election demonstrated that the Republican Party was changing into one of conservative business interests as opposed to the egalitarian ideals that historians often presume characterized Lincoln's presidency.[26] The election taught Republicans that they could rule more effectively by allying with similar white interests in the South than with black voters. At least one historian has concluded that the process of settling the 1876 election led the public to anticipate that a new Civil War was more likely in the centennial year than was generally thought by the 1860 public after Abraham Lincoln's election. Although Northern Democrats were enraged, Hayes sensed that the Southern Democrats were less angered. They had been recently disappointed that the Northern wing of the Democratic Party blocked public works in the South even though federal investments in the South had been negligible since the end of the Civil War. Hayes became convinced that Southerners felt Republican congressmen were more sympathetic to the South's economic needs than were Northern Democrats.

Throughout American history, no social class has ever been more radically and quickly debilitated than the Southern aristocracy after the Civil War. The most adroit among them partnered with the Yankee businessmen who went South in search of profit at the end of the war. Termed economic carpetbaggers—as opposed to political carpetbaggers, who were the partisan officeholders—such Northerners had access to capital as well as subsidies from the political carpetbaggers in the Southern state governments.

Although nominally Democrats, the Southern aristocrats who replaced carpetbag leaders in the years up to Hayes's election were typically former Whigs. As such, their political philosophy had much in common with the increasingly business-oriented Republican Party. Former Whigs were not the enemies of capitalism, and if the South could win its fair share of public works, it would not oppose federal spending on internal improvements as it had before the war.

Hayes perceived opportunity for his party by forging a new alliance with such white Southern leaders. He targeted the same former Whig class that Lincoln had earlier hoped to recruit into the Republican Party.

After his inauguration, Hayes toured the South accompanied by Confederate hero and Democratic governor Wade Hampton of South Carolina. In Atlanta, Hayes told African Americans that white Southerners could better protect the "rights and interests" of the region's blacks than could the federal government.

He might have been correct. Populism, however, did blow in from the West. It never took root in the North but did infect the South. To the silent applause of Northern Republican capitalists, Southern aristocrats purged it by separating poor whites from blacks along racial rather than economic lines.

EIGHT

Southern Reparations

As explained earlier, a number of federal laws enacted during the Civil War intended largely to address immediate needs ultimately had far bigger impact over the long term. The ramifications of the Pacific Railroad Acts, for example, were discussed in chapter 6. The present chapter focuses on the long-term effects of post-war government spending resulting from wartime federal financing, Union veterans' pensions, tariffs, and wartime monetary reforms.

Examination of federal budgets during Reconstruction reveal that ex-Rebels paid their share of federal taxes for sizable items that if funded by an independent defeated foe would have constituted reparations.

To be sure, reparations are not a rare form of a victor's compensation, but it should not be assumed that the Southern states avoided equivalent penalties merely because they were readmitted to the Union. In more recent times, Germany and Japan paid reparations after World War II ended in 1945. Although Japan continued to pay some Asian countries for years thereafter, both stopped paying the United States and most Western European countries in 1949. Instead, the victors focused on rebuilding the economies of their erstwhile enemies with economic aid such as the Marshall Plan. In contrast, the federal government provided little economic assistance to the former Confederate states during Reconstruction. In fact, from 1865 to 1873, less that 10 percent of all federal public works spending was in the former Confederate states despite their greater need. In combination, New York and Massachusetts got more than twice as much as the former Confederacy.[1]

Table 2 summarizes federal tax revenues and spending for a quarter century following the Civil War. As may be observed, more than half of federal tax revenues were applied to three items: (1) interest on the federal debt, (2) budget surpluses used primarily to retire federal debt, and (3) Union veterans' benefits, none of which aided former Rebels.

But the table does not tell the whole story.

First, four years after the war ended, the Republican-controlled federal government enacted a law that required federal debt to be redeemed in specie. Although the specie might technically be either gold or silver in 1869, the market commodity value of silver was greater than its monetary value. From a pragmatic viewpoint, therefore, bond redemption would be in gold. When the market price of silver later dropped, Congress adopted the 1873 Coinage Act, which abolished the silver dollar, thereby again ensuring that redemption would still be in gold. During the war, however, many investors used greenbacks, which traded at a discount to gold, to buy the bonds. The discount got to be as much as 63 percent—meaning that a greenback dollar was worth only thirty-seven cents—after Grant sustained heavy casualties in 1864 only to be stalemated at the siege of Petersburg. In short, gold redemption was a huge windfall for the bondholders.[2]

Southerners held few, if any, federal bonds. Some were held by national banks, which bought them to use as monetary reserves as mandated by the 1863 National Bank Act, but many other Northerners also owned the bonds. Additionally, bond interest had to be paid in gold, which was another windfall. Thus, until greenbacks traded at par with gold, the amount of paper currency needed to retire the bonds and pay the interest was larger than the amount of specie required. The differential was an extra cost to the taxpayer but a bonus to the bondholder.[3]

Second, the budget surpluses were caused by protective tariffs that generated more income than necessary to operate the federal government. Dutiable items were taxed at about 45 percent. The purpose of the excess was to restrict competition for domestic producers, almost none of which were in the South.

Protective tariffs were injurious to most Southern farmers, who sold primarily to export markets, which were highly competitive. Europeans,

Table 2.
Federal Tax Revenue and Spending, Fiscal Years 1866–1890

	Millions of Dollars	Percent of Total
Spending and Surplus		
Union Veteran Pensions	$1,145	12%
Interest on Federal Debt	$2,278	23%
Budget Surplus	$1,685	17%
Subtotal	$5,108	52%
Other	$4,742	48%
Total Revenues*	$9,850	100%

*Revenues were primarily taxes, mostly obtained from tariffs

Source: usgovernmentspending.com ==> spending by decade ==> individual years.

for example, needed to be able to sell manufactured goods into the United States in order to generate the exchange credits needed to buy nonperishables such as American cotton. But US tariffs motivated Europeans to buy cotton from other countries such as India, Brazil, and Egypt, where they could more competitively export their own manufactured goods to pay for the fiber. Such diversion of European buyers was detrimental to Southern cotton growers, white and black. Finally, high American tariffs had the potential to provoke Europeans into retaliation with costly tariffs of their own on American goods, including cotton.[4]

Congressman Thaddeus Stevens also hoped to strengthen protection for domestic manufacturers by imposing an export tax on raw materials, especially cotton, shipped out of the South to overseas markets. An export tax specific to cotton would increase the raw-materials costs of European textile makers, thereby making them less competitive with New England manufacturers who would not have to pay the tax by virtue of being located in the United States. Since an export tax was unconstitutional, Stevens proposed an amendment in 1864 to allow it. The proposal never gained sufficient support, partly because farmers in the present-day Midwest feared it might be applied to their grain exports.[5]

Instead, a federal tax imposed during the Civil War on the production of cotton continued until 1868. As cotton prices dropped after the end of the war, the fixed-rate-per-pound tax increased significantly as a percentage of the fiber's market value. In 1867, the $12.50 per bale tax represented over 20 percent of its $65 selling price. Since there was no similar tax on the agricultural products of Northern states, Southerners felt the tax violated the constitutional principle that taxes be evenly apportioned to states. In contrast to being burdened with geographically specific taxes, some Northern businesses actually received subsidies, such as the bounties for New England fishermen.

Despite its short life, the cotton tax generated $68 million in revenue, which was almost three times as much as the $25 million invested in the Freedmen's Bureau during the bureau's seven-year existence. The tax could not be passed along to buyers since most cotton was exported to the London market, where buyers could choose to purchase the fiber from other countries that did not impose such a tax. In 1867, the US commissioner of agriculture declared the tax to be "disastrous" partly because it hindered Southern farmers—white and black—and partly because it resulted in a steep drop in the percentage of cotton feedstock imported into Britain from America. It invited other countries to challenge America's leadership in cotton production.[6]

A third reason that the larger federal spending in Northern states after the Civil War understates the fiscal penalties paid by Southerners involves Union veterans' pensions. Yearly pension disbursements did not stop growing until 1921, when they reached $253 million annually, fifty-five years after the war ended. By 1950, a total of nearly $8 billion had been paid. As members of the opposing army, ex-Confederates naturally received no federal benefits, although they did collect much smaller pensions from their respective states.[7]

Republicans also used the pensions as a political lever to enlist voter support for high tariffs, which were the chief source of pension funding. As will be explained later in this chapter, however, the linkage between pension funding and high tariffs also enabled large industries to evolve into monopolies.

The first Union Civil War Pension Act was adopted in February 1862. Wounded veterans were entitled to a monthly payment for disabilities incurred during military service. If they had been killed, the benefits went to their survivors. The amount depended upon rank. For example, a lieutenant colonel disabled for manual labor received $30 monthly, whereas privates got $8. A couple of years later, the act was amended to provide benefits specified by an itemized schedule of disabilities.[8]

Payments commenced once an application was approved. There was no pension for merely becoming aged. About 2.2 million men served in the Union military during the war. Since three hundred sixty-five thousand died and two hundred eighty thousand survived wounds, fewer than

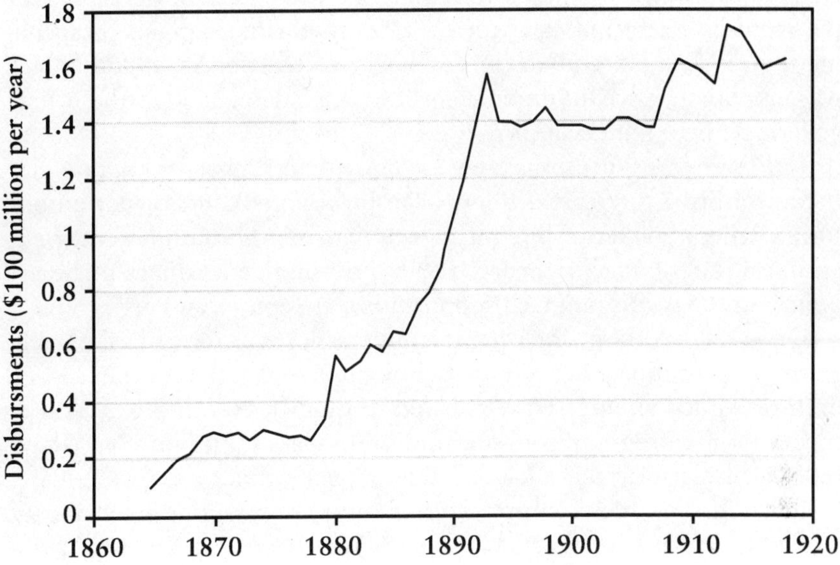

Graph 1. Growth of Civil War Union Veterans' Pensions.
Source: William H. Glasson, *Federal Military Pensions in the United States*, 273.

six hundred fifty thousand participants qualified for pensions. Ultimately, however, the active recipient list peaked at about 1 million, which implies that the accumulated number of recipients was even larger.[9]

Only eight years after the end of the war, the number of beneficiaries reached an apparent peak at around one hundred ten thousand in 1873. They numbered less than 25 percent of all eligible veterans and survivors, including the survivors of soldiers who died of wounds after the war. Apparently, there were three reasons why only a minority of qualified veterans applied for pensions. First, most were youthful men who chose to focus on building independent livelihoods after the war. Second, some were unfamiliar with the paperwork, although lawyers were permitted to collect application fees to help. Third, others considered pensions as charity and were too proud to accept them.[10]

The commissioner of pensions, James Baker, predicted that expenditures would soon stop growing when he said in 1872, "We have reached the apex of the mountain." Despite his prediction, the "apex of the mountain" was only a foothill. As indicted in the graph above, for the thirty years from 1880 to 1910, Union veterans' pensions averaged more than 25 percent of the federal budget. They peaked at more than 40 percent in 1893 and only started dropping as a percentage of the total after the Spanish-American War triggered a steady expansion of federal spending. By 1917, the accumulated pensions totaled over $5 billion, which was more than twice the amount spent by the federal and Northern state governments to fight the entire war.[11]

Union veterans' pensions grew for more than fifty years because they became a bribe to create a Republican-loyal voter constituency among former federal soldiers. The strategy was particularly fruitful in Midwestern farm states, where the party's high tariff and deflationary monetary policy otherwise discouraged support for the Republican Party.[12]

One way to enlarge the veteran constituency was to increasingly liberalize qualifications. Eventually, widows, mothers, fathers, orphans, and even orphaned siblings were allowed to qualify. Another way was to transform the program from one of disability assistance into an old age retirement platform that included able-bodied retirees.

For almost a half century after the war, only a single Democrat, Grover Cleveland, was elected president. Moreover, despite a nationwide popular vote majority, Cleveland lost his bid for consecutive terms when Benjamin Harrison narrowly beat him in Indiana and New York, where veterans supplied the Republican edge. The states had thirty-eight thousand and forty-five thousand pensioned veterans respectively and gave Harrison two thousand three hundred and thirteen thousand respective vote majorities.[13]

Pension awards started escalating in 1879 with the adoption of an Arrears Act. Previously, beneficiaries were only permitted to collect a monthly stipend after applying for a pension. The '79 act basically made the application date retroactive to the date of military discharge. Thus, soldiers who had left the army years earlier could collect the arrears as a lump sum. At a time when the average nonfarm worker earned $400 a year, the average arrears payment was $1,000. Among the factors triggering the 1879 act was a powerful lobby of attorneys who earned fees for helping applicants win pension awards.[14]

Partly because agrarian workers earned even less than nonfarm workers and partly because they contained few Union veterans, Southern states opposed the Arrears Act. Conversely, nearly all Northern Democrats and all Republicans favored it. Northern Democrats later sided with the Southerners after the Northern wing of the party became more dependent upon big city immigrants who seldom qualified for such benefits.

Even as late as 1901, Union veterans who were then living in the eleven former Confederate states received less in combined benefits than the veterans in the single state of Indiana. Per capita disbursements in

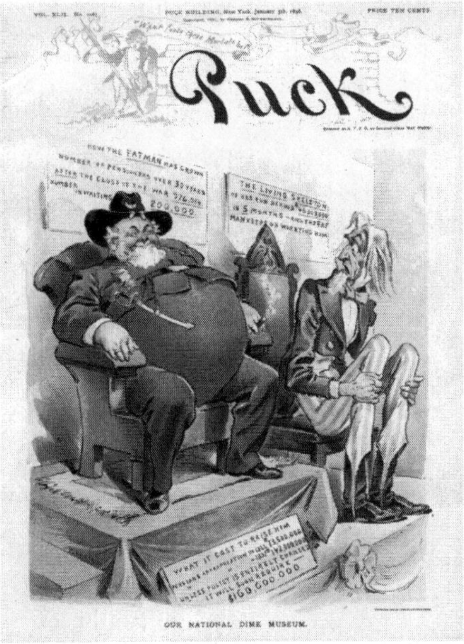

The January 5, 1898, cover of *Puck* magazine featured a bloated Civil War veteran sitting on a chair beneath a sign that states, “How the Fatman has grown. Number of Pensioners over 30 Years After the Close of the War 976,014. Number in waiting 200,000.” Next to him is Uncle Sam sitting on a chair beneath a sign that states, “The Living Skeleton. He has run behind $46,000,000 in 5 months and the Fatman keeps on Worrying him.” Beneath them is a sign that states, “What it cost to raise Him. Pensions appropriation in 1866 $13,500,000 . . . in 1897 $142,000,000. Unless policy is entirely changed it will soon require—$160,000,000.” (*Library of Congress*)

South Carolina were only 20 cents compared to $4 in Indiana. Shortly after the 1879 Arrears Act one New York City magazine editor wrote “the effect of this law is to stir-up a multitude [one hundred forty-one thousand] of people to apply for pensions . . . who had not realized they were disabled until the Government offered a premium of $1,000 or more.”[15]

By 1890, it was evident that Republicans were using veterans’ pensions as a means of keeping tariffs high in order to protect an ecosystem of Northern manufacturers. Tariffs accounted for about half of federal tax revenues even though the federal budget was consistently reporting embarrassingly large surpluses. Democrats reasoned that cutting tariffs was the best way to balance the budget and simultaneously benefit all consumers. Republicans, however, were adamantly opposed to cutting tariffs that protected domestic manufacturers.

In response, Senator Henry W. Blair of New Hampshire devised a scheme to enlist Southern support for high tariffs. In 1883, he introduced a bill to provide federal funding for public education. Since the end of the Civil War, the Southern states had complained that they were saddled with the expense of educating the children of ex-slaves even though emancipation was a national policy. Therefore, Southerners reasoned that at least some of the public education expense in the region ought to be paid for by the federal government. Blair's bill proposed that temporary federal funding be provided to all states based upon their respective rates of illiteracy. The initial amount was to be $15 million annually, but it would decline each year until it reached $1 million. Based upon the South's higher illiteracy, the region would be allocated over two-thirds of the total.

The Senate voted on the bill repeatedly over the next decade but it never came to a vote in the House. Most of the South's senators voted in favor of it. Within three years, ten Southern state legislatures also passed resolutions supporting the bill. Some Southern representatives, however, balked because they did not want to create the appearance of supporting protective tariffs. They were also concerned that once the temporary federal subsidies expired, the Southern states would be left with higher educational budgets than they could sustain from their own tax base.[16]

Meanwhile, Republicans increasingly favored reducing the budget surplus by liberalizing Union veterans' pensions. They succeeded with the 1890 Dependent Pensions Act. It enlarged the number of people who could qualify for assistance. Any soldier who served a mere ninety days and wives who married veterans anytime prior to 1890 became eligible. Any soldier injured during the war who later became unable to perform manual labor was covered. Within four years, pension disbursements doubled from $80 million to $165 million. The budget surplus vanished. Republicans dropped the Blair proposal, thereby demonstrating that protective tariffs and veterans' pensions were higher priorities than the education of youthful African Americans.[17]

In 1904, President Theodore Roosevelt released an executive order that made all veterans over age sixty-two eligible for pensions. The disability platform was essentially augmented to also become an old age assistance program. From 1862 to 1942, accumulated Union veterans' pensions totaled almost $8 billion. About $7 billion of that went to the North, and the remaining $1 billion was divided between the South and West.[18]

For more than fifty years after the war, pension policy was linked to protective tariffs. Like interest payments on Civil War federal debt and the retirement of such debts, Union veterans' pensions represented a distributive income policy that transferred income from the impoverished South to the prosperous North.

MANY, PERHAPS MOST, Reconstruction students fail to appreciate the connection between protective tariffs and monopolies because industrial trusts did not become a familiar part of the business landscape until the last quarter of the nineteenth century. As explained in the introduction, however, Southern Reconstruction extended far beyond the conventionally accepted terminal year of 1877, where historians often erroneously end the narrative.

The first federal response to monopolies was the 1890 Sherman Antitrust Act. Unfortunately, the act targeted only the apparatus of monopoly instead of the cause. Nine years later, the president of New York-based American Sugar Refining Company, which controlled 98 percent of its market, admitted in testimony to an industrial commission:

> The mother of all trusts is the customs tariff bill. . . . [Production economies of scale] . . . in the same line of business are a great incentive to [trust] formation, but these bear a very insignificant proportion to the advantages granted in the way of protection under the customs tariff. . . . The tariff bill clutches the people by the throat, and then the governors and attorneys-general of the several States take action, not against the cause but against the machinery . . . [used] . . . to rifle the public's pocket. . . . It is the Government through its tariff laws, which plunders the people, and the trusts . . . are merely the machinery for doing it.[19]

The monopolistic consequences of tariffs have long been obfuscated by the political rhetoric of those who favored the tax. Nonetheless, the danger was recognized in the US Constitution when the founders outlawed tariffs between the states. Other things being equal, the smaller the territory protected by a tariff, the more readily competitors inside the tariff wall will combine to regulate prices. Thus, to understand how tariffs foster monopolies, consider the hypothetical result if tiny Rhode Island were to build a tariff wall against the other states.

If Rhode Island adopted a steep tariff on lumber, the state's sawmills would soon start charging higher prices than mills in Connecticut and Massachusetts. Lumber would cease to be available in Rhode Island at prices lower than it could be imported from neighboring states, even though Rhode Island lumberyards would theoretically be competing with one another. Basically, such a tariff would be an invitation to the state's sawmills to raise prices to match those of the duty-burdened imports. Moreover, Rhode Island yards would have a natural tendency to consolidate their operations into a single trust.

Although the state's tariff would lift selling prices, it would not increase production costs. Thus, if they produce more lumber than Rhode Island residents need, the mills would seek to sell their excess production to buyers in neighboring states. If Rhode Island sawmill operating costs are similar to those in Connecticut and Massachusetts, where mills are operating profitably, the state's mills could sell to customers in nearby states at a lower price than in Rhode Island and still earn a profit. It is just such an ability to sell output profitably at lower prices outside a tariff wall than inside it that makes for a telltale sign of monopoly.

Rhode Island consumers and workers would be the losers. Yet the workers might be deceptively enlisted to support tariffs by offering them wages that are higher than in Massachusetts and Connecticut. As long as the higher wages do not absorb the entire excess tariff profits, Rhode Island's sawmills could continue to sell profitably into Massachusetts and Connecticut at lower prices. It's wicked. But on a national scale it basically describes Republican Party dogma well into the twentieth century. In fact, Rhode Island senator Nelson Aldrich was a leading high-tariff proponent.

Although the hypothetical tariff wall is unfair to Rhode Island consumers and workers, it is a greater injustice to the state's producers of goods that are sold primarily to other states. Suppose, for example, that Rhode Island were a leading producer of jute bags, which are used primarily for bagging cotton in the South. The state's politicians might offer to also grant the bag-makers a protective tariff, but it would be a hollow offer. Since Rhode Island grows no cotton, there would be no market for the bags within the state. Consequently, a jute-bag tariff would be of no practical value. No doubt workers making the jute bags would need to work just as hard as the sawmill employees in order to earn a living. Unfortunately, they'd likely be paid less because a jute-bag tariff could not increase the item's sales price in any sizable market, which are all beyond the borders of Rhode Island. Due to their reliance on cotton and other export commodities, such was the status in the Southern states on a national scale for more than half a century after the Civil War.

Tariffs breed monopolies like swamps breed mosquitoes. In 1904, John Moody's *The Truth about Trusts* listed almost 320 examples. All but about 20 were protected by tariffs. The biggest, United States Steel, was formed with the deliberate intent to suppress competition and re-

Table 3.
Import Tariff Rates Collected on Dutiable Items as Percent of Value of Imports by Decade, 1865–1954

Decade	Percent
1865–1874	45%
1875–1884	43%
1885–1894	47%
1895–1904	47%
1905–1914	43%
1915–1924	29%
1925–1934	46%
1935–1944	33%
1945–1954	16%

Source: *Census Bureau Historical Statistics of the United States: Colonial Times to 1970*, Part 2, 888.

strain trade. Even though at the time steel could be produced more cheaply in America than in other countries, U. S. Steel sold products overseas at lower prices than domestically. The differential averaged about $10–$20 per long ton. Wire nails, for example, which sold domestically for $2 per hundredweight, were priced at $1.55 in Britain. The beneficiaries were the steel trust and its ecosystem, which included its workers. Even though the company had relatively minor steel operations in the South, the Birmingham Differential and discriminatory railroad freight rates explained earlier intentionally penalized the region.[20]

As Table 3 illustrates, US tariffs averaged about 45 percent of the value of dutiable items from the end of the Civil War until Democrat Woodrow Wilson became president in 1913. During Wilson's two administrations, the average rate dropped below 30 percent. Rates returned to about 45 percent after the Republicans regained the White House during the Roaring Twenties. They began to drop during the Great Depression when Franklin Roosevelt was president but did not reach the low levels consistent with near-free-trade policies until after World War II. By that time, American manufacturers, which were mostly in Northern states, had little to fear from overseas competition because of the wartime destruction of European and Asian economies. It is hard to avoid concluding that US free trade advocacy after World War II at least partly reflected our country's worldwide industrial dominance that left nothing—only temporarily in hindsight—to fear from foreign competition.

Moreover, American industrial dominance was concentrated in the North. In 1944, historian Walter Webb wrote:

> Since the Civil War the tariff wall has been built higher and higher, not so much for the nation as . . . for the benefit of a section. For seventy-five years, and more, the tariff [cornucopia] hung over the North, showering it with . . . billions of dollars, bringing it . . . the greatest gift that any modern government ever bestowed on one group of people at the expense of other groups.[21]

National banking regulations and monetary policy also placed extra burdens on the South for decades after the Civil War.

As outlined in chapter 1, the challenges of financing the Civil War led the federal government to adopt the 1863 National Bank Act and its 1864 amendments. As illustrated in Table 1 on page 17, the government financed almost 60 percent of the war by issuing war bonds, which banks operating under the 1863 act could use as monetary reserves. Since the bonds earned interest, many bankers preferred them as reserves instead of gold or paper money, which did not earn interest. The bonds-as-reserve provision created a dubious alliance between the federal government and the banking industry. It transformed national banks into eager buyers of federal bonds in almost any quantity. To be sure, fiscal policy for decades after the war was conservative because it focused on retiring the Civil War bonds. After the Great Depression of the 1930s, however, the ready market for such bonds among nationally chartered banks may have contributed to habitual federal deficit spending.

The National Bank Act was discriminatory against the South because of its capital requirements, banknote limitations, operating constraints, and lending restrictions. The provisions were also commonly harmful to rural Western states, but Westerners were generally not as poor as Southerners.

First, capital requirements for national banks were beyond the means of impoverished Southerners. Equity of $50,000 was needed to form such a bank in communities with fewer than 3,000 residents while banks in towns with 6,000 to 50,000 inhabitants required $100,000. Banks in cities of more than 50,000 people required $200,000 of equity capital. New Orleans was the only former Confederate city in the third category. Not until 1900 were the capital requirements in towns of 3,000 or fewer residents dropped to $25,000, which was still high given the South's lingering poverty.

Even though state charters might permit lower capital requirements and provide more operating flexibility, the National Bank Act imposed a 10 percent tax on the notes of independent banks. The tax was a ruinous penalty for many years. Not until checking accounts became more common than banknotes were independent banks able to compete with the national banks. But that happened later in the South than elsewhere.[22]

Second, for ten years after the Civil War, few additional national banks could be chartered because of limits on the amount of banknotes allowed to be in circulation. In 1875, the limit was $354 million. About $300 million had already been issued before the end of the Civil War, and the ceiling was not raised for the remaining $54 million until 1870. When the ceiling was removed in 1875, banknotes were less profitable because the amount that could be issued was a fraction of the par value of government bonds that the banks held. In contrast, the market value of bonds issued during the Civil War was well above par because they could be redeemed in gold, which traded at a premium to paper currency, and the coupon interest rate on such bonds was higher than the 1875 market rate.

Consequently, the amount of national banknotes in circulation declined until the Gold Standard Act in 1900. The act permitted banks to exchange bonds trading at a premium to par for "refunding" issues in larger principal amounts paying lower interest coupon rates. Since the principal amounts received in exchange for the redeemed bonds were larger, the total interest earned by the banks on their government securities was unchanged. What did change, however, was the amount of bank reserves the new bonds provided because of their higher par value amounts.[23]

As an example, consider if the market rate of interest was 3 percent in 1900. Thus, a bond with a 3 percent coupon would trade at 100 percent of par value. In order to provide an equivalent interest yield on a bond with a 4 percent coupon, however, the bond's market price must equal 133 percent of par. Therefore, a bank with $1 million in principal amount of 4 percent bonds could exchange them for $1.33 million of 3 percent bonds, thereby enabling it to increase its banknote issues by 33 percent.

Therefore, the increased reserves created by the Gold Standard Act allowed national banks to issue more banknotes. From 1900 to 1901, national banknotes in circulation increased from $205 million to $310 million. By 1910, the circulation totaled $675 million.[24]

Third, with rare exceptions, national banks were only permitted to operate a single branch. The restriction was particularly hard on the South, where small towns were more prevalent, because the proscription meant that no national banking facilities could be available in such towns without meeting the large start-up capital requirements for a separate bank. For example, investors who might open a national bank in Atlanta could not open a branch in nearby Athens. Instead, they would have to create an entirely new bank for Athens and meet the steep capital stipulations a second time. Consequently, 123 Georgia counties had no bank as late as 1895.[25]

Fourth, national banks could not make mortgage loans, even though such loans were essential to the agrarian South. The provision remained in effect into the twentieth century.[26]

As a consequence of the four above factors, even as late as 1900, only about 7 percent of the America's national banks and capital were located in the former Confederate states. For decades after the war, the region's economy was dependent upon its own nearly nonexistent financial resources. The shortage increased the South's cost of borrowing and impeded efforts to industrialize. Consequently, as late as 1910, Southern manufacturing employed less than 10 percent of the area's working people.[27]

Since only a small number of national banks could be funded in the South, the region's bankers were left in a comparatively monopolistic position. They were able, therefore, to charge high interest rates, restrict loans in local markets, and exercise price discrimination. In combination with lending restrictions, the result was a transfer of funds from local agricultural uses to industrial uses in other parts of the country.

In the South, where communities of fewer than 3,000 people were common, the potential lending activities were not sufficient to enable a bank to earn a reasonable return on the required $50,000 equity capital, particularly considering the restrictions on real estate lending. The effect was to drain funds from the countryside where it was scarce, to the big cities where it was abundant. One rural banker from Kansas explained to a 1908 National Monetary Commission: "It is almost impossible for a bank in a farming community . . . to absorb loanable funds [in a manner] to avoid . . . all connection with real estate. As it [presently] stands, the country national bank may buy [interest yielding] commercial paper in [money center cities] about which it is difficult for the [bank] officers to know much, but must turn down the farm mortgage offered [by locally known citizens] at its counter."[28]

As a result, financing in the South devolved to a network of factors and country merchants each of whom took a markup in the lending rate to the ultimate borrower who was often a poor tenant farmer or sharecropper. Historian C. Vann Woodward described the arrangement:

> The farmer pledged an unplanted crop for a loan of an unstipulated amount at an undesignated but enormous rate of interest averaging about 60 percent a year. Trapped by the system, a farmer might continue year after oppressive year as a sort of peon, under debt to the same merchant and under constant oversight. The lien system imposed the one-crop system, for the merchant would advance credit only against cash crops such as cotton or tobacco. . . . The system not only impoverished the farmers but stifled their hopes and depleted their incentive.[29]

As illustrated in Table 1, the federal government relied upon its first issues of a paper fiat currency (greenbacks) to finance about 27 percent of its Civil War expenditures. Since greenbacks were not convertible into gold, a paper dollar traded at a fluctuating discount to a gold dollar. Consequently, after the war, the future of greenbacks became a subject of fierce debate.

Conservative businessmen and bankers generally wanted them removed from circulation for two reasons. First, it would put American commercial interests on firm footing internationally, where gold was the standard exchange medium. Second, bankers wanted the federal bonds they bought during the war to be redeemed in gold instead of a lower-valued paper currency they used to buy them. They wanted the windfall profit.

Conversely, farmers and some businessmen wanted the greenbacks to remain in circulation, or even increased in amount. Farmers and indebted businesses argued the unfairness of requiring them to repay their greenback-dollar debts with premium-valued gold dollars, while iron producers and other industries that wanted price protection from overseas competitors—above that provided by tariffs—realized that imported goods had to be purchased with gold. That requirement inflated the price of imports in terms of greenbacks because of the higher value of a gold dollar to a greenback dollar. It was essentially an added measure of price protection above the tariff against import competition.

Even before Lincoln was assassinated, his last Treasury secretary, Hugh McCulloch, announced his intent to gradually remove greenbacks from circulation. By October 1866, he had reduced the amount to $400 million from the $433 million when he took office in March 1865. He also converted about $300 million in short-term government debt that had functioned as a quasi currency into long-term bonds that could not readily be substituted for paper money like the short-term obligations. Since the actions triggered an economic downturn, Congress repealed the

Treasury's authority to withdraw more greenbacks in 1868 after $44 million had been removed.[30]

Due to the political difficulties in getting greenbacks retired, conservative interests modified their tactics. The first step was the 1869 Public Credit Act, which required government bonds to be redeemed in gold. Most Northern businessmen were drawn to the Republican Party in the 1868 election because they anticipated it would enact the Public Credit Bill. They were less concerned with racial justice in the South. The businessmen were similarly drawn to the party's sound money policies in 1872, which resulted in the 1873 Coinage Act that eliminated the silver dollar because of a drop in the bullion value of silver in such dollars to a level below their monetary face value. In other words, the silver in a silver dollar was worth less than a dollar. Next came the 1875 Resumption Act, which ordered the retirement of greenbacks, or their convertibility into gold, by 1879.

The depression that followed Jay Cooke's 1873 bankruptcy led to lower commodity and industrial prices, which threatened the solvency of farmers and other indebted businesses. In addition to their objections to repaying their paper money debts with premium-valued gold, they argued that decreasing the money supply by retiring greenbacks would intensify downward pricing pressure. Since the amount of money in circulation per capita had dropped from $31 in 1865 to $16 in 1878, they sought relief by reinflation, which they reasoned could be obtained by enlarging the money supply.

Instead of calling for more greenbacks, however, they proposed a politically more palatable solution. Specifically they wanted to return the United States to a bimetal standard by reauthorizing the silver dollar and coining it in large quantities. Over President Rutherford Hayes's veto, in 1878, Congress passed the Bland-Allison Act, which required the Treasury to purchase specified quantities of silver to be issued as coins.[31]

Conservative interests opposed Treasury purchases of silver because the department was required to buy the bullion at the monetary face value of a silver coin as opposed to the lower market value. Such purchases would drain the gold reserves needed to retire greenbacks in the next year. Consequently, the Bland-Allison Act prohibited the Treasury from purchasing more that $4 million of silver monthly. The department instead bought the act's stipulated monthly minimum of $2 million. Whether reflecting habitual use or public confidence, few greenbacks were presented for gold when they became eligible for redemption in 1879.

Nonetheless, the conflict was the beginning of an approximate twenty-year battle between conservative and expansionist monetary policies that would lead to the formation of the Populist Party and culminate with the 1896 presidential election between William McKinley and William Jennings Bryan. Conservatives were concentrated in the Northeast whereas the expansionists were mostly in the South and West. Due to the region's greater need, the Southern Farmers' Alliance was the first and among the most powerful advocates of expansionist policy. According to historian Lawrence Goodwyn, who specialized in the Populist movement, it was the crop-lien system in the South—not a general agriculture depression as commonly supposed—that triggered the movement.[32]

In 1890, a Southern Farmers' Alliance executive proposed a plan intended to benefit rural America. His Sub-Treasury Plan was designed to improve the credit and increase the money supply in rural areas. It would also provide facilities that would enable farmers to sell their nonperishable produce over an extended period as opposed to only at harvest time, when prices were typically at their lowest.

He proposed that the Treasury Department open a sub-Treasury office in every American county that produced more than $500,000 of farm goods. The offices were to include storage facilities, such as grain elevators, for nonperishable produce. When farmers deposited their goods at the storage facility, the Treasury Department would provide them warehouse receipts amounting to 80 percent of the value of the stored goods. The receipts could be exchanged among the people as another form of paper money. Farmers could gradually sell their produce out of the storage facilities over the ensuing year instead of being forced to sell all of it at harvest time.

Although radical in concept, the plan was basically sound. While the receipts would admittedly be a form a paper currency, readily marketable commodities would underlie their value. In that context, they were stronger than the original greenbacks. The certificates would basically become a commodity-based currency in regions where specie-based currency and greenbacks were scarce. Although the plan was rejected by Congress as too radical, it may be noted that the New Deal price support schemes of the 1930s were based on similar ideas.[33]

Historian David L. Cohn summarized the consequences to the South resulting from the tariffs, discriminatory banking laws, injurious monetary policies, taxes-as-reparations, and other factors discussed above:

> The agrarian South had been delivered over to non-agrarian interests, and had become a satellite of the banking industrial Northeast. And the already burdened cotton farmers were to bear heavier burdens in the future. They could complain in vain . . . of railroad

> rates that crippled them, of gouging by trusts and combines operating in cottonseed oil, jute bagging, farm implements, and other adversities. They might work hard, live meanly, and die in poverty to pass on to [future generations] the apparently irrevocable estate of poverty.[34]

EXCEPT FOR ONE or two vengeful decades after the war, the adverse federal policies toward the South were probably not a deliberate effort to punish the region. They instead reflected the influence of more powerful interests in other parts of the country that leveraged the government into adopting national policies that would be favorable to their regions without regard to how such policies might impact other regions. It was, perhaps, requiring too much of human nature to expect that they would decline to put their own priorities first.

Nonetheless, it is tempting to speculate whether the Southern states would have fared better as a British colony, like Canada, which was then known as British North America. The slaves would have been freed because slavery was outlawed, and owners often compensated, throughout the British Empire in 1833. Southerners could have purchased manufactured goods at better prices because Britain advocated low tariffs. Southern farmers could have exported freely to Europe without fear that Europeans might shop elsewhere in retaliation for high American tariffs. Within twenty-five years after the Civil War, the British Empire evolved into a commonwealth as a culmination of increasingly cooperative commerce among its members, which would have benefitted the Southern states had they been organized as one such member.[35]

NINE

Sharecropped

The earliest efforts to employ ex-slaves in cotton-growing ventures were supervised by federal agents and the US Army while the Civil War was still in progress.

The first instance was in the South Carolina Sea Islands after Port Royal was occupied in November 1861. At the start of the April 1862 cotton-planting season, the US War Department took charge of the region's plantations and former slaves. Generally, worker-management methods varied little from slavery. Blacks were forced to work in a gang system that divided them into groups such as plow gangs, hoe gangs, and trash gangs. They could not travel from one plantation to another without passes. A total of three thousand four hundred acres were planted and harvested before the end of the year, but the results were disappointing. The 1862 yield was less than 26 pounds per acre compared to an average of 137 pounds before the war.[1]

The disappointing results reflected inexperienced management, a clash of cultures, and poor treatment of the former slaves. New Englanders, who managed many of the federal plantations, were accustomed to supervising the twelve-hour workdays characteristic of the textile industry back home. Former slaves, however, valued the unstructured time available after tasks were completed on prewar plantations. One ex-slave announced in a church meeting, "The Yankees preach nothing but cotton, cotton," while the ex-slaves wanted to spend at least some time planting corn and other edibles. Conversely, many Northern supervisors thought the ex-slaves were lazy. One commented, "The [blacks] are very wayward—now they work and then they stop—and some stop before they begin." Supervisors retaliated by evicting, or cutting the rations of, former slaves who failed to work "diligently."[2]

The second wartime opportunity for Northern leaseholders to manage ex-slaves in a plantation environment came with Union military control of the lower Mississippi River valley after New Orleans was occupied in May 1862 and the Confederate fortress at Vicksburg fell in July 1863. Six months after Major General Benjamin Butler occupied New Orleans, he allowed Union-loyal planters in adjacent parishes to hire ex-slaves as salaried workers. When Major General Nathaniel Banks replaced Butler in December 1862, Banks extended the practice throughout all of occupied Louisiana.

Since Banks resolved that former slaves must avoid vagrancy and idleness, he established regulations to govern their employment. The resulting policies, however, resembled slavery. Ex-slaves were "induced" into yearly contracts with planters. Their compensation was fixed at either three dollars monthly or 5 percent of the crop's sales proceeds after harvest. After they were hired, the former slaves were forbidden to leave their plantation without the permission of supervisors. Critics complained that the federal provost marshals who rounded-up "vagrant" blacks functioned more like slave patrols than agents of emancipation. Historian Lawrence Powell wrote, "The entire apparatus was really a system of vagrancy laws that left black people with the choice of working on the plantations or laboring on the public works."[3]

The blacks, however, had no option to avoid the system by migrating to Northern states. Like Southern whites, the Northerners wanted blacks to concentrate on cotton production. Secretary of War Stanton ordered Major General Ulysses Grant to recruit freed slaves to "military service or put them to work picking cotton for the government." The Senate scorned an 1864 proposal by a Kentucky senator that Congress redistribute blacks to the Northern states in "proportion to their white population." When a West Virginia senator proposed that the Freedmen's Bureau negotiate with northern governors and mayors to accept black refugees, even the author of the 1875 Civil Rights Act, Massachusetts Senator Charles Sumner, rejected it. Instead, the federal government

Plantation superintendent David Franklin Thorpe with a group of ex-slaves tending a field on Saint Helena Island, South Carolina, c. 1863. (*Library of Congress*)

hoped to "line the banks of the Mississippi River with a loyal population . . . and give employment to freed negroes."[4]

Northern opportunists seeking to line those banks and lease plantations at bargain rates swarmed into the lower valley after the fall of Vicksburg. A reporter for the *New York Herald* who traveled among them wrote of the adventurers:

> The desire of gain alone prompts them and they care not whether they make it out of the blood of those they employ or from the land. . . . The majority . . . were unprincipled men, who understood the enterprise solely as speculation. They had as little regard for the rights of the negro as the most brutal slaveholder had ever shown. Very few of them paid the negroes for their labor, except in furnishing them small quantities of food, for which they charged five times the value.

Nonetheless, such examples of federally managed wartime cotton cultivation laid the foundation for postwar cotton growing and black employment schemes.[5]

Having known nothing but slavery until emancipation, most ex-slaves at the end of the war were prone to wander about the countryside or perhaps visit long lost relatives who had moved into distant Southern states. Many congregated idly in the towns and cities. Most exercised such freedoms simply because it was the first time in their lives that they could.

About five years after the Civil War, Englishman Robert Somers visited the South. Based upon his interviews and research during the trip, he wrote about conditions in Mississippi in the months after the war ended:

> The negroes, after the Confederate surrender, were disorderly. Many of them would not settle down to labour . . . but roamed about with arms in their hands and hunger in their bellies; and the governing power, with the usual blind determination of a victorious party, was thinking only all the while of every device of suffrage and reconstruction by which "the freedmen" might be strengthened, and made, under Northern dictation, the ruling power in the country. Agitators of the loosest fiber came down among the towns and plantations, and, organizing a Union league, held midnight meetings with the negroes in the woods, and went about uttering sentiments which . . . were . . . destructive. A real terror reigned for a time among the white people.[6]

It was under such circumstances that Mississippi's white legislature responded in 1865 by adopting Black Codes, which had two objectives. The first was to prevent black vagrancy and put the ex-slaves back to work in a manner similar to the regulations applicable to the federal wartime plantations. The second was to define the legal status of ex-slaves who were not yet citizens despite the abolition of slavery by the Thirteenth Amendment. The Fourteenth Amendment, which would make blacks citizens, would not be adopted for three years. Republican politicians overlooked, or did not understand, the first objective. They saw only that the second objective resulted in codes that seemed little different from slavery.

Consequently, the occupying military forces and the Freedmen's Bureau prevented the codes from ever taking effect. According to historian Avery Craven, "neither northerners nor southerners understood the thinking of the other. One group faced a society in economic and social chaos, the other a society madly reveling in prosperity and progress."[7]

After the Black Codes were rejected, Union League agitators arrived, and some Freedmen's Bureau agents started spreading irresponsible rumors that led many former slaves to erroneously believe that the federal government would give each family forty acres and a mule. The expectation may have originated with a provision in the March 1865 Freedmen's Act. The applicable section empowered the Freedmen's Bureau to rent up to forty acres of abandoned or confiscated land to each Union-loyal refugee or freedman. Annual rents were set at 6 percent of the property's value, and lease terms were for up to three years. Occupants would be permitted to buy the land anytime during the rental period. Although the properties were not stipulated as gifts, some Republican politicians later made such promises to freedmen in order to get their votes and drive a wedge between Southern blacks and whites.

In September 1865, Representative Thaddeus Stevens proposed confiscating almost four hundred million acres of Southern land—exceeding the total area of Texas and California—to give forty acres to each adult freedman and sell the rest to pay off the national debt and reduce taxes. Judging from his mail, Stevens got most of his support from those who wanted to cut the debt and lower taxes. One witty observer remarked that if Northern voters could be convinced "that all our taxes are to be removed . . . there will be but one solid vote for the [Republican] party." Despite persistent attempts, Stevens could not get his plans through Congress, even though there was a large Republican majority. The party was pivoting toward its capitalist principles, which were inconsistent with government paternalism toward individuals and would dominate its future dogma.[8]

Through a multitude of sources, some merely irresponsible and others originating from bored federal occupation soldiers with wicked tastes for humor, freedmen were falsely told to expect a great distribution of lands and mules on the first Christmas after Appomattox. When rumors swept through Louisiana, some blacks threatened an uprising if the dream was not fulfilled. But a local Freedmen's Bureau agent, General J. S. Fullerton, cut them short, saying, "The Government will not do more for you than the white laborers who are your neighbors."[9] Fullerton reported on the conduct of other bureau agents more fully through official channels:

> [T]he idea was constantly held out to the freedmen that they were a privileged people to be pampered and petted by the government and the effect was most pernicious. . . . The acts of a few local agents of the Bureau were such as to destroy the confidence that should exist between these planters who were endeavoring to give free labor an impartial trial and the freedmen who worked in the fields. These acts were done through a mistaken notion of kindness to the blacks.[10]

The expected free parcels were presumed to be reserved within lands taken from Southern whites through the wartime confiscation acts, particularly the July 1862 act. As explained in chapter 1, however, Lincoln objected to the act until Congress passed a resolution clarifying that confiscation could not extend to the owner's heirs. Lincoln also pledged at the February 1865 Hampton Roads peace conference that he would be liberal in restoring Southerners to ownership of confiscated lands. President Johnson sought to fulfill Lincoln's intent in a September 1865 circular to Freedmen's Bureau agents. Circular 15 clarified the steps through which pardoned landowners could reclaim their lands or, conversely, how the parcels might be irrevocably declared confiscated or abandoned and thereby eligible for lease to freedmen.[11]

After Christmas 1865 came and went without a grant of forty acres and a mule, sharecropping and tenant farming quickly supplanted the federal wage-based contract system at the next spring planting because Southerners did not have enough money to simultaneously pay wages and provide worker subsistence during the long growing season. Those who tried could only pay inadequate wages, thereby inducing workers to abandon the fields, leaving the crops uncultivated and unharvested. In addition, freedmen did not like the constant supervision of the wage system. It was too much like slavery. Sharecropping allowed them to work on their own time.

SHARECROPPING is an ancient practice commonly adopted to produce cash crops in instances when there is an abundance of landless workers and a shortage of capital. In the post-Civil War South, the cropper and his family typically cultivated a twenty-acre plot. The landowner provided the plot, seeds, tools, and work stock at no charge. He also gave the cropper a cabin, water, and a place to cut firewood, plus an acre or two of land upon which to raise barnyard animals and grow vegetables. Additionally, the landlord normally agreed to provide the cropper with food and clothing valued at stipulated sums until harvest time. Medical services and medicines might also be included.

The cropper's responsibility was to raise the crop and turn over half the cotton and cottonseed to the farmer at harvest time. He kept the other half for himself. He also agreed to pay the farmer, with interest, for funds advanced in the form of food, clothing, and related items. A cropper who supplied his own work stock and tools normally kept more than half of the crop.

Tenant farming is similar to sharecropping except that the cultivator rents the tilled land. If he supplies all of his tools, work stock, and other family needs, he may not be required to share any of his harvest with the landlord. Like sharecroppers, however, he generally bought his family supplies at a store often owned by the landlord. Such merchants typically sold merchandise on credit and held a lien on the tenant's crop in order to ensure payment at the end of the season.[12]

In 1880, one observer described how sharecropping evolved on a former one-thousand-acre plantation near Oglethorpe, Georgia:

> [After the war, most] of the twenty-five Negro families [remained] living in the [former slave] quarters centered around the big house. For several years following emancipation the force of laborers were divided into two squads . . . [in] the same manner as in antebellum days. . . . The laborers were paid a portion of the crop. . . . After a while . . . the two squads split up into smaller and smaller squads. The mules were ill-treated, the crop was frequently badly worked and in many cases not honestly divided.
>
> It became necessary to reorganize the plantation. The owner sold his mules to the Negroes on credit, thus placing the risk from careless handling on the tenants. The gang system was abandoned and the land was divided so as to give each family its individual tract. When some of them had to walk a mile, it became impractical to keep the cabins closely grouped.[13]

Although commonly identified with African-American culture, sharecropping and tenant farming was also common among many whites. Every census from 1870 to 1940 showed that white sharecroppers outnumbered blacks. In 1860, slaves produced 80 percent of the cotton, but in 1899, blacks accounted for less than half the crop. At a time when whites represented 71 percent of the South's population, in 1937—seventy-two years after the end of the Civil War— two-thirds of the region's tenant farmers were white, as were half of its sharecroppers. According to an economic report prepared for President Franklin Roosevelt, white sharecroppers "were living under economic conditions almost identical with those of Negro sharecroppers." Southern tenant farmers cleared an average of $73 annually, compared to $63 for sharecroppers.[14]

A British company, Delta & Pine Land (D&PL), owned the largest Southern cotton farm during the first half of the twentieth century. It eventually totaled almost forty thousand acres and was located in the delta near Greenville, Mississippi. After confessed bribe taker and former Grand Rapids, Michigan, district attorney Lant K. Salsbury moved to Mississippi, he became a cotton farmer. In 1911, he journeyed to England, where he persuaded a British cotton textiles consortium to acquire the inactive D&PL and use its charter to purchase large tracts of Mississippi cotton land. The British sent over a delegation to investigate. Local planters who would sell the British some of the land charmed the buyers with hospitality and entertained them with goose hunting.

A sharecropper family in Hale County, Alabama, summer 1936. (*Library of Congress*)

After completing the purchase, the British quickly discovered how difficult cotton growing could be. Floods in 1912 and 1913 took a toll, as did the persistent boll weevil. The company did not earn a profit until 1917 and did not pay a dividend until 1920. Nonetheless, in the 1920s, the plantation grew from twelve thousand acres to eighteen thousand. Due to overproduction, the cotton market crashed in 1926. The disastrous 1927 flood, however, led to a cotton shortage the following year from which D&PL benefitted primarily by speculative buying early in the futures market. In the ensuing years, the company's operating efficiency steadily improved. It also pioneered the breeding of superior cotton types that could better withstand insect infestations and provide higher yields.

By the time of the Great Depression, D&PL was not only America's largest cotton farm, it was also perhaps the most efficient at utilizing its sharecroppers, who were almost entirely blacks. In 1937, the company was the subject of a *Fortune* magazine article, "Biggest Cotton Plantation." In 1936, it produced 15,000 bales at a yield of almost 640 pounds per acre, whereas the typical cotton farmer obtained a yield of only about 190 pounds per acre. Due to its superior qualities, D&PL cotton sold on the market at an average price premium of 10 percent. Its cottonseed was in demand throughout the world, and three thousand five hundred tons were exported. Net income in 1936 was $153,000, a 30 percent margin.[15]

The company provided farms and homes to a dozen managers who were paid a salary of $150 monthly with the potential for a 10–15 per-

A sharecropper family in Little Rock, Arkansas, autumn 1935. (*Library of Congress*)

cent year-end bonus. Each supervised about 100 sharecropping families with an average of three children. In order to maximize production, managers gave croppers detailed cultivation instructions obtained from the company's scientific research and experience. For example, croppers were provided D&PL's high-yield cottonseed, which matured about six weeks earlier than normal. Managers commonly rode through their respective territories daily to look for problems and provide assistance. Crop-dusting airplanes applied insecticides. D&PL also distributed a half ton of yeast annually to worker families in order to prevent pellagra, which was a common ailment among malnourished Southern farmers of the era.

Beyond these advantages, however, working conditions were little different from those of the earliest post-Civil War sharecroppers. A farmer who used one of the company's one thousand mules was entitled to a half share at harvest time. If he provided his own mule, the share was typically three-quarters. However, D&PL often did not permit three-quarter shares, because management did not believe that most sharecroppers cared properly for their mules. Each farmer was provided a dwelling unit, free fuel, and a half-acre parcel for growing fruits and vegetables. D&PL also paid for half of the fertilizer costs. The entire cultivating season totaled only 125 days. At other times, croppers might work for cash wages of a dollar a day on other company projects, if available.

D&PL offered croppers a company-owned store to provide food, clothing, and other essentials. The currency of the store was company scrip because of, as *Fortune* put it, the sharecropper's tendency to "blow

[cash] rapidly for unnecessaries such as whisky." Knowing the potential for captive stores to charge high prices and impose steep interest rates, *Fortune* concluded that D&PL's success partly resulted from the "intangible . . . treatment of [its] labor," which included reasonable terms at the company store. The company also provided a school and hospital for the workers. The school operated five months annually at no charge. The hospital had a doctor on staff and was available for a fee of $9 a year.[16]

In 1936, the average cropper consumed $200 in store credits and was paid $320 in cash, resulting in total earnings of $520. If one ended the year with a deficit at the store, D&PL normally canceled the debt. The cash was typically paid on "settlement day" at the end of the harvest. Almost immediately thereafter, used car salesmen, prostitutes, and bootleggers arrived in the neighborhood from Greenville. A cropper's entire year's earnings might be wasted in a single day.

Between 1930 and 1932, D&PL reported one thousand cases of syphilis. The best treatment available at the time cost $14,000, which was shared by D&PL and the nonprofit Rosenwald Foundation. Thus, over a two-year period, D&PL invested more than twenty-two times its 1936 income to treat venereal disease among its sharecroppers. Assuming only $320 of clear cash income a year as in 1936, the average cropper would have otherwise required forty-four years to pay for the treatment costs alone.

D&PL's presence was generally regarded as benevolent to African Americans of the region. Even though labeling sharecropping as a "national disgrace," *Fortune* concluded, "[A]ny practical solution . . . is hard to see and, even if seen, hard to preach. . . . It is possible that at Delta and Pine, you see sharecropping at its best, or say, its least objectionable." An independent 1939 Harvard University study added scientific evidence to support *Fortune*'s opinion. It stated that the good diet and excellent medical care encouraged by D&PL lowered the death rate among the croppers. In response to the study, the *New York Times* wrote, "The Harvard experiments not only teach a valuable physiological lesson but [also] point to the sociological moral that working for an enlightened company on a sharecropping basis need not be another form of slavery."[17]

According to *Fortune*, Delta & Pine supplied "better than average cabins with tight-fitting walls [and] grooved and tongued floors." Tenants were not, however, provided window and door screens, because "the croppers normally punch holes in the screens to let the dogs in or throw trash out."

When *Fortune* asked local whites why D&PL's black sharecroppers failed to use their earnings to purchase lands and improve their economic status, the whites replied that the croppers earned enough money to do so but were not thrifty and lacked initiative. They compared the blacks unfavorably to Italian families who had migrated to the area after the Civil War to become cotton workers. Some second generation Italians, they said, "had become Memphis doctors and lawyers . . . or otherwise improved themselves." At the time, however, black sharecroppers occupied such a low social rank that it may have seemed impossible to many—even among the young and ambitious—to improve their position. There were few examples to serve as role models. Those who tried faced obstacles from racial discrimination as the tiny number who succeeded often described.[18]

Presently, Delta & Pine Land is a subsidiary of Monsanto Chemical. It is the world's largest developer of cottonseed and controls about 70 percent of the market. Its breeding, gene-splicing, and selection technologies provide seeds that are setting new records in terms of yield, infestation resistance, and fiber quality. The genetically engineered seed is reducing the need for pesticides. It is also hugely profitable for Monsanto because insecticide costs about $150 per acre, whereas conventional seed is priced at about $8 per acre. D&PL can earn a generous profit margin by pricing its transgenic seed at $32 an acre and still lower a farmer's overall cultivation costs. The company sold most of its cotton lands in 1978 and no longer operates the plantation.[19]

The 1939 claim by the *New York Times* that D&PL's methods indicated that sharecropping "need not be another form of slavery" warrants analysis. Sharecropping was not a choice freely made by Southerners after the Civil War. As explained earlier, it was compelled by a regional capital shortage when the only alternative was starvation. Federal aid, or investment by outside capital, might have enabled more satisfactory arrangements, but neither was forthcoming. The South's economic recovery was to be by its own bootstraps. Moreover, it would need to be accomplished within an environment of injurious federal policies such as protective tariffs, unfair freight rates, industrial monopolies, and discriminatory banking rules that favored the Northern states. There were consequences.

First, post-Civil War cotton growers evolved into a multitude of itinerate families encompassing millions of whites and blacks who were living an existence little different from homelessness. Since sharecropping and tenancy contracts were typically for a single season, tillers were motivated to optimize output for the present year only. The practice steadily diminished soil productivity, thereby often prompting croppers and tenants to move annually in search of mythical greener pastures to new locations the following season.

In 1938, almost two million families were caught in the nomadic web. Their annual moving costs of $25 million were basically a recurring economic waste. Given the temporary character of the landlord contracts, the tillers had little or no incentive to invest in capital equipment, barnyard animals, land improvements, or even enhancements to their dwellings. One result was the ubiquitous pattern of identical-looking sharecropper shacks common in the rural South for a hundred years. For thirty years after the Civil War, Southern farmers worked with tools "that were as primitive as those in use in India and the Balkans."[20]

It would be many decades before cotton growing could be mechanized. Picking of the bolls was the most labor-intensive part of the job. Since the bolls do not mature simultaneously, it was necessary to use people as pickers for many years in order to bag only the ripe ones. Mechanical pickers could not distinguish between ready and unready bolls. If they were used, laborers were still needed to discard the immature bolls.[21]

Sharecropping and tenant farming detached the Southern farmer from his traditional connection to the land. It discouraged plowing in contours to prevent soil erosion or crop rotation to avert soil depletion. The disconnection precipitated a fundamental cultural change that was forced upon the South by losing the Civil War. The 1938 report to President Roosevelt noted above stated that 61 percent of all the nation's badly eroded land was in the South. Historians Thomas Clark and Albert Kirwan concluded, "Erosion and soil wastage were high crimes, which robbed the region of more wealth than half a dozen Yankee armies marching to the sea.[22]

A second consequence of the discriminatory federal policies following the Civil War that resulted in sharecropping was that the only form of funding available to farmers was expensive merchant financing. Sharecropping also locked growers into a perpetual cycle of cultivating mostly inedible cash crops such as cotton and tobacco. Consequently, the region was forced to purchase grain, meat, and other foodstuffs from Northern states, creating a second recurring capital drain. Funding merchants granted merchandise credits on lien notes and thereby became virtual overlords to their customers. Since cash crops such as cotton, tobacco, and rice could be sold on established regional markets, store managers insisted that their patrons plant such crops.

Nonetheless, given the unpredictability of farming and the nomadic nature of store customers, merchant financing was a risky business. It could be hard, for example, to collect from a cropper who moved away without paying his debt to the merchant. Consequently, store items sold on credit were tagged at a 25–100 percent premium over cash prices. When account balances were settled at the end of the season after the growers had collected their share of the crop sales, unscrupulous merchants might overstate the balances due particularly from customers who were not educated enough to tally the balances themselves.[23]

Historians Samuel Eliot Morison and Henry Steele Commager concluded that the sharecropping system which "appeared at first to be mutually advantageous was really disastrous to all. The sharecropper was rarely able to escape from the tenant class into the farm-owning class; the planter was seldom able to farm profitably or scientifically with [itinerate] sharecrop labor. With every year the number of tenant farmers increased [while] the profits of farming and the fertility of the soil decreased. In 1880 . . . one-third of the cotton belt farmers were tenants; forty years later the proportion had increased to two-thirds."[24]

A third consequence of postbellum federal policies was that most blacks were unprepared for free-market responsibilities. Four months after Lee's surrender at Appomattox, a group of nine hundred freedmen assembled near Mobile, Alabama, and passed a resolution complaining that their status as freedmen was worse than slavery. They voted to return to their plantation homes and work for their former owners.[25]

One ex-slave, Sylvia Cannon, explained her disillusionment:

> Times was sure better long time ago than they be now. . . . Colored people never had no debt to pay in slavery time. Never hear tell about no colored people been put in jail before Freedom. Had more to eat and more to wear then, and had good clothes all the time 'cause white folks furnish everything, everything. . . . [Freedom] let the white people down and let us down, too. Left us all to about starve to death. . . . Land went down to a dollar a acre.

A male freedman, Charlie Davenport, echoed Cannon's conclusions:

> Like all the fool niggers of that time, I was smartly bit by the freedom bug for a while. It sounded powerful nice to be told: "You don't have to chop cotton no more. You can throw that hoe down and go fishin' whenever the notion strikes you. And you can roam around at night and court girls just as late as you please." . . . I was foolish enough to believe all that stuff. But to tell the honest to God truth, most of us didn't know ourselves was no better off. Freedom meant we could leave where we'd been born and bred. But it also meant we had to scratch for ourselves."[26]

In *Up from Slavery,* Booker T. Washington recalled when the nine-year-old heard his former master announce that all the slaves had been set free:

> For some minutes there was great rejoicing and thanksgiving and wild scenes of ecstasy. But there was no feeling of bitterness. In fact, there was pity among the slaves for our former owners. The wild rejoicing . . . lasted but for a brief period, for I noticed that by the time [the freedmen] returned to their cabins there was a change in their feelings. The great responsibility of being free, of having charge of themselves . . . and their children, seemed to take possession of them. . . . Was it any wonder that within a few hours the wild rejoicing ceased and a feeling of deep gloom seemed to pervade the slave quarters?[27]

While freedmen increasingly learned to adapt, sharecropping turned out to be a school taught by the hardest of knocks, and racial discrimination put additional obstacles on their learning curve. Like many Southern whites, black sharecroppers were held in a system of debt peonage for almost a hundred years. To the perpetually impoverished Southern farmers, the Great Depression of the 1930s was nothing new, since most had been familiar with nothing but hard times all their lives.

In sum, sharecropping was a system that destroyed culture, land, and families. If not chattel slavery, it was a peonage system that enslaved the cropper to a cycle of annual debts and perpetual backbreaking labor. Children as young as four regularly worked in the fields. Poor health was a consequence. Ailments such a pellagra, rickets, and hookworm that were almost unknown in other parts of the country and could be prevented by cheap dietary changes, better sanitation, and shoes, plagued the South for almost a century after the Civil War. So short was the life expectancy in South Carolina that as late as 1930, half the state's population was under twenty.[28]

Only the region's financiers, landlords, and professional classes gained. Except for a brief challenge from Populists in the late nineteenth century, they would dominate Southern politics for nearly a century. The North, however, benefitted from the region's production of cheap raw materials as well as the international gold inflow resulting from Southern exports, without which the United States would have been unable to repay its Civil War debts in gold or return the country to the monetary gold standard much loved by Northeasterners. Before World War I, about two-thirds of the US cotton crop was generally exported and was therefore a major source of gold settlements.[29]

TEN

Redeemed

Northern businessmen began to doubt the wisdom of Radical Reconstruction before the end of President Grant's first term. Many believed that carpetbag regimes were retarding Southern economic development and were even harmful to the overall American economy. They wanted Southern conditions to be more adaptable to economic penetration by Northern businesses. Nearly all wanted the South's traditional cotton-export engine to recover because America had trade deficits for ten of the first eleven years after the Civil War. Cotton recovery, however, was slow and might be postponed indefinitely if the region remained burdened with misgovernment. Not until 1879 did the cotton crop match that of 1860, which was the last year before the war. Horace Greeley's *New York Tribune* bluntly disclosed that Northern businessmen "preferred economic to political exploitation of the South."[1]

In 1875, the co-founder of the Phelps, Dodge mining empire who had also invested in Southern timberlands after the Civil War, William Dodge, convincingly explained: "What the South needs is capital to develop her resources, but this she cannot obtain till confidence in her state government can be restored, and this will never be done by federal bayonets. . . . As merchants we want to see her gain her normal condition in the commerce of the country; nor can we hope for a general revival of business while things remain as they are." Regarding the freedmen, Dodge added that it was a mistake to make them feel "that the United States government was their special friend, rather than . . . [Southern whites,] . . . among whom they must live and . . . work. We have tried long enough. Now let the South alone."[2]

In addition to businessmen, Northern politicians gradually began to appreciate that white Southerners might have legitimate complaints about Radical Reconstruction. One example surrounded many of the most influential political leaders when they regularly convened in Washington City.

As an object lesson for the rest of the country, in January 1867 the Republican-controlled Congress granted blacks the right to vote in Washington and that same year also mandated racially segregated public schools in the city. Three years later, the city government was so impoverished that creditors seized the mayor's furniture to pay municipal debts. In response, Congress organized a unified territorial government for the District of Columbia.

After serving as executive vice president of the district's Public Works Board, Republican Alexander "Boss" Shepherd was appointed by President Grant to be the District of Columbia's territorial governor in 1873. Among Shepherd's initiatives popular with voters who paid little in direct taxes was an ambitious spending program to modernize the capital city. Partly because of strong support among black voters, Shepherd was able to get a bond referendum approved to finance the expenditures. Although a vote was not officially required, the victory enabled Shepherd to cite it as evidence that the local residents endorsed his program. The district's mostly white taxpayers and property owners, however, were horrified by the implications of the ballooning debt.

A year later, the $6 million initiative had already exceeded $9 million. When local taxpayers complained of losing properties for tax deficiencies caused by the unsustainable spending, the House of Representatives formed a bipartisan investigative committee. It learned that the program's chief beneficiary was a ring of Shepherd business associates and real estate developers.

While Republicans were unwilling to perpetuate a censured government that might continue to irresponsibly manipulate black voters, they did not want to backtrack on African American suffrage. As a matter of consistency, Congress might otherwise be compelled to spread the retrenchment to the former Confederacy, thereby disfranchising the Republican Party's largest and most reliable voting bloc in eleven states. Consequently, the committee recommended unanimously that the district's territorial government be abolished and replaced by a presidentially appointed board of commissioners. That action disfranchised *all* of the district's voters, black and white.

The district went into bankruptcy after an audit revealed its bills were $13 million in arrears. Among the casualties was the Freedmen's Savings Bank, whose chief depositors were ex-slaves. The bank had invested heavily in Washington real estate in response to the temporary boom triggered by Shepherd's untenable spending. When its doors closed in 1874, it had only $31,000 to cover the deposits of 61,000 accounts. Boss Shepherd moved his family to Mexico in 1876 after declaring personal bankruptcy. The district did not completely repay the Shepherd-era debts until 1916.

After the commission government was functioning, Congress agreed to pay half the district's municipal operating expenses. Elected government would not return to Washington, DC, until the 1960s civil rights era. Shepherd's mismanagement, partly enabled by manipulation of poorly educated black voters, brought some of the governmental evils common in Southern carpetbag regimes to the capital city, where congressmen from the rest of the country could witness it firsthand. The sobering experience was one factor that prompted Northern politicians to increasingly question the wisdom of Radical Reconstruction and to consider the potential merits of Southern home rule, a term that meant the return of Southern state government to the traditional white ruling class and its allies.[3]

Evidence of Northern opposition to Radical Reconstruction appeared as early as 1870 in a number of popular publications. In addition to the *New York Tribune*, the *Commercial & Financial Chronicle* and the *Nation* urged an end to Radical policies because they were paralyzing Southern business and discouraging capital investment in the region. The *Nation* wrote that Northern "businessmen of the highest character" who had investigated matters in the South were discouraged by the situation. Congressional elections later that year swung toward the Democrats when the Republicans lost their two-thirds majority in the House.

The Republican Party split initially appeared in Missouri because Grant continued to back the corrupt federal internal revenue collector, John McDonald, who was located there. The president's stubbornness enabled Democrats to win the legislature and reenfranchise the state's numerous Confederate veterans. In response, Missouri Republican senator Carl Schurz began to organize a Liberal wing of the Republican

Party to oppose Grant's Stalwarts. (According to historian Eric Foner, Stalwarts were Republicans for whom, "The . . . [party] . . . itself, not the . . . [antislavery] . . . crusade that once created it, commanded their highest loyalty.") Essentially, Stalwarts were politicos whose primary concern was winning elections. Since their chief tool was the political spoils system, they opposed civil service reform.[4]

The Schurz movement soon expanded nationwide. Its goal was to purge the Republican Party of corruption and vindictiveness toward the South. Among the converts was Horace Greeley, whose *Tribune* was rivaled only by James Gordon Bennett's *Herald* in terms of political influence. (The two later combined to form the *New York Herald Tribune*, which was published until a fatal labor strike in 1966.) Another convert was Charles Francis Adams, who was a son and grandson of two American presidents and had been Lincoln's minister to Great Britain during the Civil War. A third, Senator Charles Sumner, brought to the Liberal wing impeccable credentials as a proponent of black equality.

In May 1872, the Liberal Republican convention nominated Greeley on a platform that included universal amnesty of former Rebels and an end to military rule in the South. As a maneuver to steal the Liberal thunder, Congress responded later that month by passing a general amnesty that restored voting privileges to all but a few hundred ex-Confederates disfranchised by the 1867 Reconstruction Acts. Nonetheless, two months later, the Democratic Party convention also nominated Liberal Republican Greeley.[5]

Greeley traveled to Texas and sent *Tribune* representatives to evaluate conditions in other parts of the South. His informants reported that although the Ku Klux Klan was active in some areas, confiscatory carpetbag taxes that deterred the migration of capital partly justified the vigilantes. Ultimately, he concluded that the South could not prosper until the Ku Klux Klan and the carpetbaggers had been driven out. The region, said Greeley, was suffering from "decayed aristocracy and imported rascality." The *Tribune* also reported that Northern investors were deterred by racial friction, which the newspaper averred resulted from the agitations of dishonest adventurers.[6]

At a Pittsburgh campaign stop in September, Greeley summarized his stance on sectional reconciliation and Reconstruction:

> Fellow citizens, are we never to be done with this? We demanded [that] our adversaries . . . surrender their arms and go home. They surrendered them. We demanded that they abandon slavery and they abandoned slavery. We demanded that they enfranchise the blacks,

> and the blacks are enfranchised. None but white men now stand disenfranchised . . . You cannot afford to teach a part of your country to hate you, to feel that your success, your greatness is identical with their humiliation. . . . The war is ended, let us again be fellow countrymen and forget that we have been enemies.[7]

Greeley, however, was a weak candidate. Support among Northern Democrats was tepid because he was historically among the party's most vicious opponents. He had previously declared, for example, that Democrats were "murderers, drunkards, adulterers, cowards, liars, and thieves." Despite encouraging postwar reconciliation, he was also unpopular in the South because of his long-term hostility toward the region, which culminated with his denunciation of its residents as traitors during the Civil War.[8]

Grant's campaign in the South relied upon the Union Leagues to corral black votes, an activity facilitated by three federal enforcement acts in 1870 and 1871. The laws put national elections in the region under federal supervision and forcibly suppressed possible disruptions by the Ku Klux Klan. By the end of 1871, the Klan was virtually nonexistent.[9]

The president's spokesmen in the North triggered hostility toward Greeley by emphasizing his endorsement by Democrats, a party held in contempt by many Northerners because of its alliance with former Confederates. Alluding to the Klan, for example, Grant supporter and Massachusetts representative Benjamin Butler, said, "Go vote to burn school houses, desecrate churches and violate women, or vote for Horace Greeley, which means the same thing." *Harper's Weekly* cartoonist Thomas Nast inflamed such rhetoric with provocative illustrations. In one, Greeley is shown shaking hands with a Confederate after shooting a Union soldier. In another, Greeley is pictured clasping hands with John Wilkes Booth over Abraham Lincoln's grave. In a third, he is depicted turning over a frightened freedman to the Ku Klux Klan.[10]

At the end of the campaign, Grant won 55 percent of the popular vote and an even larger percentage of the electoral vote. Congressional Republicans also regained a two-thirds majority in the House and retained it in the Senate. Greeley, who had been mercilessly ridiculed during the campaign, returned to New York in October to be with his fatally ill wife. She died at the end of the month, and the despondent Greeley followed her less than a month later. The Republican victory, however, was only temporary.[11]

Although President Grant and the Stalwart Republicans won the 1872 election, the depression that followed the Panic of 1873, combined with the growing number of Grant administration scandals, prompted a sharp reversal in the mid-term elections of 1874. Twenty-three of thirty-five states holding elections went Democratic. Stalwart Republicans in the House were transformed into a minority party because the Democrats held 63 percent of the seats after the election. Stalwart control in the Senate dropped from 70 percent to 57 percent.

Home-rule candidates defeated carpetbag nominees in Arkansas, Alabama, and Texas. Voters had restored home rule earlier in Tennessee, North Carolina, Virginia, and Georgia. Remaining carpetbag governments held onto power only in Mississippi, Louisiana, South Carolina, and Florida—all states in which almost half, or more than half, of the voters were black. In April 1874, Northern hostility toward former Confederates was partly arrested by an impassioned eulogy from Mississippi congressman Lucius Lamar for abolitionist Senator Charles Sumner who had been one of the South's bitterest opponents most of his life. Republican political losses, the continuing depression, and additional Grant-related scandals set the stage for the end of all carpetbag governments following the 1876 election, as explained in chapter 7.[12]

After expelling Northern opportunists and their scalawag sidekicks, most native white Southerners rejoiced that the state governments had been "redeemed" to the proper electorate, which they defined as their own kind. Thereafter, they reasoned, the South would be given more freedom to manage its own affairs.

Many of the region's new leaders came from the former Whig Party that Lincoln had originally hoped to ally with the Republicans. They were augmented by growing numbers of reenfranchised former Confederates with other political backgrounds. Although Radical Reconstruction had poisoned all against the Republicans, many of a political coalition known as the "Redeemers" were initially reluctant to take up the Democrat label. In Virginia, for example, the Conservative Party was the antipode to the GOP for ten years. Sometimes, as in Arkansas, white Southerners attached first to a conservative wing of the Republican Party before joining with Democrats after a split had weakened the Republicans.[13]

Contrary to popular belief, the Redeemers' first objective was to reduce the cost of operating the state governments, not to segregate or disfranchise black voters. That would come later, after two classes of Southern whites came into conflict during the Populist era. The last Southern black congressman before modern times served until 1901. By comparison, the first black from a Northern state did not get into Congress until 1928, sixty-three years after the Civil War had ended.[14]

Louisiana's post-carpetbag 1879 constitution stated "no qualification of any kind for suffrage or office . . . on account of race, color, or previous condition of servitude shall be made by law." Consequently, the state's black voters continued to outnumber white voters until about 1880. Blacks were continually represented in the state's legislature until 1900. Nine blacks were in the Tennessee House of Representatives during the 1880s and 1890s. Black voters also outnumbered whites in Mississippi until the early 1890s and often supported the Democratic Party, through which some became officeholders. Post-carpetbag blacks were a majority in South Carolina as well until the mid-1890s and were elected to the legislature from both parties. All across the South, white politicians solicited the black vote with dances, picnics, and an abundance of distilled spirits.[15]

Arkansas's 1878 Democratic Party platform stated, "it is the sense of the convention that the colored population . . . are identified in the interests of the great Democratic party of the state" and "we embrace this opportunity of inviting them . . . to an active cooperation with us in furthering our common interests." Until the advent of the Populist Party, post-carpetbag blacks generally aligned with the conservative wing of the Democratic Party, which was led by comparatively wealthy whites.

One such plutocrat was South Carolina's first post-carpetbag governor, Wade Hampton, who stated, "as the negro becomes more intelligent he naturally allies himself with the more conservative of the whites, for his observation and experience both show him that his interests are identified with those of the white race." In November 1886, the *Fort Smith (AR) Weekly Elevator* wrote, "Talk with the people who have lived in the rural districts of the Gulf States, or go and reside there yourself, and you will learn that the negroes generally vote the democratic ticket."[16]

Most of the redeemed Southern states adopted new constitutions that sharply cut government services and expenses. They reduced officeholder salaries, set short limits for legislative sessions, and slashed property taxes. Even in the 1880s, only two Southern governors were paid as much as $5,000 yearly. If the Texas legislative session lasted beyond sixty days, the daily pay for members dropped from $5 to $2. Six years after redemption, Louisiana had cut state government expenses from $8 million annually to $2 million. Alabama took two years to cut government expenses from $2.2 million a year to $0.9 million. Even as late as 1900, Alabama's expenses were still under $2 million.

During the ten years following Mississippi's 1875 home-rule restoration, the state cut government operating costs by 50 percent. As a result of the consequent reduction in property taxes, millions of acres of land threatened with forfeiture for tax deficiencies were restored to their owners. Florida's first home-rule governor advised his legislature, "Spend nothing unless absolutely necessary." Two years later, the governor pronounced that the government "that gives the greatest protection to the taxpayer" is the one that should be most highly regarded.[17]

Due to fiscal abuse during the carpetbag era, the new constitutions also restricted the power of states to issue additional bonds. At the start of congressional Reconstruction in 1868, the debts of the eleven former Confederate states totaled about $75 million, which did not include $40 million in Confederate debt that had been repudiated by the Fourteenth Amendment as well as by President Johnson's earlier Reconstruction program. Only five years later, in 1873, the total debt was about $218 million, which translated into a compound annual growth rate of 24 percent. An estimated $100 million of the 1873 debt had never been authorized.

Most of the bonds were issued to fund projects that barely got off the ground or never existed except on paper. Since they were commonly issued as bearer bonds, anyone holding such a security was considered to be the owner by default. As a result, the bonds could be traded like cash and illegally given to people for dubious services, or no service at all. One New York courtesan boasted of owning $100,000 in state bonds given to her by a railroad company president. Interest payments alone required such high property levies that Southern landowners considered the taxes to be an indirect form of land confiscation. Virginia's annual debt service was almost equal to the state's entire tax receipts. Georgia and Louisiana were so traumatized by the burden of such borrowings that their Redeemer constitutions stipulated the states could only borrow money to repel invasion or suppress a revolt.[18]

Initially, Southern bonds were a boon to Wall Street investment firms and others who distributed the securities for generous fees. In one example, South Carolina was only able to sell bonds on Wall Street for 25 percent of their face value, thereby leaving a large profit margin for distributors who resold them at prices closer to par value. The assumed ownership of the bearer facilitated intentionally poor record keeping, especially if distributors and politicians kept some of the bonds for themselves. As the probability of default increased, Gilded Age securities brokers increasingly sold the bonds to poorly informed European investors.[19]

As the economic depression materialized after the Panic of 1873, even some of the carpetbag governments started trying to cut debts, spending, and real estate taxes. Contrary to popular belief, they were the first postwar Southern state governments to repudiate debts by replacing some outstanding bonds with new ones bearing lower interest rates and smaller principal amounts. Once in control, however, Redeemers accelerated the trend after verifying that the applicable bonds were illegally issued or otherwise fraudulent. Some were wholly repudiated while others were exchanged for new issues with smaller face amounts and lower interest rates. Eventually, all the former Confederate states except Texas and Mississippi repudiated at least some of their debts.[20]

Unlike the District of Columbia after its carpetbag-induced bankruptcy, Southern states received no congressional subsidies. After a temporary loss of credit, however, the remaining Southern state bonds started trading at par because the interest and principal amounts were faithfully repaid according to schedule. The speed with which Redeemer governments cut extravagant carpetbag-era spending was a key factor in restoring credit. Frugality almost became an obsession. At least initially, legislative appropriations were too small to allow for much theft by corrupted officials. Things changed in the following decade when the treasurers of Alabama, Arkansas, Louisiana, and Tennessee managed to steal a combined total of almost $3 million. State treasuries in Georgia, Mississippi, and Virginia were similarly scandalized. [21]

As noted earlier, white Southerners resented their financial burden to educate ex-slaves. Since abolition was a national policy, many felt that the federal government should partially subsidize the expense. Such resentment, however, was merely a secondary reason that the Redeemers slashed public education spending for both races. The impoverished states simply could not afford the expense.

In Virginia, the governor argued that public education was a luxury that should be paid for by those who use it. Although the reaction of Redeemers in other states was not as severe, the average length of the region's school terms dropped by 20 percent. The one-hundred-day term common in the carpetbag era did not return until the start of the twentieth century. In 1880, per pupil spending in the heart of the South was only about 60 percent of the amount in 1871. Even by 1890, per pupil spending in the South was less than $1.00 annually, compared to $2.24 for the entire nation, a figure that would have been higher had it not included the South.[22]

Nearly all other services were also cut. Institutions caring for the blind, insane, and other state dependents were wretchedly underfunded as were the prisons. Some states tried to revert to the antebellum doctrine of local responsibility by shifting as much burden as possible to the local governments that were even less able to fund schools and other services. Florida abolished its penitentiary and allowed private contractors to lease convicts as unskilled labor, thereby transforming a $25,000 annual expense into a revenue source. Convict leasing, however, quickly evolved into a sinister business. Some states granted leases of up to thirty years. Worker health care was often shameful. In 1881, for example, the death rate among Arkansas prisoners was about 25 percent annually. Planters, Northern syndicates, mining companies, and wealthy businessmen were the chief beneficiaries of convict leasing.[23]

Since planters, business professionals, and other capitalists were the principal leaders of redeemed governments, tax cuts and exemptions favored their interests. Railroads, utilities, and insurance companies were often granted franchises that exempted them from taxes. Property assessments on the businesses that were taxed tended to be below true value. New manufacturing capital was regularly granted tax exemption to encourage and placate Northern investors. In contrast, taxes on citizens without property, such as poll taxes, were increased. After a Texas governor vetoed public school funding in 1879, he urged the state's legislature to exempt new manufacturing capital from all taxes for ten years.[24]

Many students of the era regard the Redeemers as mere reincarnations of the antebellum aristocracy, but the comparison has limited validity. Comparatively few of the new leaders were chiefly focused on agriculture. By 1880, for example, less than 40 percent of Georgia's legislators were planters or farmers. Although they had nominal connections to agriculture, most were members of the middle class, focused on general industrial and capitalistic pursuits. Many invested in railroads but gladly sold their shares to better capitalized Northern companies whose interests they were thereafter incentivized to guard perpetually.

In short, a few at the top of the Southern food chain profited handsomely while the region's economy increasingly became characterized by absentee ownership. As former Virginia senator and author Jim Webb wrote in *Born Fighting*, when the Yankees left, "they did so with their ownership of the Southern economy firmly in place so that their businesses could be controlled from outside the region thereby sucking generations of profits out of the South and into their own communities."[25]

Redeemer retrenchment left at least two lasting consequences, both magnified by the region's near-colonial economic status, which lasted well into the twentieth century. First, laissez-faire economic philosophy became so engrained that it was practically transformed into a test of Southern patriotism. Post-carpetbag state constitutions typically limited government authority. Deep suspicion of government power was widespread. Second, Southerners became habituated to government parsimony, even to the point of rationalizing their neglect of the needs of handicapped and destitute citizens. With minor exceptions from private charities, white Southerners received almost no assistance in recovering from the Civil War. Liberal spending by corrupt carpetbag regimes merely worsened the situation by leaving the South heavily indebted.[26]

Redeemer governments were eventually challenged by a split between Southern white classes as opposed to a shift in black loyalties. One reason Redeemers did not initially try to curtail black voting was because they could often control such votes in regions where large percentages of voters were African American. Conservative white minorities generally controlled the economy in such areas, known as the black belts. Resident blacks tended to support politicians who favored the interests of the economic engines in the black belts as opposed to the interests of regions that were chiefly composed of poor whites. Southern blacks voted in large numbers until the late 1890s. Their participation started declining after poor Southern whites started agitating for a political divorce from conservative whites in the late 1880s. Black voters were caught in the crossfire.[27]

ELEVEN

Divorced

Populism split Southern whites along class lines. In 1887, a North Carolina editor wrote, "There is something radically wrong in our industrial system. There is a screw loose. The wheels have dropped out of balance. The railroads have never been so prosperous and yet agriculture languishes. The banks have never done a better or more profitable business, and yet agriculture languishes."

Even though America's population doubled from 1860 to 1890, crop and livestock production grew even more rapidly. Eventually corn was burned as fuel in Kansas because it was cheaper than coal. Similarly, Dakota wheat remained unharvested because market prices could not support the cost of hauling it to grain elevators and railroad depots. By the 1890s, world markets were buried in commodity surpluses.

Wheat sold for $1.06 a bushel in 1870, dropped to $0.71 in 1890, and dipped below $0.65 in the mid-1890s. Declining prices were an even bigger problem for cotton farmers because the impoverished South could not invest in up-to-date production equipment. Cotton sold for fifteen cents a pound in 1870, eight cents in 1890, and six cents in 1895.[1]

Since the costs of the products they purchased were also dropping, farmers might have had no special complaints except for their indebtedness. The petroleum and steel industries, for example, steadily reduced prices as production volumes increased, although prices might have been even lower without the monopolies of John D. Rockefeller and Andrew Carnegie. Even though they could not generally afford capital equipment, Southern farmers regularly borrowed for seed and fertilizer, while farmers elsewhere also borrowed to buy better production tools and more land. A farmer's only source of revenue to repay such debts was the sale proceeds of his harvest, which was partly dependent upon market prices. When proceeds were stubbornly insufficient to cover costs, farmers became trapped in a perpetual annual cycle of increasing indebtedness.[2]

The Farmers Alliance was the first organization to effectively address the economic needs of American agriculture in the second half of the nineteenth century. It came to power after the earlier organized Grange movement had faded. The secret alliance was formed in 1875 in central Texas by a group of ranchers to cooperatively combat horse thieves and round up strays. It also generally tried to protect the interests of smaller operators when they came into conflict with large ranchers and landowners. After spreading to other parts of the South, it became known as the Southern Alliance. By the mid-1880s, it had fifty thousand members when a brief return to prosperity interrupted its growth.

A similar Northern Alliance also formed in the 1870s. By 1881, it had twenty-five thousand members, which leaped to one hundred thousand the following year. The Northern Alliance mostly represented farmers in the upper Mississippi River valley and its western tributaries. Like the Southern Alliance, however, it lost influence until economic conditions worsened in the second half of the 1880s.

Historically, during hard times, western farmers were able to liquidate their debts by selling their farms and moving farther west to start over by purchasing cheaper lands. Since the closing of the frontier around 1890 eliminated that option, many western farmers who might have otherwise remained independent joined the Northern Alliance.[3]

Although black farmers confronted the same economic problems, few joined the Northern Alliance because of their low percentage of the region's population. While the Southern Alliance remained racially segregated, it encouraged black farmers to form a tandem organization that could help advance the interests of farmers from both races. The resulting Colored Farmers National Alliance and Cooperative Union was formed in 1886.

In 1889, the Southern and Northern Alliances held concurrent annual meetings in St. Louis as discrete organizations in separate buildings. Although the two alliances did not merge, their leaders met and agreed to seek common goals. Both wanted railroad-rate regulation and more convenient access to new lands by small farmers. In hopes of lifting commodity prices, they wanted the federal government to increase the amount of currency in circulation. Convention delegates returned to their respective regions intent on electing proponents of such goals to political office.

Southerners generally tried to accomplish the mission within the established Democratic Party. Since many Northern Alliance members were Union army veterans, they did not want to associate with the Democratic Party, which generally opposed increases in veterans' pensions. Northerners, therefore, more readily considered forming new political parties that ultimately consolidated into the Populist Party. Some of the Populist objectives were first articulated in the 1890 campaign.

"We want the abolition of National Banks and we want the power to make loans directly from the government," said spokeswoman Mary Elizabeth Lease of Kansas. Other campaigners attacked the railroads and grain elevator operators. One South Carolina Alliance member and Democratic gubernatorial candidate, Benjamin Tillman, told audiences how creditors bankrupted him. "The devil tempted me to buy a steam engine and other equipment amounting to $2000, all on credit." A drought-induced crop failure forced him to sell his farm.[4]

Populists initially won congressional representation in 1890 by gaining nine House seats. Although most Southern Alliance members officially remained Democrats, they gained more than forty seats, including three in the Senate. The alliance won control of the legislatures in eight Southern states. Members were elected governors in South Carolina, Tennessee, and Georgia, while an ally was elected governor in Texas. The Northern Alliance gained control of the Nebraska legislature and the lower house of the Kansas legislature. Populist congressmen elected from both states were heading to Washington.

Energized by such successes, the Northern and Southern Alliances held a joint convention in Ocala, Florida, in December 1890. Northern Alliance members wanted to consolidate all congressmen into the Populist Party right away. Southerners were reluctant because of the Democratic Party's traditional dominance in the South. They did, however, indicate an increased willingness to consider a third party in the future by resolving, "If the people by delegates coming directly from them agree that a third party move is necessary, it need not be feared."[5]

In July 1892, the Populist Party held its first presidential convention in Omaha. During the preceding two years, some Southern Democratic congressmen, such as Thomas Watson of Georgia, had left their party to join the Populists. The convention nominated Iowan James Weaver for president and Virginian James Field for vice president. Salient platform points were:

1. Unlimited coinage of silver with a statutory equivalency of sixteen silver ounces to a single ounce of gold.
2. An increase in the value of currency in circulation to an amount equal to fifty dollars per capita.
3. A graduated income tax.
4. A restriction of federal taxes to only the amounts necessary to operate the government (an antiprotective-tariff plank).
5. Postal savings banks.
6. Public railroad ownership and return of railroad land grants to the public.
7. A government-supported (sub-Treasury) financing plan for farmers of nonperishable goods.[6]

The first plank aimed at increasing the money supply as a way of reversing long-term price deflation, particularly for farm commodities. It would remove restrictions of the 1890 Sherman Silver Purchase Act that instructed the Treasury to buy no more than 4.5 million ounces monthly above the modest minimums previously set by the 1878 Bland-Allison Act. The 16–1 exchange ratio placed the monetary value of silver above the bullion value, thereby inducing silver producers to sell to the Treasury, where the supplies would be coined, instead of the open market, where prices were lower.

The second plank set a specific per capita target to which it aimed to increase the money supply. The fourth plank thrust at minimizing, or abolishing, protective tariffs. The fifth plank attacked federal banking policies that tended to concentrate national banks in the Northeast. Federal capitalization requirements and lending restrictions often made such banks uneconomical in rural areas. Consequently, loans in agricultural belts were often only available through factors and merchants who were basically high-cost tributary distributors of Northern capital. The arrangement perpetuated a near financial monopoly for the Northern money centers.

The sixth plank targeted the high freight rates of railroad monopolies and hoped to make more land available for farmers to purchase at reasonable prices. As explained in chapter 8, the seventh plank's sub-Trea-

Benjamin Tillman, left, Democratic governor and later senator from South Carolina; Thomas Watson, right, Georgia congressman and Populist Party vice-presidential candidate in 1896. (*Library of Congress*)

sury plan was a proposed network of government owned warehouses to store harvested cash crops, such as cotton, to function as collateral for temporary government loans to farmers. It was the forerunner of the agricultural support programs of the Great Depression.

In addition to its platform, the Populist convention declared "sentiments" designed to attract voters from industrial states. Among them were the eight-hour workday, immigration restrictions, and a prohibition of hiring strikebreakers. It also endorsed selective boycotts of products from industries experiencing strikes. Among its good government proposals were the secret ballot and advocacy for referendums. Contrary to Southern interests, however, it promised to continue liberal Union veterans' pensions, which tended to keep tariffs high as a means of paying for the pensions.[7]

The Populist Party's ultimate objective was to replace the Democrats as the principal opposition party to the dominant Republicans. The party defined a society through its membership base instead of its apex members. It wanted, therefore, to level the economic and social playing field for the disadvantaged. In the South, that compelled an attempt to include the black man. Georgia's Tom Watson wrote, "Why should the colored man always be taught that the white man of his neighborhood hates him, while the Northern [capitalistic] man loves him?"[8]

Given its stronger 1890 showing with Farmers' Alliance candidates compared to the West, the South might become the key to Populist gains in 1892. If the Democratic Party failed to adopt a Populist agenda, Southern Alliance politicians might switch to the Populist Party. Due to Grover Cleveland's previously demonstrated policies, the Democratic Party showed that it rejected the Populist agenda in 1892 when it nominated him for president a third time.

In order to offset party defections that Cleveland's nomination might cause in the South, the region's conservative Democrats played the race card to divert the attention of poor whites from the benefits of populism. If poor whites would not unite with the conservative whites on economic principles and thus deny the conservatives continued regional control, they might vote the conservative ticket if offered a racially superior legal status—laws that would promote whites over blacks—as a method of preventing the black voter from becoming the balance of power between any two competing white groups.

Much like Republicans waved the "bloody shirt" toward former Confederates to remind Northerners that the Democratic South was responsible for the Civil War and thus keeping them loyal to the GOP for years afterwards, around 1890, aristocratic Southern Democrats started reminding poor whites of the role black voters played in sustaining the evils of the carpetbag era. Thomas Watson identified and publicly exposed the situation:

> You might beseech a Southern white tenant to listen to you upon questions of finance, taxation, and transportation . . . you might have him almost persuaded to the truth, but if the merchant who furnished him farm supplies . . . or the town politician . . . came along and cried "Negro rule!" the entire fabric of reason and common sense . . . would fail . . . and the poor tenant would joyously hug the chains of . . . wretchedness rather than do any experimenting on a question of mere sentiment.[9]

Watson accused the Republicans of adopting a similar strategy with blacks. The result, he lamented, was a "solid black vote against a solid white vote." Since blacks were in the minority, the outcome was predictable. Watson would later recant his liberal views on African Americans, perhaps because of a legitimate change of heart, but more likely as a political survival mechanism in the wake of the Populist collapse.[10]

It was, therefore, no coincidence that legal segregation and indirect suppression of black voters began around 1890. In fact, the incident that resulted in the "separate but equal" validation of segregation by the US Supreme Court *Plessy v. Ferguson* case occurred in Louisiana the same year that Watson wrote the words quoted above. While segregation confered a lower social status on the black man, finessed voter suppression almost eliminated his political influence in the South for decades to come. Black political power also remained insignificant in the North chiefly because African Americans long represented only a small proportion of the population outside the South. For example, in Massachusetts, which was the cradle of abolitionism, blacks represented only about 2 percent of the population in 1960.

Disfranchisement began in Mississippi in 1890 and was triggered by two factors. First, the House passed the Federal Elections Bill that would empower federal courts to mandate supervision of congressional elections. The chief sponsor was Republican Massachusetts congressman Henry Cabot Lodge, who wanted to increase the black vote in the South, which he presumed would normally go Republican. Like most informed observers, Lodge anticipated that Republican president Benjamin Harrison would be in a tough fight for reelection against Grover Cleveland in 1892. Although Northern weariness toward the seemingly perpetual federal intervention in local Southern affairs caused the Lodge bill to fail in the Senate, Mississippians met to form a new state constitution the month after it passed the House in July 1890, without waiting to see what happened next in Washington.

The second trigger was a growing split among the state's white voters. White yeomen farmers inclined toward a Populist agenda while a combination of planters and business professionals tended toward a conservative program. Although neither side wanted black voters to hold the balance of power, the yeomanry took a stronger stand because of persistent evidence that conservative Democrats had generally controlled African American votes. Conversely, author Wilbur Cash concluded that Populist attempts to "carry out a program . . . [in behalf of the yeomanry] would inevitably be to raise class conflict, and to raise class conflict would inevitably be to split the Democratic Party into irreconcilable factions. And that . . . would be . . . to lay the way open to the return of [the] Negro in politics," which was also anathema to the conservative wing of the Democratic Party.[11]

Simultaneously, many blacks concluded that, contrary to initial expectations, political participation was more harmful than helpful. Since the end of the Civil War, the black voting bloc was mostly a political football fought over by opposing white groups who put their own interests first. Initially, carpetbaggers manipulated the freedmen. Later, conservative Democrats controlled black votes by fraud, bribery, or suggestions of economic penalties such as hints to deny sharecropper contract renewals. Perceptive African American leaders like Booker T. Washington urged the race to concentrate on economic and educational progress through which it could hope to eventually command respect and win fairly administered suffrage.[12]

Even though the last of the carpetbag regimes collapsed in 1877, black voters continued to outnumber whites in South Carolina, Louisiana, and Mississippi. If voting as a block, they might also control the political destinies in Alabama, Florida, and Georgia by throwing their support to a minority party among whites. In 1892, for example, Georgia and Alabama would have voted the Populist ticket except for the black voters who aligned with the plutocratic wing of the Democratic Party, much to the annoyance of the white yeomanry. Many post-Civil War Southern white voters, therefore, increasingly came to feel that their region was at the mercy of "Negro Supremacy," which they concluded must be replaced with "White Supremacy."[13]

Initially, other Southern states only slowly followed Mississippi's lead. South Carolina's Farmers' Alliance gubernatorial candidate in 1890, Benjamin "Pitchfork" Tillman, was hostile to black voters mostly because his opponent solicited their support in a losing effort to beat Tillman. When he left office in 1894 to become a US senator, Tillman urged his successor to organize a new state constitutional convention partly in order to adopt regulations to limit black voter participation. The result was the state's 1895 constitution that required voters to pass a literacy test and pay a poll tax six months before scheduled elections. Many poor, improvident, and illiterate blacks were persistently ineligible to vote thereafter.

Indirect disfranchisement of Southern blacks accelerated after 1898 for two reasons. First, in *Williams v. Mississippi*, the US Supreme Court basically upheld Mississippi's 1890 voter restrictions in a unanimous decision. Interestingly, only one of the nine justices was from a former Confederate state. Second, after America occupied the Philippines at the end of the Spanish-American War, our country demonstrated that white supremacy was a national—not a regional—principle. President William McKinley had taken up the so-called white man's burden implicit in America's new imperialism.

When commenting upon the Supreme Court's *Williams v. Mississippi* decision, the New York-based *Nation* magazine wrote, "an interesting coincidence is that this important decision is rendered at a time when we are considering the idea of taking in a varied assortment of inferior races in different parts of the world, which of course could not be allowed to vote." Boston's *Atlantic Monthly* wrote, "If the stronger and cleverer race is free to impose its will upon 'new-caught, sullen peoples' on the other side of the globe, why not South Carolina and Mississippi?" Columbia University professor John W. Burgess concluded "that the Republican party, in its work of imposing the sovereignty of the United States upon eight millions of [Filipinos], has changed its view in regard to the

Populist Party candidate William Jennings Bryan, left; Republican candidate William McKinley, right. (*Library of Congress*)

political relations of races and has at last virtually accepted the ideas of the South upon that subject."[14]

From 1898 to 1910, Louisiana, North Carolina, Alabama, Virginia, Georgia, and Oklahoma indirectly disfranchised blacks in their constitutions or by amendment. Over the same years, Tennessee, Arkansas, Texas, and Florida got the same result in other ways, chiefly the poll tax. Contrary to popular belief, a number of Northern states had already enacted similar laws, but they did not have the effect of disfranchising many voters because few blacks lived outside the South. From 1865 to 1900, for example, both Pennsylvania and Massachusetts required voters to pay a poll tax.[15]

In 1896, the Populist Party gambled everything on a fusion with the Democrats to back the charismatic William Jennings Bryan for president against Republican William McKinley. The 36-year-old Bryan had electrified the July Democratic convention with his "Cross of Gold" speech advocating expansion of the money supply by the unlimited coinage of silver. Bryan closed his speech by indirectly addressing the Republicans about their insistence upon primarily restricting coinage to gold, saying, "You shall not press down upon the brow of labor this crown of thorns. You shall not crucify mankind upon a cross of gold."

When the Populists later also nominated Bryan for president, all other party principles took a back seat to the "free and unlimited coinage of silver" plank underscored by Bryan. Tom Watson foresaw the dilemma.

"If we fuse, we are sunk; if we don't fuse all the silver men will leave us for the Democrats." Watson agreed to run on the Populist ticket as vice president only because he hoped it would keep the party from being absorbed by the Democrats.[16]

From a legal perspective, Bryan had a sound case. Partly due to the failure of the fiat-based Continental dollar prior to the formation of the United States in 1789, the US Constitution specified that the individual states could not make anything legal tender except gold or silver specie. Unlike the fiat money (greenbacks and national bank notes) adopted by the Republicans during the Civil War, silver was explicitly mentioned as an acceptable metal for coinage even though Republicans in 1896 were intent on restricting its use. Twenty-first century readers may think it odd that circulating money could ever be in short supply—like gasoline during the 1973 Arab oil embargo—but it was scarce in rural areas during the second half of the nineteenth century. Farmers, therefore, reasoned that an increase in the silver coinage would stimulate prosperity and higher commodity prices. In 1896, the Democrats and Populists gambled everything on that single principle.[17]

They could not, however, win the election without taking some of the Northern states, and they adopted some party planks to appeal to factory workers and labor unions. Historian Walter Webb explained:

> The interest of northern labor was almost the same as the interest of the South and the West, but the pressure on labor was too strong. . . . The chief weapon to bludgeon labor out of Bryan's camp was fear, the specter of lost jobs. Factory superintendents posted notices . . . that if Bryan were elected the factories would shut down. Men were offered positions contingent on McKinley's election. Such pressure cannot be resisted by men whose loved ones depend upon their daily labor for daily bread and so northern labor did not join with the farmers of the South and the West.[18]

The Populists lost in two ways. Bryan was defeated and, as Watson feared, both the Republicans and Democrats thereafter selectively adopted Populist principles.

After McKinley was assassinated during his second term, Vice President Theodore Roosevelt became president. Roosevelt quickly gained a reputation as an antimonopoly trustbuster. His first target was the railroad industry, which resulted in the breakup of the Northern Securities Company that controlled several trunk lines between the Midwest and the West Coast. When Democrat Woodrow Wilson became president four years after Roosevelt left office, he cut tariffs, established the Federal

Reserve banking system, and presided over the adoption of a graduated income tax and popular election of senators. Shortly after Bryan was defeated, gold discoveries in the Canadian Yukon and elsewhere began to increase the money supply without resorting to unlimited silver coinage.[19]

After thirty years of limited participation, Northerners began to invest aggressively in Southern industries following the Panic of 1893, thereby strengthening the region's output and economic diversification. Although native Southerners had already formed a growing textile manufacturing business, New England owners started taking their cotton mills to the cotton fields in the 1890s. During that decade, the number of spindles in the South increased from 11 percent to 23 percent of the US total. By 1910, they had increased to 39 percent, and they were 60 percent by 1930. Since most were raised in poverty, Southern employees were glad to have such jobs, even though they worked longer hours for lower pay than did the New Englanders. Poverty also made Southerners more prone to put their children to work. An 1887 Alabama law that limited a child's workday to eight hours was repealed at the behest of a Massachusetts mill that had expanded into the state and wanted the children to work longer days.[20]

The demise of the Populist Party that drove most of the Southern Farmers' Alliance and Populists into the Democratic Party had good and bad effects. Among the good was the incorporation of key alliance and Populist reform agendas into the Democratic Party. Among the bad was the marginalization of African Americans through indirect voter restrictions and de jure segregation, which fostered a culture of racism. South Carolina's Benjamin "Pitchfork" Tillman is an extreme example of the Jekyll-Hyde white Southern politician that sometimes resulted. Although he was progressive on economic matters, he was also an inveterate racist.

Tillman was the last of seven children belonging to an up-country South Carolina family and was fourteen years old when the Civil War broke out. Up-country families along the Appalachian foothills were typically less prosperous than the aristocrats of the low country along the Atlantic Seaboard. Initially, he was too young to enlist as a Confederate soldier. When he later joined the army toward the end of the war, Tillman suffered an infection that required his left eye to be removed. The war was over by the time he recovered.

In his late twenties, he helped former Confederate lieutenant general Wade Hampton win the governorship during the disputed 1876 presidential election discussed in chapter 7 that ended the last of the carpetbag regimes. Hampton genuinely sought a mutually beneficial alliance with the state's black voters. Many African Americans, however, were suspicious of his motives or were habituated to manipulation by lingering carpetbag Republicans.

Therefore, some Hampton supporters formed "Red Shirt" rifle clubs, which paraded around the state to lift the morale of Hampton voters and discourage—even intimidate—his opponents. Tillman was one Red Shirt who was prepared to go beyond mere intimidation. He participated in an unplanned skirmish with a unit of the Republican-controlled black militia in Hamburg after area whites protested the failure of militia members to appear at a court hearing. Seven blacks and one white were killed.[21]

Tillman's hostility toward blacks partly reflected the role they played in sustaining corrupt carpetbag governments from 1868 to 1876. No state had a greater percentage of African Americans than the 57 percent of South Carolina. They accounted for 61 percent of the members in the state's House of Representatives and 27 percent of its state senators elected with carpetbag governor Robert Scott in 1868. Only twenty-two members of the 1868 South Carolina legislature were literate.[22] The combined members of both chambers paid less than $700 in taxes to support the state government. Governor Scott organized fourteen regiments of black militia shortly before the 1870 election, partly to intimidate opposition voters and partly to spread patronage among black voters. He thereby unintentionally inspired the later formation of the Red Shirts.

Scott's administration was characterized by such wasteful spending that later investigators could not even determine how much the state's debt had increased. When he took office in mid-1868, South Carolina's debt totaled about $6 million, but three years later it was estimated at $17 million to $29 million. Scott also fraudulently acquired state-owned shares in a major railroad and encouraged the state to buy land from political allies at inflated prices. The purchased lands were worthless for the ostensible purpose of distributing farmland to freedmen in exchange for low interest borrowings. Scott's successor, Frank Moses, was "entirely devoid of moral sense." He later moved North of the Mason-Dixon line, where he became a petty criminal and died in poverty.[23]

Despite his general animus toward blacks, Tillman evolved into a progressive advocate for small farmers and an opponent of the low-country aristocracy. He organized South Carolina farmers into a state association that later became part of the Farmers' Alliance. Although he stayed within the Democratic Party, he promoted the Alliance's progressive agenda. He spoke to his constituents in an earthy language that accentuated his differences with the party's elite.

As noted, Tillman candidly admitted his failures at farming, which, he asserted, were partly because of financial debts to the economically privileged. He was ever after convinced that farmers were permanently disadvantaged when political conservatives gave free reign to powerful capitalists. When the party's penny-pinching conservative wing opposed accepting a land gift for an agricultural college from John C. Calhoun's late son-in-law, Thomas Clemson, Tillman rallied the yeomanry to back the funding required to operate the new school. He shot back at the aristocracy by suggesting that the state-supported Citadel in Charleston was a "military dude [dandy] factory" that might be more useful if transformed into a school for girls.[24]

When he decided to run for governor in 1889, he wrote a policy statement that was released by G. W. Shell, president of the state's farmers association. Known as the "Shell Manifesto," it argued that the African American voting bloc had compelled poor whites to acquiesce to white conservative leadership, which largely controlled the black vote after the end of the carpetbag rule. According to historian John Ezell, however, the manifesto also opposed lynching and advocated a number of progressive actions:[25]

> The agricultural college had to be established; the fertilizer trust in the state broken; and protection be given against the "greed of the gigantic corporations owned by the North. . . . " [It complained that] the railroad commissions had been tamed [to the injury of shippers;] the penitentiary was mismanaged and the legislature should be apportioned according to population. . . . "Can we afford . . . [to any longer leave the state] in the hands . . . of a few families and for the benefit of a selfish ring of politicians?"[26]

Tillman emerged as the state's political boss after winning elections as governor in 1890 and US senator in 1894. During his time in office, he secured a number of progressive measures. Despite an earlier reputation for violence, he frequently called out militia to prevent lynches. Although his antilynching policy was sometimes violated, the frequency of such atrocities declined. Other progressive actions included higher royalties from companies mining the state's phosphate deposits; more money for education, including Clemson University; state control of the sale of alcoholic drinks; and better alignment of the state's railroad commission to the interests of shippers. He inspired the 1895 convention that gave South Carolina its post-carpetbag state constitution.

Despite such progressive measures as popular election of US senators, however, the South Carolina constitution included a number of indirect methods for limiting black votes, including property ownership, literacy tests, and a poll tax. When addressing the convention, Tillman reminded its delegates of the Reconstruction-era evils, which he argued were caused by black voters who "put the little pieces of paper in the box that gave . . . commission to these white scoundrels [carpetbaggers and scalawags] who were . . . [the freedmen's] leaders and the men who debauched them." Tillman did, however, support provisions to remove sheriffs who permitted lynching and financial penalties for each county in which a lynching occurred.[27]

Predictably, at the 1896 Democratic presidential convention, Tillman was an outspoken Free Silver advocate. When earlier running for the Senate, he promised that upon arrival in Washington, he'd take a pitchfork to Grover Cleveland to underscore his objection to the president's proposal to repeal the Sherman Silver Purchase Act. When he publicly proclaimed that the Free Silver delegates would rule the convention, Cleveland supporters hissed. Tillman characteristically volleyed back, "There are only three things . . . that can hiss; a goose, a serpent and a man." He might have won the nomination instead of Bryan except for his belligerent language and racist attitudes.

After engaging in a fistfight in the Senate a few years later, Tillman lost an invitation to dine at the White House with President Theodore Roosevelt. He later played a key role in passage of the Hepburn Act that gave the Interstate Commerce Commission authority to set "just and reasonable" rates and fares. The pioneering 1907 Tillman Act that prohibited corporations from making donations to candidates for congressional or presidential elections was named for him. He remained in the Senate until his death in 1918.[28]

AFTER MISSISSIPPI AND SOUTH CAROLINA established black voter restrictions, other Southern states followed. The two most common methods were literacy tests and property requirements. When it became apparent that such restrictions also affected uneducated whites, some Southern states adopted grandfather statutes that permitted the descendants of earlier (e.g., pre-1868) voters to retain the privilege. In 1915, however, the Supreme Court ruled in *Guinn v. United States* that such laws violated the Fifteenth Amendment. Meanwhile, Southern voter participation among all races declined significantly. Many blacks had been pragmatically disfranchised, and fewer whites felt the need to vote because of blacks being forced out of the picture and the dominance of a one-party (Democratic) system.

In Louisiana, for example, voter registrations dropped from about three hundred thousand in 1897 to under one hundred thousand in 1904.

The decline among blacks was about one hundred thirty thousand, compared to seventy-five thousand whites. Mississippi lost forty-two thousand white voters and one hundred forty thousand of its one hundred forty-seven thousand black voters. Participation in congressional elections dropped sharply across the region, with declines ranging from 80 percent in Georgia and Louisiana to 35 percent in North Carolina. In the 1912 elections that put the first Democrat in the White House since Grover Cleveland, voter participation in the South averaged about 33 percent, compared to 60 percent nationally.

Since only small numbers of endemic whites were Republican, the disfranchisement of Southern blacks left the Democratic Party in control by default. Thus, it became evident that a second way to limit blacks' political power was to bar them from Democratic primaries. It mattered little if they voted in the general election because the region's office holders were essentially selected in the earlier primaries. By 1930, all but three of the former eleven Confederate states had banned blacks from Democratic primaries, generally by statutes that permitted each party to set membership rules as though they were private clubs. The US Supreme Court eventually outlawed such "white primaries" with a series of rulings that began in 1927 and ended with *Smith v. Allwright* in 1944.[29]

Five years later, historian Herbert Agar wrote:

> It was wicked to force the Negro to rule the disfranchised white man [during the carpetbag era] when everybody knew the position would be reversed as soon as Northerners grew sick of governing their fellow Americans with the sword. It was wicked to turn the Negro free . . . without thought for his future except that he must be bullied or brought into voting Republican. It was extra wicked to commit both these cruelties at the same time. . . . There is a limit beyond which only mad moralists and the truly corrupt will go. It was the fate of the Negro . . . to be sacrificed to an alliance between these two. He didn't want to run the South. . . . But his Northern friends wanted to prove their political theories, or they simply wanted his vote. The moralists thought he could eat freedom . . . the others didn't think at all, beyond the next election. But . . . he gave them his vote, since they asked for it. And the white South has not forgiven him in eighty years.[30]

The less-pronounced disfranchisement of impoverished and uneducated whites left the South's Democratic Party controlled by its conservative wing until the 1960s. Memoirist Shirley Abbott described the last remnants of such rulers as "mostly southern civilized gentlemen who advocated peace and good will and good manners, except when threatening their opponents with financial ruin, stealing elections, or bribing governors." Such plutocrats increasingly allied with the Republicans on economic matters, especially after the Franklin Roosevelt and Harry Truman presidential administrations. During the long interval between the McKinley and Richard Nixon administrations, the South paid a heavy price for its one-party system. Nationally, the Democratic Party took the region's votes for granted, and Republicans felt no obligations toward the South because they had no constituency there.[31]

TWELVE

Racial Adjustment

Often the biggest problems of war emerge during the ensuing peace. Two major challenges surfaced in the wake of the Civil War. First was racial adjustment, which Southern whites did not want to face and Northern whites did not want to share. Second was the rebuilding of the Southern economy.

During most of the postwar period in the nineteenth century, the federally dominant Republican Party's attitude toward the South focused chiefly on racial matters before letting them fall into neglect toward the end of that era. In contrast, not until the Great Depression of the 1930s did a Democratically controlled federal government give much thought to Southern economic development. As the two political parties competed more equally for national power after World War II, the South's race and economic problems received more attention.

Prior to the Civil War, slaveholders had two basic goals for their slaves: to extract labor and prevent servile insurrections. Both required that blacks and whites remain in close contact. Overseers directed black work gangs. After work, owners tried to keep slaves from congregating in groups where rebellion might be discussed and encouraged. On smaller farms, slaves and owners often worked shoulder to shoulder. Blacks and whites constantly mingled in towns and cities. Visitors from other regions to cities like New Orleans were often surprised in the casual way the two races mixed. Since most blacks were slaves, there was no need for segregation to remind everyone of their lower status. In a master-slave relationship, segregation was literally unworkable.

After the war, white racial attitudes bifurcated along economic lines. Since virtually all freedmen were poor, white aristocrats did not need segregation to be assured of their own superior status. The same was not true for poor whites. In the antebellum period, slavery always conferred a superior social rank to all whites, including poor ones. Once the slaves were freed, however, poor blacks and whites competed for the same jobs. Neither could claim a superior station to the other if economics were the defining characteristic. Poor whites, therefore, were the prime advocates of Southern segregation. The Northern laboring class felt much the same way.[1]

Although leading proponents of black suffrage such as Thaddeus Stevens and Charles Sumner are generally regarded as among the Republican leaders most sincerely interested in black-white racial equality, GOP concern for ex-slaves also had much to do with perpetuating the party's power by creating a reliable voting constituency in the South. Even Stevens and Sumner admitted that their efforts to secure voting rights for black men was partially motivated by such political considerations.

When speaking in Congress in January 1867, Stevens said, "If [black] suffrage is excluded in the rebel States then every one of them is sure to send a solid rebel representative delegation to Congress. . . . They, with their kindred [Northern] Copperheads, would always elect the President and control Congress." He also stated that the Southern states, "ought never . . . be . . . counted as valid states until the Constitution shall have been amended . . . to secure perpetual ascendancy to the party of the Union [the Republican Party]." Similarly, a Rhode Island Republican complained to Sumner, "Without [black suffrage in the South], Southerners will certainly unite . . . with Democrats of the North, and the long train of evils sure to follow their rule is fearful to contemplate . . . [including] . . . a great reduction of the tariff."[2]

Harvard and Columbia historians Samuel Eliot Morison and Henry Steele Commager conclude that Stevens was more interested in punishing white Southerners than in helping African Americans:

> Stevens is one of the most unpleasant characters in American history. A harsh, somber, friendless old man . . . with no redeeming

> spark of magnanimity, he was moved less by sympathy for the Negro than by cold hatred of the Southern gentry. . . . [H]e would humiliate, disfranchise, and despoil . . . all . . . landed [property owners] in favor of the freedman. [Stevens sought retribution saying,] "I have never desired bloody punishments to any great extent . . . but there are punishments quite as appalling and longer remembered than death. They are more advisable because they would reach a greater number. Strip a proud nobility of their bloated estates; . . . send them forth to labor and teach their children to enter the workshops or handle a plow . . . and settle [their states] with new men and drive the present rebels as exiles from this country."[3]

Massachusetts's junior senator and Sumner's colleague, Republican Henry Wilson, who later became vice president under Ulysses Grant, was even more explicit: "[Given universal black suffrage in the South] . . . a majority of [the former rebel] States will within twelve months, send here Senators and Representatives who think as we think, speak as we speak, and vote as we vote, and will give their electoral votes for whoever we nominate for President in 1868."[4]

Even if Republican leaders like Stevens, Sumner, and Wilson are credited with wanting racial equality for its intrinsic merit, they realized that the scarcity of blacks in the North would make racial adjustment inconsequential in their region as compared to the South. As noted earlier, in 1860, only 1 percent of the population of free states was black, compared to 34 percent of the slave states and 40 percent in the eleven states that would join the Confederacy.[5]

Equality advocates also understood that racial prejudice was common throughout the United States, not just the South. When the Civil War began, blacks were not permitted to vote in sixteen of the twenty-two Union-loyal states. In most of the remaining six, they could only vote by meeting property and education tests that were more stringent than those applied to whites. In 1868, three Northern states put black suffrage on the ballot, and all failed to pass it. Even though slaves were freed in Washington, DC, during the war, the district voted 7,337–36 against granting them suffrage in 1867. Despite the vote, Congress granted black suffrage in the district.[6]

William H. Seward, an impeccably credentialed abolitionist and early Republican party leader who served as secretary of state under Lincoln and Johnson, said, "The North has nothing to do with negroes. . . . I have no more concern for them than Hottentots. They are God's poor; they always have been and will be so everywhere." In 1862, Massachusetts governor John Andrew refused to accept black refugees because he said they would become paupers. That same year, former slaves sent from the lower Mississippi River valley to Illinois prompted riots upon their arrival. Consequently, they were returned to the South.[7]

Perhaps the four-day New York City draft riot in July 1863 best illustrates Northern racial prejudice. A new draft call provoked many of the city's working class to riot. They particularly objected that wealthy men could avoid the call by paying a three hundred dollar commutation fee, or by hiring a substitute.

Initially mobs targeted the draft centers and the outnumbered police. The Emancipation Proclamation signed six months earlier, however, had left a smoldering resentment that suggested that blacks should be blamed for the war. Moreover, the city's whites had been losing jobs to free blacks, and they worried that such competition would intensify if ex-slaves migrated north. Consequently, the crowds soon targeted African Americans, even though only 1.5 percent of the city's population was black. A black orphanage was destroyed. Blacks discovered in the riot regions were pursued and killed, often by lynching. About one-fourth of the city's blacks were left homeless. Estimates of the killed varied widely, from 74 to 1,200 for all races. Whatever the correct figure, the July 1863 New York draft riots proved to be bigger than any Southern Reconstruction era race riots.[8]

Senator Thomas Hendricks of Indiana, who was the Democratic minority leader in 1868 and later became vice president under Grover Cleveland, said of African Americans:

> I say we are not of the same race; we are so different that we ought not to compose one political community. . . . I say . . . this is a white man's Government, made by the white man for the white man. . . . I am not in favor of giving the colored man a vote, because I think we should remain a political community of white people. I do not think it is for the good of either race that we should attempt to make a Government a mixed Government of white and black. . . . I am not in favor of attempting to mix these races. I want to see the white race kept a white race and the power in this country without mixture and without attempt at mixture.[9]

For eight months after the Civil War, from September 1865 through March 1866, New England journalist and former Andrew Johnson aide Benjamin C. Truman toured the South to investigate conditions. During his trip, Northerners were chiefly concerned with whether Southerners were secretly plotting to continue the rebellion, which meant that the existing peace would be only temporary, and the matter of "the freedmen and their affairs." Truman visited eight of the rebel states, missing only Virginia and the Carolinas. He summarized his findings in a report, which President Johnson sent to the Senate on May 7, 1866.[10]

Benjamin C. Truman, later in life.

Truman compared the attitude of Southerners toward the federal government, which they tried to leave, to that of the Northerners toward President James Buchanan's administration on the eve of the Civil War. While Northerners generally "hated and despised" Buchanan, they never seriously considered rebelling against his government. Similarly, Truman concluded, "now that war has swept over the South there is no more disposition . . . to rebel against the national government than there was in the north . . . [in Buchanan's] time." Southerners were "indifferent" toward the federal government. "Fully one half of the southern people never cherished . . . any government that was over them and the war has left them very much as it found them." He felt that loyalty to the old flag was growing. "It is my belief that the south . . . is more loyal now than it was at the end of the war . . . and that it will be more loyal to-morrow than to-day." Southerners accepted defeat. The war would not continue.[11]

He also concluded that the former Confederate soldiers were likely to be the best source of the region's future leaders. Those who dutifully remained with their armies to the end "are the backbone . . . of the south. . . . Around . . . [them] . . . gathers the same circle of friends that we see around the millions of [Northern] hearth-stones . . . and from [them] they are slowly learning the lessons of charity and brotherhood." Although hard feelings toward Yankees remained, Truman wrote, "rumors to the effect that northern men are bitterly persecuted and compelled to abandon the country, I pronounce false." [12]

As to the freedmen, Truman averred that the typical Southern white regarded blacks as a perpetual servant and working class. Most believed the end of slavery would be more calamitous to blacks than whites. They were skeptical that former slaves could develop the initiative of successful free whites. Planters mostly assumed that freedmen would require care and instruction, if not the disciplinary whip sometimes used previously by ruthless overseers. Truman concluded that the Black Codes adopted in some states were a "corollary" of such beliefs and condemned them. He particularly objected to those of Mississippi, which were the harshest of the eight visited states.

Truman perceived that Southern hostility toward freedmen was concentrated among the white working class. Addressing the situation in Mississippi, where blacks represented more than half the population, he wrote:

> Petty, unjust, and discriminating licenses are levied in the State upon [black] mechanics, storekeepers, and various artisans. . . . What are known as "poor whites" sustain . . . this legislation, upon the insane dread they share in common with certain skilled laborers at the north, of competition. . . . That folly and injustice on the part of law-makers is being corrected in many sections.[13]

Truman also concluded that former slaveholders had more constructive attitudes toward freedmen than did the lower classes. Since planters also regarded blacks as racially inferior, however, they did not readily provide blacks with opportunities for self-improvement.

Nonetheless, planters generally treated freedmen better than the Northern fortune hunters who migrated South after the war, planning to strike it rich in cotton growing.

> It is my observation . . . that the planters are . . . better . . . than the majority of northern men who go south to rent plantations. . . . [To] the northerner the negro is slow, awkward, wasteful and slovenly; he causes his new employer to lose patience. . . . It is the almost universal testimony of the negroes themselves . . . that they prefer to labor for a southern employer.[14]

Truman's claim that previous slaveholders were more sympathetic toward freedmen than nonslaveholders is echoed in an 1866 address to the Georgia legislature by the plantation owner and former Confederate vice president, Alexander H. Stephens:

> Wise and humane provisions should be made for [freedmen] . . . ample and full protection should be secured to them, so that they may stand equal before the law, in possession and enjoyment of all rights of person, liberty, and property. Many considerations claim this at your hands. Among these may be stated their fidelity in times past. They cultivated our fields, ministered to your personal comforts; nursed and reared your children; and even in the hour of danger and peril, they were, in the main, true to you and yours. To them we owe a debt of gratitude, as well of acts of kindness.[15]

Proposals for immediate black suffrage, Truman reported, should be evaluated in light of whether they would provide any substantial benefit to blacks "which they are now denied or . . . avert . . . any evil that threatens their welfare. So general . . . is the opposition of whites to this measure that I am fully persuaded that . . . [forcible] enactment, at this time, would" be seriously detrimental to the ex-slaves. Poor Southern whites appreciated that suffrage was one of their few privileges over blacks. Consequently, they guarded it fiercely. Truman was hopeful, however, that the surviving planter class could persuade working-class whites to accept gradual black suffrage if a delay of perhaps five years was allowed. (His report did not clarify whether it contemplated universal, or partial, black suffrage at the end of the interval.)

According to Truman, freedmen were far less concerned with voting than with achieving justice in legal cases. Such disputes were often with poor whites. Since former slaveholders generally controlled the courts during his tour, Truman believed they would provide a type of guardianship toward the ex-slaves in such cases. Nonetheless, as explained in chapter 3, Congress basically forced the South to accept universal black suffrage the following year. It also blocked many former planters from serving as judges and other civil officers.[16]

Booker T. Washington, who became one of the most prominent of all freedmen, agreed with Truman. He pointed out that the ex-slaves were given more rights than they knew how to use constructively and paid a penalty for decades thereafter. When Radical Republicans abruptly gave blacks full citizenship privileges, the freedmen didn't have time to develop leaders or a code of ideals and goals. Washington wrote, "In many cases it seemed to me that the ignorance of my race was being used as a tool with which to help white men into office, and that there was an element in the North which wanted to punish the Southern white men by forcing the Negro into positions over the head of the Southern whites."[17]

Washington was not alone in his viewpoint. In 1871, Mississippi's black secretary of state, James Lynch, advised African Americans to deemphasize the "enjoyment of political honors . . . [as a] . . . means of our elevation" and instead concentrate on their own abilities. A delegate to an 1876 national black convention argued that his race must first demonstrate it was worthy of the desired rights by gaining an education and demonstrating skilled-work capabilities. Emerging black businessmen, such as Mississippi's Robert Gleed, who served on the central committee of Mississippi's 1871 Planter's Convention, held similar opinions, as did relatively prosperous African Americans in Louisiana and South Carolina.[18]

Booker T. Washington
(*Library of Congress*)

Nonetheless, white carpetbaggers and scalawags who promised blacks more than could be provided grabbed the reins of leadership. Ultimately, their unfulfilled promises fueled disillusionment among blacks and left white neighbors resentful of the black man's false expectations. Racial animosity was the inevitable result.[19]

In *The Mind of the South*, Wilbur Cash explained, "Had there been no Reconstruction the result would have been unhappy. . . . But mark how the Yankee was heaping up the odds. In his manipulation of the unfortunate black man he was . . . generating a terrible new hatred for him."[20]

In August 1868, a month after the Fourteenth Amendment was ratified and blacks were permitted to vote in all Southern states, former Union major general William Rosecrans and former Confederate general Robert E. Lee met by chance while vacationing at White Sulphur Springs, West Virginia. During a conversation about conditions in the South, Rosecrans asked Lee to provide a written summary of the latter's views.

In the matter of black suffrage, Lee's reply—signed by twenty-five other vacationing Southerners—opposed any system that would put ex-slaves in charge of the state governments. "[T]his opposition springs from no feelings of enmity, but from . . . conviction that at present the negroes [lack] the intelligence [and] other qualifications . . . necessary to make them safe depositories of political power. They would inevitably become the victims of demagogues, who for selfish purposes would mislead them, to the serious injury of the public."[21]

One early advocate of Southern black suffrage was Carl Schurz, who was briefly Lincoln's ambassador to Spain before becoming a Union major general in the Civil War. When he later became a Republican senator from Missouri, Schurz criticized the already adopted Republican policy of disfranchising former Confederates:

> The stubborn fact remains that the negroes were ignorant and inexperienced . . . that in spite of the best intentions they were easily misled, not infrequently by the most reckless rascality. . . . [W]hen universal suffrage was granted . . . [to blacks] . . . universal amnesty ought to have been granted [to ex-Confederates] to make all the re-

sources of political intelligence and experience available for the . . . welfare of all.[22]

Harriet Beecher Stowe, who wrote *Uncle Tom's Cabin* before the war, opposed abrupt African American suffrage in the South. In February 1866, she wrote in a letter to the Duchess of Argyll:

> My brother Henry has talked with [Andrew Johnson] earnestly. . . . Henry takes the ground that it is unwise . . . to force negro suffrage on the South. His policy would be to hold over the negro to the protection of the Freedmen's Bureau until the great law of free labor shall . . . draw the master and servant together. . . . [Senator] Charles Sumner is simply looking at the abstract right of the thing. Henry looks at the actual probabilities.[23]

General William T. Sherman felt much the same way when he wrote in May 1865:

> I have reason to believe that Mr. Johnson is not going as far as Mr. Chase in imposing negro votes on the Southern States or any States. I never heard a negro ask for that and I think it would be his ruin. . . . I believe the whole idea of giving votes to the negroes is to create just that many votes to be used by others for political uses because I believe the negro don't want to vote now when he is mixed up with whites in nearly equal proportion, making [the] ship dangerous.[24]

The same month that Truman's report reached the Senate, the first of two Southern race riots that would swing Northern public opinion toward the Radicals erupted in Memphis. Since Union armies captured Memphis early in the war, it suffered little military damage. In fact, the city's wartime commerce thrived because it was a cotton-trading center. Its population grew rapidly, from twenty-three thousand in 1860 to forty thousand in 1866. About half of the total were African Americans and about a quarter were Irish. The Irish soon dominated civil administration, including the police department, because ex-Confederates were prohibited from holding public office or even voting. Consequently, the Irish were apprehensive that growing Republican advocacy for mandatory black suffrage in the South would cause them to lose their political power.

After the war, a nearby military post was garrisoned by troops who were mostly blacks. Memphis residents suspected that War Secretary Stanton, an enemy of President Johnson's, deliberately selected the blacks in hopes of provoking a race riot. Johnson's opponents could then cite such violence as evidence to discredit his Reconstruction plan. No less an authority than General Ulysses S. Grant had warned against using black occupation soldiers throughout the South because of his concern that they would provoke racial violence. Tensions between the two Memphis newcomer groups grew as they competed for jobs and the ex-slaves sometimes raucously celebrated their new freedom while the Irish enforced order. After one black regiment was mustered out on April 30, 1866, its celebration resulted in a clash with the police.

Shooting started the next day after the celebrating ex-soldiers failed to disperse as ordered. The initially outnumbered cops retreated, and two were shot. The following morning, the Irish police and firemen, along with a one-hundred-man armed white posse deputized by the sheriff, assembled, only to find that the former soldiers were gone. The whites went on a rampage against other blacks and black neighborhoods that did not stop until the local army commander declared martial law two days later, even though the Memphis mayor had asked that commander to intervene two days earlier. An estimated forty-six blacks and two whites were killed.[25]

One consequence of the Memphis riot—as Stanton perhaps intended—was to strengthen momentum behind the formation of what would become the Fourteenth Amendment.[26]

Two months later, in July, another riot exploded, this time in New Orleans. Basically, it resulted from an attempted coup d'état by the Radical wing of the state's Republican Party under the leadership of James Madison Wells, who had been the state's Republican lieutenant governor during the Civil War under Lincoln's 10-percent plan. When the 10-percent-plan governor became one of Louisiana's senators (never seated by Washington Republicans), Wells replaced him as governor. After the war, when returning Confederate veterans were pardoned and given the vote, Wells appointed many to government offices. He was, however, disappointed that most appointees failed afterward to support him politically.

Consequently, he resolved to take control of Louisiana's Republican Party in another way. His plan was to convene a new constitutional convention to be composed of his white supporters. He attracted the black support by promising that the new state constitution would grant them suffrage. The convention was set to meet on July 30, 1866, in New Orleans. White Louisianans reasoned, probably correctly, that the new constitution would make them almost powerless in the government, which would be controlled by Radicals and blacks. They also concluded, again probably correctly, that there was no legitimate reason for holding the convention. It was merely an attempt by Radicals to take over the government.

A *Harper's Weekly* illustration of the July 30, 1866, assault on the Republican convention in New Orleans by the police and citizens. (*Library of Congress*)

As the convention approached, Wells realized that whites were going to resist it—violently if necessary. Consequently, he was not in attendance when a group of delegates attempted to call the meeting to order, while about 200 blacks supported them outdoors.

The mayor of New Orleans asked the local military commander to intervene and block the convention to prevent violence. The commander wired Secretary Stanton for instructions, but Stanton did not reply. He failed to even mention the tense New Orleans situation to President Johnson. His silence on the matter, and similar duplicitous actions, eventually led Johnson to request the secretary's resignation. Meanwhile, a New Orleans mob broke up the convention before military units arrived to end the violence. Thirty-four blacks and one white were killed.[27]

Wells later became a figure in the controversial 1876 election of Rutherford Hayes as president despite the fact that Hayes had significantly fewer popular votes than his opponent. After Hayes became president, Wells was appointed federal tax collector for the port of New Orleans. The post had long been a source of wealth for each director who yielded to the temptation of corruption.[28]

Prior to the end of the Civil War, such urban race riots were concentrated in the North. From 1832 to 1849, there were five such disturbances in Philadelphia. Most notorious, however, was the four-day 1863 New York City draft riot discussed earlier.[29]

After Congress rejected President Johnson's Reconstruction plan and set a new course with the 1867 Reconstruction Acts passed over his veto, white Southerners were hopeful that the Supreme Court would judge the congressional plan to be unlawful. Since voter qualifications were historically a matter of a state's right, they were hopeful the court would rule as unconstitutional the congressionally imposed requirement that former Confederate states grant universal black suffrage and simultaneously limit participation by former Confederates according to specifications of a new, untested federal law.

The first test case originated in Mississippi in 1867 when a newspaper editor, William McCardle, published articles critical of congressional Reconstruction. He was arrested and jailed by the commander of the military district. However, since the Supreme Court's *Ex Parte Milligan* decision a year earlier ruled that military courts had no authority over civilians in areas where civilian courts were operating, McCardle argued that his case should be transferred to the civil courts. The appeal (*Ex Parte McCardle*) did not reach the Supreme Court until 1869, when the justices ruled against McCardle. They concluded that a law passed by Congress *during the appeals process* denied them jurisdiction.[30]

It was a dangerous precedent that essentially empowered Congress to limit the court's authority retroactively. From the demoralized Southerner's perspective, the Republican Congress was demolishing the protections implied by the three-branch structure of the federal government. It was shrinking the independent powers of the executive and judicial branches simultaneously. If the trend continued, the country would be ruled by congressional tyranny. Four factors created suspicion among the most fearful of Southerners that congressional Republicans wanted to force whites out of the South and leave the region segregated for blacks.

First were repeated attempts by Congressman Stevens and others to confiscate Southern lands and give them to freedmen. Since Stevens was known to be the prime architect of congressional Reconstruction, Southern fears that he would succeed with confiscation were reasonable—at least for a time. Second were the high carpetbag-era property taxes constituting the primary source of state tax revenues. They forced many white landowners to forfeit their properties, which could then be purchased by ex-slaves at low prices. Third, illiterate blacks and corrupt whites were prevalent officers in many of the carpetbag regimes. In 1865, illiteracy among Southern blacks was 97 percent. Fourth, fair elections were difficult to hold under the glitter of federal bayonets and the manipulation of black votes through graft and organizations such as the Union Leagues, Loyal Leagues, and Freedmen's Bureau.[31]

George Boutwell, who was a leading Radical Republican congressman from Massachusetts and later treasury secretary under President Grant, admitted that one reason he advocated civil and voting rights for ex-slaves was to keep them out of the North. He even recommended that Florida, Georgia, and South Carolina be reserved exclusively for African Americans. Suspecting that Boutwell's attitude was common in the North, in December 1867, one contributor to a popular Southern magazine wrote, "The whole legislation of Congress for the last two years, which has been under the guidance and direction of the New England radicals, shows the deliberate purpose . . . artfully concealed of Africanizing the . . . Gulf States." The object, he reasoned, was to motivate whites to leave the Deep South so that blacks could be isolated in the region instead of migrating to the North.[32]

One Republican recruitment tool in the South was the local chapters of the Union League, which was sometimes referred to as the Loyal League. In Alabama, for example, league lodges were largely responsible for getting over 95 percent of the black electorate registered to vote by October 1867. Unfortunately, they also "had much to do with putting life into" the Ku Klux Klan as it evolved from an obscure social club into a violent anti-Republican, and therefore anti-black, vigilante group.[33]

The first league chapters were formed in the North to support Republicans after Democratic gains in the 1862 wartime elections. According to historian Christopher Phillips, the league lodges "demanded undiluted loyalty to the wartime policies of Abraham Lincoln." They believed there was no such thing as a loyal opposition. Voters either supported Lincoln or they were traitors. "Western Loyal Leaguers fought dissent with more than words. In central Illinois, one woman claimed that Republicans 'were forming Vigilance committees to . . . [identify] every man and woman . . . not loyal to Lincoln.'" Even nonvoters had no immunity from league violence. In 1863, Union Leaguers tarred and feathered seven Ohio women, including one who was a widow of a recently deceased Union soldier.[34]

At the end of the war, league chapters opened in the South to serve as rallying points for whites that had opposed the Confederacy. After Southern blacks were permitted to vote for state constitutional conventions by the authority of the 1867 Reconstruction Acts, most Southern whites dropped out as blacks flooded into the leagues. Some of the remaining whites became scalawags and were soon joined by Northern carpetbaggers. The new goal for the Southern lodges—shared with the Freedmen's Bureau—was to register blacks to vote Republican. After ratification of the Fourteenth Amendment, blacks composed a majority of voters in five of the eight former Confederate states permitted to vote in the 1868 presidential election. They were also a sizable minority in the other three. At their peak, the Southern Union Leagues had about two hundred fifty thousand members, which was over one-third of the seven hundred thousand black voters.[35]

The leagues recruited members with a cult of secrecy and exaggerated promises. Members were indoctrinated to believe that their interests were perpetually at war with Southern whites, who were falsely accused of wanting to put blacks back into slavery. Blacks were told their continued freedom depended upon the supremacy of the Republican Party. One member explained that the Union League was the "place where we learn the law." Another member said that he always voted Republican because "I can't read and I can't write. . . . We go by instructions. We don't know nothing much." One North Carolina chapter was falsely told that if Republican Ulysses S. Grant won the 1868 presidential election, lodge members would be given public offices, farms, and mules. The state voted for Grant.[36]

Black female supporters vowed that they would not consort with, or marry, men who were not league members. Ex-slaves who were reluctant to join because of friendship with their former masters were beaten and some were murdered. Some lodges organized military units that trained regularly and inevitably clashed with armed whites. Often, lodge organizers were employees of the federally funded Freedmen's Bureau, which had the trust of most Southern blacks by spring 1866. Consequently, the bureau failed at what should have been its primary objective: to promote understanding and tolerance between Southern blacks and whites. Unfortunately, its political tactics and racial agitation backfired to the disadvantage of blacks with the formation of the Ku Klux Klan.[37]

Two years after the end of the Civil War, the one-million-man Union army dwindled to about fifty thousand. Although about twenty thousand federal troops remained deployed in the South to enforce martial law and mitigate Northern fears that Rebels might try to renew the war, Congress wanted a stronger force in place after the region once again held elections. Since Washington Republicans wanted to spend the least amount of federal funds, however, they devised a two-step approach.

First, in 1867, they effectively abolished the white militias of the unreconstructed Southern states. Second, after the 1868 elections put carpetbag governments in the Southern states, a number of the states created new militias composed almost entirely of former black Union League members. As with all militias, they were funded by revenues from the respective states, thereby obviating the need for a federal subsidy.[38]

Author John Chodes writes, "[These] militia [were] to be used as the private armies of the carpetbag governors. . . . In addition to insuring that voting by terror kept them in power, these militia forces defended against other ambitious carpetbaggers who attempted to usurp illegal power with illegal force." Such Republican Party splits led to the demise of carpetbag governments in Arkansas, Tennessee, and Louisiana. Two opposing black militia forces even fought one another during the Arkansas division, known as the Brooks-Baxter War, which was named for the two contending Republican gubernatorial candidates, Joseph Brooks and Elisha Baxter.[39]

The militias may have done more to alienate Southern whites from the carpetbag regimes than did the Union Leagues, per se, since they had the authority of government behind them, even when exercised in an irresponsible or racially discriminatory manner, and impoverished whites had to pay most of the taxes required to fund them.

The biggest episode of Reconstruction-era racial violence involved such a militia and occurred in Colfax, Louisiana, in April 1873, where about sixty blacks and three whites were killed. Understanding the calamity requires contextual background about Louisiana Radical Reconstruction.

After Louisiana formed a new constitution under the 1867 federal Reconstruction Acts, the state had a total of one hundred thirty thousand voters. Although slightly more whites than blacks populated the state, disfranchisement of former Confederates gave blacks a decisive 65–35 percent majority among registered voters. Consequently, after ratifying the Fourteenth Amendment, the state was readmitted to the Union with a carpetbag Republican governor, Henry C. Warmoth, a Union veteran and native of Illinois. In four years as Louisiana's governor, he accumulated a $500,000 fortune on an $8,000 annual salary. In describing the Louisiana carpetbag environment, he said, "Corruption is the fashion and I do not pretend to be honest, but only as honest as anybody in politics."[40]

Graft was common throughout Warmoth's government. One state senator sold his votes for $600 each, and a New Orleans tax collector received over $60,000 in fees annually. The state's printing budget totaled almost $1.2 million over three years, although it had never been over $60,000 a year previously. The state paid $250,000 for a private building valued at $84,000. Its debt grew from $7 million to $40 million. Spending rose by 500 percent and taxes by 800 percent.

Warmoth's political machine relied upon black votes and was supported by James F. Casey, a brother-in-law of President Grant's. The Warmoth-Casey machine manipulated elections with a canvassing board that jiggled figures to get the desired results. After Warmoth left office, Grant appointed Casey as New Orleans customs collector, and Casey pocketed excessive fees.

The corrupt largess eventually led to a falling-out among thieves. In the 1872 elections, Casey supported former Lincoln friend (and carpetbagger) William Kellogg for governor. Warmoth backed the Democratic candidate, John McEnry. Following the vote, the Warmoth returning board declared McEnry the winner. In response, Kellogg declared himself the winner by creating a returning board of his own, although it had no ballots or returns to count. When a corrupt federal judge sanctioned Kellogg's vote count, McEnry declined to accept the decision.[41]

To compound the problem, Washington refused to recognize either claimant. The result left Louisiana with two rival governors and legislatures. Consequently, many citizens favoring one claimant refused to pay taxes to the collectors of the other. The resulting chaos ultimately triggered the Colfax tragedy in April 1873.

The village's courthouse became a battleground after Kellogg appointees and their black allies occupied it. In response, McEnry supporters resolved to remove them, forcibly if necessary. McEnry's troops attacked on Easter, April 13. There were few casualties until the attackers deployed a cannon that could demolish the courthouse structure. Kellogg's men fled. Some were killed in the act of surrender, although most were executed after surrendering. Fatalities totaled about sixty, predominately blacks.[42]

Although Colfax was the worst racial atrocity of the era, it was not the last. There were numerous smaller episodes as well as some big ones. The tumultuous Louisiana situation prompted another one in New Orleans six months later. In September 1873, eight thousand McEnry supporters attacked three thousand five hundred black Kellogg militia and policemen in Jackson Square under the command of former Confederate lieutenant general James Longstreet. The general was pulled from his horse and forced to surrender. After a few days, President Grant sent federal troops to force McEnry's supporters out of the buildings seized from his friend Longstreet. Thereafter, no Republican could be elected in Louisiana without the intimidating presence of federal troops or marshals at the polls. As discussed in chapter 7, the end of Radical rule in Louisiana came with the controversial 1876 presidential election.[43]

The Colfax and Jackson Square incidents were counterrevolutionary actions by white paramilitary groups such as the Ku Klux Klan, Pale Faces, Knights of the White Rose, White Brotherhood, Knights of the

White Camelia, and Constitutional Union Guard. Much like the Italian Mafia, their histories and dimensions are shrouded in mystery because they were generally outlawed in the states where they operated and were soon thereafter banned by federal authorities as well. Due to its secrecy, night riding, and use of disguises, the Klan became the most infamous among them and was sometimes exaggeratedly characterized as an "invisible empire."

The rise and fall of the Tennessee Ku Klux Klan, where the order began, was typical. It originated in December 1865 as a secret fraternity for youthful Confederate veterans prone to mischievous practical jokes. One was to ride about in ghostly costumes at night to call in silent serenade at the homes of admired young ladies. Originally, the club had no political agenda, but it started to become a tool for resisting Radical Reconstruction in the spring of 1867.[44]

When Andrew Johnson left Tennessee to become Lincoln's vice president in 1865, William "Parson" Brownlow replaced him as governor. In February 1867, Brownlow's legislature adopted universal black suffrage. The state also tightened voter restrictions on "rebels and rebel sympathizers" by requiring that all whites seeking a voter certificate provide at least two witnesses to verify that they had been Union-loyal during the Civil War. Brownlow-appointed election and voter registration officials would settle disputes. The new governor ominously vowed that he would strictly enforce the white disfranchisement law even "[i]f to do it, it becomes necessary that there shall be violence and bloodshed."[45]

In March, over President Johnson's veto, Congress passed the First Reconstruction Act. It revealed the Republican Party's unmistakable intent to deny the former rebel states permission to reenter the Union until they provided universal black suffrage and restricted the number of ex-Confederates who could vote or hold office.[46]

Many Tennessee landowners worried that property taxes would be increased under Radical rule because the state needed to fund more services than were provided in the antebellum era, such as public education for ex-slaves; and since few blacks owned land, the property tax was a greater burden on the whites. The whites feared they might be forced to forfeit their properties in tax deficiencies, thereby making the lands available at bargain-priced tax sales. Tennessee's Union and Loyal Leagues were armed, militant, and apparently at the threshold of promoting the confiscation of lands from formerly wealthy ex-Rebels.[47]

As a result of a combination of white disfranchisement, black suffrage, and the transfer of police power in Memphis, Nashville, and Chattanooga to Brownlow-appointed commissioners following the 1866

Reconstruction Era Southern Paramilitary Organizations

	Union and Loyal Leagues	Ku Klux Klan
Leadership	White Carpetbaggers	Ex-Confederates
Members	Ex-Slaves and Former Union Black Soldiers	Southern Whites
Meetings	Secretive, Ritualistic, and Social	Secretive, Ritualistic, and Social
Political Choice	Republican	Anti-Republican
Year Formed	1865	1865
Reason Formed	Elect Carpetbag Governments	Social[a]
Ended	1869; evolved into Black Militias	1871[b]

[a]Transformed after the 1867 Reconstruction Acts into resistance to Radical Reconstruction and promoting white supremacy.

[b]By law only; the Anti-Defamation League estimates current versions have fewer than 3,000 members, no central leadership, and declining in stature.

Memphis riots, some ex-Confederates concluded that their only option to oppose despotism was to step outside the law. Prior to the Civil War, plantation owners authorized night riders to patrol the countryside for unauthorized slave movements. Any caught off their owner's plantation without permission were returned and could be physically punished. Given their postwar racial paranoia and presumed need for blacks to work the land in order to reignite the South's economy, some white Southerners renewed night patrols through groups such as the Ku Klux Klan. It was the beginning of the Klan's politically motivated activities.[48]

Historians generally agree that former Confederate lieutenant general Nathan Bedford Forrest became the Klan's leader during the first half of 1867, although he never admitted it. The Klan laid low in the 1867 elections in hopes that blacks might vote for conservative Democrats, which was the ticket of their ex-masters. Partly due to Union League activities, however, such hopes proved to be futile.

Governor Brownlow was reelected with more than 75 percent of the votes. In a letter to a newspaper editor the following summer (1868), Forrest wrote that the "only hope for . . . good government is in the success of" the Democratic Party. Soon thereafter, Klan violence spread across the South. Although Forrest and other Klan leaders expressed a preference for attacking Radical white agitators who encouraged blacks to hate Southern whites, the cult used outlaw methods such as threats, whippings, and murder to suppress blacks and whites from voting for carpetbag governments.[49]

In early August 1868, Governor Brownlow requested that the legislature arm a new state militia to give battle to the Ku Klux Klan. Since Tennessee's finances were already stretched too thin, however, he had to settle for aid from federal troops. In a newspaper interview later that month, Forrest acknowledged that some Klan violence had gone too far but claimed that it was being restrained. He stated, for example, that three Klan members had been court-martialed for unauthorized violence. If he was not actually the head of the cult, he talked like it. Whatever his station, his remarks suggest that Klan leaders had poor control over their members, probably as a logical consequence of the fraternity's secretiveness and its use of disguises, which would appeal to a lawless element.[50]

When Brownlow was appointed to the US Senate by Tennessee's legislature in 1869, De Witt Senter succeeded him as governor. As was common in the carpetbag states, Radical rule in Tennessee ended by a split in the Republican Party, as opposed to a direct challenge by Democrats. Initially, Senter was as hostile to ex-Confederates as was Brownlow. Ultimately, however, he transformed them into allies in the 1869 election, when his only opponent was a Republican from the rival wing of his party. Consequently, Senter-appointed election officials were not as strict as under Brownlow in blocking suspected ex-Confederates from voting. The former Rebels helped Senter beat his Republican rival by a vote ratio of more than 2–1. But he paid a price because the ex-Confederates attracted to his banner also voted for conservative legislators who enabled Tennessee to approve a post-carpetbag constitution the following year.[51]

The election of Senter and a conservative legislature eliminated most of the reasons for the Ku Klux Klan. Accordingly, Forrest called for it to disband in 1869. He complained, however, of men who had joined the order set on matters of private vengeance and racism. The hood enabled such renegades to operate secretively in their pursuit of terror.

Although Tennessee's Klan disbanded in 1869, the order continued for a few more years in other Southern states that remained under carpetbag rule. The sketchy, hearsay evidence about the Klan hierarchy started to vanish after 1869. Thereafter, its activities were sometimes more vicious, but scattered. When called to testify before a congressional panel in 1871, Forrest opined that "wild young . . . [and] . . . bad men" were responsible for the more recent outrages attributed to the Klan. As early as 1868, the more genteel white Southerners concluded that the Klan's time was over and that its continuation jeopardized political gains.[52]

Partly because of Klan activities, by 1870, conservatives had either been successful or appeared to be on the verge of success in several Southern states. Consequently, the Republican Congress began to enact laws to strengthen African American suffrage. At the time, the laws represented a sweeping shift toward the supremacy of federal authority over the individual states. (As noted in the introduction, the laws would later provide the authorization for using federal troops to suppress striking labor unions.)

First was the 1870 Enforcement Act. It permitted the president to appoint election supervisors in states where he suspected local whites were preventing blacks from voting. The supervisors were authorized to bring legal cases in federal courts against whites accused of violating the act. So long as the president was a Reconstruction-era Republican, there could be little doubt about the practical rulings of such supervisors. The second act came early in 1871, after Republican losses in the autumn 1870 elections. It strengthened the enforcement mechanisms of the first act in elections involving federal offices.[53]

The most sweeping of the acts, however, was the third, which was passed in April 1871. Known as the Ku Klux Klan Act, it empowered the president to suspend the writ of habeas corpus in regions where he believed African Americans were prevented from voting. Consequently, federal authorities in such regions, including the army, could arrest whites and hold them in jail indefinitely. Those arrested had no recourse to question whether they were legally arrested. Later, the arrested whites might be charged with the crime of interfering with black voters. The charges would be tried in federal, instead of state, courts.

Many suspected Klansmen were arrested under the acts. Hundreds were indicted in North Carolina, where federal troops were used to apprehend them. Many served prison terms. Seven hundred people were indicted in Mississippi, although most were given suspended sentences. President Grant declared martial law in nine South Carolina counties where federal troops made hundreds of arrests and thousands of whites fled the state out of fear of arrest.

A few dozen of the presumed worst offenders were brought to trial before predominantly black juries. Furthermore, the newly formed US Justice Department and solicitor general's office aided the prosecution at the expense of federal taxpayers. According to historian Eric Foner, "By

1872 . . . [such actions] . . . had broken the Klan's back and produced a dramatic decline in violence throughout the South." Most Klan activities thereafter were limited to renegades, and are the origin of the Klan's revival in the twentieth century.[54]

During the past half century, there has been considerable research to document and itemize violent incidents involving Southern white paramilitary units. In contrast, little has been written about violent episodes practiced by similar Republican-controlled freedmen's organizations such as the Union and Loyal Leagues. Although most Reconstruction-era students are aware of Ku Klux Klan voter suppression, few seem to recognize that Republican control of the election apparatuses in carpetbag-era Southern states—amplified by the presence of federal troops—suppressed votes on the opposite side.

After the 1877 collapse of the final three carpetbag governments in Florida, Louisiana, and South Carolina, the Republican Party forsook Southern blacks. Although the Fifteenth Amendment perpetually assured black suffrage, it wasn't until well into the twentieth century that Southern blacks had meaningful political influence or economic power. With a few inspiring exceptions, they would long remain an underclass of sharecroppers, farmers, laborers, and servants. They paid a heavy price for the deliberate Republican strategy of putting them at odds with their white neighbors only to be abandoned by the architects of the strategy after only a dozen years.

As in the antebellum era, political control of the Southern states remained with the conservative white politicians from the regions with the highest concentration of blacks. After blacks were given the vote, such areas had even greater representation than before the war. In South Carolina, for example, the first Redeemer governor openly courted black votes in 1876. Six years later, fifteen members of the state's General Assembly were African Americans. Typically, the Redeemers sought to control black votes instead of disfranchising them.[55]

As whites regained power over the destinies of their states, they had less reason to resent the black voters who lost influence when the carpetbag regimes vanished. Constructive racial mixing was initially more common than often supposed. In 1885, for example, a black Boston-based journalist named McCants Stewart toured the South to report on racial conditions. Although Stewart confirmed the obvious examples of the racial discrimination he expected, he was more surprised by a greater underlying sense of equality than he anticipated.

One time, when the cars of a Virginia passenger train became increasingly crowded, no whites asked him to forfeit his seat, even though some of the later-arriving white passengers were sitting on their luggage in the aisles. After arriving in Columbia, South Carolina, he wrote, "I feel about as safe here as in Providence, Rhode Island." He could ride railroad first class cars as freely as in New York. He could enter saloons and order drinks. Stewart even wrote that merchants and soda shops were more polite than in some parts of New England. In the same year, another traveler in New Orleans recalled that "White and colored people mingled freely." A North Carolina black wrote, "The best people of the South do not demand this separate car business . . . this whole thing is but a pandering to the lower instincts of the worst class of whites in the South." No Southern state enacted a segregation law on trains until twenty years after the Civil War ended. Whites and blacks were often buried in the same cemeteries for years after the war.[56]

The Redeemer governments that followed the carpetbag era were probably initially more sincere in their wishes to protect African Americans than is popularly believed today. Since the first post-carpetbag leaders were from the upper classes, they were less threatened by potential economic competition with black laborers. Many were previously slaveholders who were eager for freedmen to work cooperatively in the fields and elsewhere. They had much to gain from a political alliance with ex-slaves. Ironically, it was the spread of political power among landless whites that triggered statutory racial discrimination.

As freedmen and poor whites started competing for subsistence employment and the Populist movement gained influence, poor whites voted for antiplanter and antiblack candidates. It is no coincidence that the first seven Southern states to require segregated railcars adopted their statutes in the years 1887–1891, when the pre-Populist Farmers' Alliance started to gain strength. Historian C. Vann Woodward concludes, "The barriers of racial discrimination mounted in direct ratio with the tide of political democracy among whites. In fact an increase in Jim Crow laws . . . is almost an accurate index of the decline of . . . the Redeemers and triumph of the white democratic movements."[57]

Perhaps intentionally, many of the first Jim Crow laws were based upon statutes and ordinances from Northern states and cities. Since the North abolished slavery decades earlier than the South, white Northerners were the first to legislate an inferior status on freed blacks. Northern African Americans were often barred from the best restaurants and hotels, isolated in separate sections of theaters and churches, and required to use segregated railway cars, while their children were forced into segregated schools. Some regions, such as New England, were more lenient, whereas others in the Midwest and West were less tolerant.[58]

Landmark US Supreme Court rulings in the 1870s and 1880s had important implications for the future of race relations. First was the 1873 New Orleans *Slaughter House* case after the city's independent butchers challenged the abattoir monopoly granted by Louisiana's carpetbag government. When the plaintiffs argued that the monopoly was a violation of their "privileges and immunities" under the Fourteenth Amendment, the court ruled that the Thirteenth, Fourteenth, and Fifteenth Amendments were narrowly focused and did not widely alter the relationship between a state and its citizens. The "privileges and immunities" applicable to US citizens did not pertain to the citizenship "privileges and immunities" that were properly the domains of the states individually. The ruling ominously implied that the federal government could only intervene to protect a small number of federal rights that would benefit blacks. Put another way, blacks would have to obtain most of their rights from the states. In the 1876 *US v. Cruikshank* appeal, the court ruled that the postwar amendments only permitted the federal government to protect blacks from violations by the states, not individuals. Generally, only states could prosecute individuals for crimes. Consequently, federal convictions against whites who had participated in the 1873 Colfax massacre were overturned. The decision was consistent with contemporary interpretations that most powers were reserved for the states. All of the majority justices in the 5–4 decision were from Union-loyal states or had established their political careers in such states.[59]

In 1883, the court relied partly upon *Slaughterhouse* and *Cruikshank* when judging the 1875 Civil Rights Act to be unconstitutional. The ruling was an 8–1 decision in which the eight majority justices were from Northern states and the lone dissenter was from Kentucky. The lone Democrat voted with the majority. While the act attempted to support social equality by outlawing racial school segregation and discrimination in public accommodations such as restaurants and hotels, the court ruled in a series of seven cases that the Constitution did not vest the federal government with the power to enforce social justice. Only two of the seven cases were from Southern states.[60]

In combination, the rulings made it almost impossible for the federal government to enforce racial equality. Such responsibility devolved upon the states individually. On paper, the Southern states provided blacks with about as much civil justice as whites of the same economic class. Since blacks would soon be relegated to an even lower social station through Jim Crow laws, however, they would often be unable to transform paper entitlements into pragmatic realities.[61]

Southern antiblack racism grew to a crescendo in the 1890s, when white politicians with Populist agendas challenged aristocrats for control of the regional Democratic Party. Blacks caught in the crossfire were sometimes victims of its most evil expression of racism: lynchings. From 1882 to 1951, an estimated four thousand nine hundred Americans were executed by vigilante mobs. About four thousand—predominantly blacks—were Southerners, and about three thousand of them were executed before 1908. Perpetrators were seldom arrested. Contrary to the commonly cited justification for the practice, less than 20 percent of the incidents involved alleged "protection of Southern womanhood" against sexual violence by black men.

White-black relations were strained to a breaking point as the depression of the 1890s put the two races into stiffer competition for mere economic survival. Simultaneously, the first generation of freeborn blacks came of age, many with greater expectations and less-subservient attitudes than their parents. As explained in the previous chapter, poor Southern whites responded politically by challenging the wealthier whites for control of the state governments. A prime objective—soon shared with conservative whites—was to remove blacks as a potential balance-of-power voting bloc between contesting white classes. Thus, Southern blacks were increasingly disfranchised during the 1890s and early twentieth century through a variety of poll taxes, literacy requirements, and whites-only primaries.

Segregation laws were also adopted during the same period instead of shortly after the carpetbag regimes collapsed in the 1870s, as is often believed. Jim Crow brought order, albeit an oppressive type. Lynchings declined. Elections were more orderly although less democratic. There was, however, no mass genocide, forced concentration, or mass removal of blacks as sometimes happened with other racial minorities in world history, including Native Americans. Unlike in South Africa, American blacks had legal rights that could not be ignored by Southern whites.[62]

The collapse of the William Jennings Bryan Free Silver movement so weakened the Democratic Party nationally that Republicans no longer needed the black vote to retain control of the federal government. Despite Wilson's presidency, Republicans generally dominated national politics from the mid-1890s to the Great Depression of the 1930s. Moreover, they did so without any reliance upon Southern voters of either race. Consequently, Republicans had little interest in blacks after Bryan's defeat.[63]

Booker T. Washington best demonstrated how blacks might succeed in the post-carpetbag and Jim Crow eras.[64] In 1881, Alabama's legislature allocated $2,000 to form the Tuskegee Institute as a black teachers college. Twenty-five-year-old Washington was quickly appointed principal. He had learned his trade at Virginia's Hampton Institute, which loaned him enough money to buy 100 acres of land for Tuskegee. Seven years later, the 540-acre school had over 400 students. In addition to academics, students were trained in skills such as carpentry, cabinetmaking, printing, and shoemaking. Girls learned how to cook and sew while boys were taught farming and dairying.

Teachers and students provided a large part of the institute's needs through their own labor. They produced and sold bricks, lumber, furniture, wagons, tools, and clothing. To those who felt that such labor was beneath the dignity of teachers and students, Washington answered, "No race can prosper till it learns that there is as much dignity in tilling a field as in writing a poem." He worked in the fields alongside such critics.

A year after forming the school, Washington traveled north of the Mason-Dixon line seeking donations. Although he was initially received coolly, potential benefactors gradually warmed up, impressed by the school's work to contribute to its own financial needs. At Madison, Wisconsin, he gave an address to the annual convention of the National Education Association in 1884, which was scarcely three years after Tuskegee was organized. In 1893, an esteemed magazine profiled him, along with white teachers at Harvard, Yale, and elsewhere, as a top American educator. He quickly became a prominent African-American leader who spoke often to Southern blacks and mixed racial groups in the North.

Finally, at age thirty-nine, in 1895, he was invited to speak to an audience of black and white Southerners in Atlanta. The occasion was the Cotton States International Exposition, which was a Southern version of the World's Columbian Exposition in Chicago three years earlier that had celebrated the four hundredth anniversary of Columbus's discovery of America. Since the Atlanta exposition was partly funded by a congressional appropriation, convention managers wanted to show that the South was not as racially blighted as some Northerners presumed.

Although Washington was the opening day's last speaker, a mixed but segregated audience packed the auditorium. At first he was only received politely, but as he explained that his students were encouraged to concentrate on becoming productive artisans to promote economic progress, the audience became increasingly attentive and began to show good feeling.

He conceded the reality of persistent racial tension but chose not to blame whites for their part. Instead he admitted black errors. "Ignorant and inexperienced, it is not strange that in the first years [of freedom] . . . a seat in Congress or the legislature was more sought [by freedmen] than real estate and industrial skills." The entire South had suffered from

Clockwise from upper left, the original buildings purchased for the Tuskegee Institute in 1881; students constructing a brick wall; framing a roof; a sewing class; and a chemistry lab. These photographs were taken about 1904. Academic classes, such as mathematics, were attended by both men and women. (*New York Public Library*)

such mistakes. As a result, some Southern blacks advocated emigration, and others wanted Northerners to provide financial aid. Although possibly well intentioned, Washington rejected such solutions. He explained his position with a parable.

When a ship that had exhausted its potable water after being lost at sea first saw the masts of a potential rescuer, the crew hoisted signal flags asking for water. The second ship replied, "Cast down your bucket where you are." Thinking they had been misunderstood, the imperiled crew replied, "We die of thirst!" The presumed rescue ship repeated, "Cast down your bucket where you are."

When the thirsty crew finally complied and threw a rope-connected canvas bucket overboard, they discovered that it contained fresh water when pulled on deck. Even though they were beyond the sight of land, both ships were off the coast of the mighty Amazon River, which spread fresh water far out to sea. Washington concluded: "To those of my race who depend upon bettering their condition in a foreign land, or who underestimate the importance of cultivating friendly relations with the Southern white man, I would say: 'Cast down your bucket where you are!'—cast it down in making friends in every manly way of the people of all races by whom we are surrounded."

He went on to give the same advice to white Southerners who wanted to import foreigner workers. "Cast down your bucket among . . . [us] . . . who have tilled your fields, cleared your forests . . . [and built] . . . your railroads and cities. . . . In the future . . . we shall stand by you with a devotion that no foreigner can match . . . interlacing our industrial, commercial, civil, and religious life with yours."

Washington went on to boldly address social segregation. He raised his right arm high into the air with the fingers initially outstretched before closing them into a fist. "In all things that are purely social, we can be as separate as the fingers, yet one as the hand in all things essential to mutual progress." Conceding disappointment among blacks with the lower social status enforced by segregation, he nevertheless added, "The opportunity to earn a dollar in a factory just now is worth infinitely more than the opportunity to spend a dollar in the opera house." The speech was received enthusiastically. Presumably, whites liked the conciliatory message, whereas black reaction was amplified by the favorable white reaction and the simple fact that a black man was on the stage.

Washington remained a leading spokesman for the African American community for the rest of his life. In 1901, President Theodore Roosevelt invited Washington as the first African American to join an official White House dinner. He still headed up the Tuskegee Institute when he died in 1915.

Soon after the Atlanta speech, however, some younger black leaders started questioning Washington's wisdom in shunning black attempts to gain political power. One example was W. E. B. Du Bois, who was twelve years younger. Du Bois grew to adulthood in western Massachusetts, where the number of blacks was too small to provoke much white racism. Consequently, he experienced little social discrimination until he attended college at Nashville's Fisk University, where he learned of the deep racial divide. After graduation, he toured Europe for two years and then went on to Harvard, where he became the first black PhD of America's oldest college.

The year after Washington's 1895 Atlanta speech, Du Bois became a teacher at Ohio's Wilberforce University. Although he agreed with Washington that blacks needed to better prepare themselves as skilled workers in order to participate in the American economy, he also believed that the "talented tenth" should seek to become professionals such as teachers, ministers, scientists, doctors, lawyers, writers, and even political activists. Such examples were required, he argued, in order to lift the aspirations of the entire race. As evidenced by his practice of hiring the best teachers, Washington basically agreed with Du Bois. The difference between the two was a matter of emphasis.

W. E. B. Du Bois.
(*Library of Congress*)

While Du Bois's emphasis suggests that his beliefs foreshadowed the Black Power mantra of the modern era—especially in contrast to Washington's comparative "Uncle Tom" attitude—Du Bois did not hesitate to fault black culture. In 1897 he wrote, "Unless we conquer our present vices, they will conquer us. We are diseased, we are developing criminal tendencies and an alarmingly large percentage of our men and women are sexually impure." On another occasion he said, "[I] believe that the first and greatest step toward settlement of the present friction between the races . . . lies in the correction of the immorality, crime, and laziness among the [blacks] themselves, which still remains as a heritage from slavery."

The divide between Washington and Du Bois bifurcated the evolution of the African-American experience in much of the twentieth century. During much of the first half, Washington's go-along-to-get-along approach seemed to yield the best results for African Americans. The sacrifice of blacks in common cause with whites in World War II, however, began to convince whites that blacks merited better opportunities to earn career success and social mobility. By the civil rights era of the 1960s, the Du Bois philosophy had the greater influence, which continues to grow.

THIRTEEN

Protracted Consequences

Seventy-three years after the end of the Civil War, the National Emergency Council's 1938 *Report on the Economic Conditions in the South* for President Franklin Roosevelt provided the federal government's first report card that essentially measured the economic results of Reconstruction. It was not one to make parents proud.

The South was America's poorest sector. In 1937, its per capita income of $314 was only about half of the $604 for the rest of the country. Moreover, it confronted systemic problems that threatened to perpetuate its poverty forever. Those problems—some endemic to the region and some imposed upon it—were addressed in the preceding chapters. Although the South also had a lower cost of living since residents paid one another less than elsewhere for local goods and service, the differential did not offset the lower incomes. A 1935 survey that placed America's average monthly family income poverty line at $75 determined that it was $72 in the South.

Poverty bred poor health. Pellagra, which was rare elsewhere, was common among Southern farmers even though it could be prevented by adequate diets. Even 60 to 88 percent of the poor families in Southern cities did not have enough money to afford the preventative diets. Only 74 percent of the residents in Southern towns had flush toilets, compared to 87 percent for America as a whole. The situation was worse among farmers with whom hookworm was a constant plague because only 80 percent had toilets or privies, whether indoor or outdoor. Of three million farm structures surveyed in 1930, only 6 percent had piped-in water and only 3 percent had it piped into bathrooms. More than half of the homes were unpainted. Only about one-third had screens. Roosevelt's economic study concluded that half of Southern families needed new housing.[1]

Conditions were worst among the farmers who powered the South's principal economic engine. In the last year before the Great Depression, Southern farmers in 1929 earned an average of $186, which was about 65 percent below the $528 average of other American farmers. Yet the $186 was a gross income out of which operating expenses such as fertilizer, seed, and interest on debt had to be paid. As a result, there was little money left for food and clothing, and none for luxuries that sometimes included such common articles as books and radios. Cotton and tobacco provided two-thirds of Southern farm income.

As late as the 1930s, more than half of Southern farmers depended upon cotton alone. Price fluctuations in the world cotton markets were sheer gambles, yet they were often the key determinant of the one-crop farmer's income. Cotton prices that were 20 cents a pound in 1927 dropped to 16 cents in 1929 and declined further to 6 cents in 1931 before rising to 10 cents in 1933. Only once during the ten years from 1927–1937 did the price change less than 10 percent annually.

Tenant farmers and sharecroppers, who composed 53 percent of all Southern farmers, were at the bottom of the heap. Many lived in circumstances comparable to the Russian serfs of the nineteenth century. Their per capita incomes ranged from $38 to $87 annually, which equaled 10 to 25 cents per day—well below the dollar-per-day poverty line of the 1870s. Black and white sharecroppers were nearly equally destitute. Since cotton was the cornerstone of the South's economy, nearly all residents shared the farmer's hazards to some degree. Financing the farmers, for example, was more costly than elsewhere because of the greater risk of failure. One 1934 study revealed that 10 percent of Southern farmland was owned by lenders who had been forced to foreclose on mortgages.[2]

Southern industrial wages also trailed those in the rest of the country. Despite working longer hours, the Southern industrial employee had an average annual wage of $865, 30 percent below the $1,219 average elsewhere. Even within the cotton textile industry, where the South had taken the production lead away from New England, only 10 percent of Southern workers were paid more than 53 cents per hour, compared to 25 percent in the rest of the country. Ninety percent of the 200 largest corporations in 1937 were headquartered north of the Ohio and Potomac Rivers.

Since many Southerners lived near or below the poverty line, the region had difficulty providing schools and other community services. In 1935, Southern taxable property values were only $463 per person, compared to $1,370 in the Northeastern states, which, therefore, had three times as much property per capita to support their public schools. Since much of the profit from Southern industries went to outside financiers and absentee owners, and Southern personal income was so low, state income taxes could do little to generate more tax revenue. Consequently, Southern states raised about 60 percent of their revenues from regressive sales taxes, whereas not a single state in the Northeast relied upon the sales tax for more than 45 percent of its revenue. "The efforts of southern communities to . . . spread the tax burden more fairly [were] impeded by the vigorous opposition of interests outside the region, which control[ed] much of the South's wealth."[3]

Although the South had one-third of America's schoolchildren during the Great Depression it had only one-sixth of the education revenues. Teachers in Arkansas were paid about $500 annually, compared to about $2,400 in New York State. Moreover, since Southern teenagers often worked to help support their families, only 16 percent of the area's children were high school students, compared to 24 percent elsewhere. About 11 percent of Southern children ages 10–15 worked, while the average for the entire country was only 5 percent. The South's illiteracy rate was 9 percent, compared to 2 percent in the Midwest and 4 percent in the Northeast. Southern states spent an average of about $25 per child in schools. That was only half of the amount for the entire country and only about one-fourth of the amount spent in New York State.[4]

The report identified absentee ownership as a major problem and traced its origins to the poverty and lack of credit that followed the Civil War. Even in the 1930s, a "very large share" of the region's natural resources and industry were owned by companies domiciled elsewhere. The situation could retard Southern economic development in two ways. First, "a monopolistic corporation in another region . . . [might] purchase and leave [as] unused resources in the South, which otherwise might be developed in competition with the monopoly." Second, "absentee ownership . . . makes it possible for residents elsewhere to influence greatly the manner in which the South is developed and to subordinate that development to . . . interests outside the South."

Examples of absentee ownership included such essential industries as electric utilities, railroads, steel manufacturing, and even cotton textile mills. Outsiders also controlled most of the area's natural resources such as coal, feldspar, iron ore, zinc, sulfur, and bauxite (for aluminum.) Moreover, the more prosperous work of converting the raw materials into finished goods was located elsewhere. The South typically retained only the lower economic value-added cost provided by extracting and shipping the raw materials.[5]

The competition between butter and oleomargarine provides an example of attempts to strangle a Southern industry in the cradle. Northern dairy farmers were the primary butter suppliers, whereas margarine was often made from cottonseed oil. Unlike butter, basic margarine has an unappetizing white color. When margarine producers began mixing in a yellow dye in the late 1880s, dairy farmers successfully lobbied for laws prohibiting the sale of premixed yellow margarine. Consumers were compelled to buy white margarine and manually mix attached packets of yellow dye. It was a laborious process that held back the growth of the oleomargarine market.

Led by Wisconsin, a number of Northern states also passed margarine-specific sales taxes to make it less competitive with butter. Dairymen even got the federal government to tax oleomargarine. Yellow margarine was taxed at two-and-a-half times the per-pound rate of white margarine. Moreover, oleomargarine was the only food product taxed by the federal government at the time. Perhaps nothing would have changed except for a shortage of butter during World War II. Thereafter, housewives all over the country complained about the troublesome mixing process. One grandmother even gave a mixing demonstration to the New York State Assembly that showed the messy, laborious mixing procedure. The last of the discriminatory laws, however, was not repealed until 1967.[6]

Finally, due to its impoverished economy, the South had provided a steady stream of de facto immigrants to other parts of the country ever since the end of the Civil War. Many of its ablest people left because of the better economic opportunities elsewhere. Other regions of the country benefitted from their abilities, although the South paid for their public education. Consequently, the South had a greater demographic concentration of the young and aged who were less productive from an economic perspective. For example, one-third of the South's population was school age and, therefore, in need of public education. By comparison, school age children amounted to only one-fourth of the combined population of the industrial states.[7]

Despite the National Emergency Council's economic report, which Roosevelt sent to Congress, the territory failed to receive its fair share of federal works projects. Since Roosevelt knew he could rely on Southern electoral votes due to the Democratic Party's dominance in the region, the Works Progress Administration distributed more developments in the West, where they might tip some states into the Democratic column during federal elections.[8]

Conclusion

Although nothing erases the lingering Southern racism and lynchings that followed the Civil War, it is well to recognize that historical interpretation is often more influenced by the zeitgeist of the age in which it is written than by objective evaluation of all the facts.

Many modern histories of the Civil War and Reconstruction reflect misrepresentations rooted in a narrow interpretation of Southern society in bygone eras, and even the present. Confederate monuments that have stood for decades are interpreted as symbols of hate that must be removed. If not removed, vandals often deface them with impunity, excused by the tyranny of popular opinion.[1]

In 1935, the United Daughters of the Confederacy constructed a memorial hall as a residence for girls at Nashville's Peabody College. Originally, residents who were descendants of Confederate veterans and agreed to become teachers were granted free room and board. Vanderbilt acquired the school and dormitory in 1979. In 2016, the university sandblasted the word "Confederate" off the building. Ironically, however, if it hadn't been for the Confederate sympathies of Cornelius Vanderbilt's second wife—Frank Armstrong Crawford Vanderbilt—and the contributions of countless Confederate descendants over the years, it is unlikely that any of Vanderbilt's prominent graduates would have even attended the university.

Through the husband of one of her cousins, the Mobile, Alabama, native persuaded the Commodore to donate $1 million to fund the university in 1873. Among the few who attended their wedding was a former attorney general of the Confederacy and a former Confederate lieutenant general. Six years earlier, the Commodore was among several prominent Northerners who posted bail for the prison release of former Confederate president Jefferson Davis. Vanderbilt hoped his generosity to the university would promote a spirit of reconciliation. His gift, he said, was intended to "contribute to strengthening the ties which should exist between all sections of our common country."[2]

No doubt the present animus toward Confederate icons and traditional white Southern society reflects the region's historical racism, which many who came of age during the 1960s civil rights era judge to be the South's defining characteristic. Southern whites, however, were not altogether unresponsive to the movement. Gradually selected members began to combat racism.

Some of the earliest contributors were artists such as Alabama's Harper Lee, who wrote *To Kill a Mockingbird,* and even Mississippi pop star Elvis Presley, whose sympathetic hit song *In the Ghetto*, written by Lubbock, Texas, native Mac Davis, was released in 1969. Southern voters joined the trend when Winthrop Rockefeller was elected Arkansas's governor in 1966 and Bill Clinton followed a dozen years later in 1978. No top-forty music hit lamented the poverty of Mississippi whites; instead, hits like Canadian Neil Young's 1970 *Southern Man* criticized the South as nothing but a racist region.

Since then, educators have increasingly defined the legacy of the Civil War and Reconstruction in racial terms. The result has been a growing misunderstanding, or even hostility, toward white Southerners—primarily among Americans who have little regular contact with people of the region—caused partly by ignorance about the length and nonracial characteristics of Reconstruction.

English author Tom Fremantle provides an example. He is a descendent of British lieutenant colonel Arthur J. L. Fremantle, who visited all but two Confederate states in spring and summer 1863. The officer entered at Brownsville, Texas, and finished by observing the battle of Gettysburg from the rebel side. (He was a character in both Michael Shaara's novel *The Killer Angels* and the corresponding film, *Gettysburg*.) About

140 years later, Tom retraced his ancestor's steps in the company of a pack mule, which he chronicled in his book *The Moonshine Mule*. By the time Tom reached northern Virginia, he noticed certain people were

> dismissive of the South. [Some were on a lark while others] were . . . stuffy types whose opinions had nothing to do with political morality and everything to do with smugness. "My dear, you *walked* through Alabama—I wouldn't even *drive* through there! The South's an embarrassment, it's worse than the Third World." When I asked these people if they had ever been to Mississippi or South Carolina, they usually replied, "Lord, no! Never!" . . . To my surprise I often became passionate in my defense of the South.[3]

The preceding chapters explain that the South's lingering poverty is at least as much a consequence of Reconstruction as was sectional racism. The discriminatory economic policies that have been partly—possibly largely—responsible for the region's enduring poverty remained even as its racism declined. Among the forty-four American cities with populations over fifty thousand having black mayors, twenty are in the former Confederacy. Thus, with 32 percent of America's population the former Confederate states have 45 percent of its black mayors. Even when adjusting for a larger number of African Americans in the South, there is still no discernible racial discrimination. The 46 percent of the country's blacks who reside in the former Confederate states is nearly identical to the 45 percent of the country's black city mayors who serve there. Finally, from former president Barack Obama on down, many political leaders increasingly assert that racism is prevalent throughout America and not just the South.[4]

Until recently, the South's demographics changed only gradually compared to the rest of America. In 1938, for example, 98 percent of its residents were born in the region. Today the number remains high, with native born residents of the eleven former Confederate states at 78 percent, impressive considering the immense popularity of Florida, South Carolina, and other Southern states for Northern and Midwestern retirees. Therefore, to many Southerners, the history of the area is not an abstraction but is more of a living thing. It is a vivid record of family stories. In town squares throughout the territory, the ubiquitous Confederate soldier monument stands as an ever-present reminder. Despite a century of ensuing poverty, the dignity of the Confederate soldiers has been a source of regional pride. Consequently, in times of emergency, the postbellum South provided more than its share of our country's soldiers. Even 135 years after the Civil War, one study showed the South provided 42 percent of military recruits, compared to having 36 percent of America's population. Conversely, New England was singled out for below-average volunteerism.[5]

Family connections to the history of the land are one reason William Faulkner famously wrote, "In the South the past is not dead, it is not even past." It is also a reason why white Southerners might object to modern race-centric Reconstruction interpretations that basically render the South as America's dark side. Since such narratives don't tell of the national policies that led to "The Mess the Yankees Made" (as former senator Jim Webb puts it), the offense is also justified. Emancipation, for example, was a national policy, but it fell to the impoverished Southern states to pay the bill for educating the freedmen.[6]

Much like the zeitgeist of the Vietnam era that belittled American soldiers eventually ended and the country gradually came to respect their sacrifices, the demonization of white Southerners may yet run its course. Just as the hippie and intellectual elites who dominated public opinion during the Vietnam War while they disparaged America's soldiers have fallen into obscurity, so also might those portraying Reconstruction as a South-as-evil-twin story might eventually fade in the face of the larger national narrative. If so, countervailing accounts like the one in this book must be told, shared, and expanded.

Appendix

Money Supply Theory During Reconstruction

In 1976, economist Milton Friedman won the Nobel Prize for work on monetary theory that can be revealing when applied to Southern Reconstruction.

One measure of a country's economic wealth is the total value of goods and services it produces annually, termed the gross national product (GNP). Friedman's insight was to express GNP in terms amenable to monetary analysis. To illustrate, our GNP might also be expressed as the product of America's money supply multiplied by the rate at which the average dollar changes hands. In algebraic terms: $(M) \times (V) = GNP$

That equation is an algebraic tautology where (M) represents the supply of money and (V) is the velocity-of-money, which is the pace at which dollars are spent. The equation is illuminating because it may be applied to any region. Thus, other things being equal, the parts of America with larger bank deposits create greater economic output. Similarly, regions with faster rates of dollar turnover generate more economic output. Geographic areas with both greater bank deposits and quicker rates of dollar turnover benefit doubly.

For decades after the Civil War, national banking policy favored the North over the South—and to a lesser extent the West—on factors affecting both bank deposits and money velocity. The 1863 National Bank Act authorized a maximum of $354 million in national banknotes. Banks located in the Northeast had already issued $300 million by the end of 1866, and the ceiling was not raised for the final $54 million until 1870. Although the ceiling was removed altogether in 1875, it was no longer profitable for banks to issue new national banknotes because of technicalities relating to the reserve requirements that did not affect preexisting banknotes, as explained in chapter 8.[1]

As a result, at the turn of the twentieth century, thirty-five years after the Civil War, the South had only 6 percent of America's bank deposits, although the eleven former Confederate states had 18 percent of America's population. Like Westerners, Southern politicians sought remedies to the persistent overconcentration of banking in the North, but to no avail.[2]

Unfortunately, the lower population density in the South and West also tended to cause a detrimental lower velocity-of-money in such geographic areas. Even though Milton Friedman would not win his Nobel Prize for another century, US Senator Oliver Morton of Indiana in 1869 recognized the consequences of a slow money velocity: "The ten-dollar bill which is used in a county in Iowa will not change hands half a dozen times while the same ten-dollar bill would change hands a hundred times in Massachusetts . . . because the [Western] population [is] comparatively sparse, money does not pass from hand to hand so readily, and the actual currency must supply the place of bank credits, bank checks, and savings institutions."[3]

Despite repeated Southern objections to the geographic maldistribution of the money supply, little help was obtained until after 1900, when the bond refunding terms of the Gold Standard Act provided at least modest relief to the technicality noted above involving banknote reserve restrictions. Even though Republican Westerners like Senator Morton were aware of the harm to their states caused by Northeast banking concentration, their support for the banking status quo was secured by protective tariffs, federally funded public works, and generous Union veterans' pensions. Persistent Northeast banking concentration by means of discriminatory restrictions against other regions is one example of seldom discussed Reconstruction injustices that lasted far beyond 1877, which is the year conventionally—but misleadingly—accepted as the end of the era.

Notes

INTRODUCTION

1. William Cooper and Thomas Terrill, *The American South: A History*, vol. 2, 4th ed. (Lanham, MD: Rowman & Littlefield, 2009), 571.
2. William McFeely, *Grant: A Biography* (New York: W. W. Norton, 1981), 367.
3. Jean Edward Smith, *Grant* (New York: Touchstone, 2001), 542, 547.
4. John Y. Simon, ed., *Grant*, 31 vols. (Carbondale: Southern Illinois University Press, 1967), 22:188; Claude Bowers, *The Tragic Era* (Cambridge, MA: Riverside Press, 1929), 396, 398; McFeely, *Grant*, 373.
5. McFeely, *Grant*, 372-73; Smith, *Grant*, 584.
6. McFeely, *Grant*, 373.
7. Avery Craven, *Reconstruction* (New York: Holt, Rinehart & Winston, 1969), 166.
8. Bowers, *Tragic Era*, 371.
9. McFeely, *Grant*, 368-69.
10. Matthew Josephson, *The Robber Barons* (New York: Harcourt, Brace, 1934), 367; Sean Cashman, *America in the Gilded Age*, 3rd ed. (New York: New York University Press, 1993), 131.
11. James Randall and David Donald, *The Civil War and Reconstruction* (Boston: D.C. Heath, 1961), 579-80; Louis Hacker and Benjamin Kendrick, *The United States Since 1865*, 4th ed. (New York: Appleton-Century-Crofts, 1949), 167-68; Walter Webb, *Divided We Stand* (Austin, TX: Acorn Press 1944), 36-37.
12. Kenneth Stampp, *The Era of Reconstruction* (New York: Alfred A. Knopf, 1965), 137; Hacker and Kendrick, *United States Since 1865*, 167.
13. Eric Foner, *Reconstruction: America's Unfinished Revolution* (New York: Harper & Row, 1988), 604.
14. Gary Gallagher, *The American Civil War: The War in the East 1861–May 1863* (Oxford: Osprey Books, 2001), 22.
15. Kathleen and Scott Morgan, eds., *State Rankings in 2014: A Statistical View of America* (Thousand Oaks, CA: CQ Press, 2014), 262; James Kibler, *Our Fathers' Fields* (Columbia: University of South Carolina Press, 1998), 195; US Census Bureau, *Statistical Abstract of the United States* (Washington, DC: Government Printing Office, 2003), 67.

16. David Cohn, *The Life and Times of King Cotton* (New York: Oxford University Press, 1956), 244-45, 247-48; National Emergency Council, *Report on Economic Conditions of the South*, prepared for President Franklin Roosevelt, July 22, 1938, 46. https://archive.org/stream/reportoneconomic00nati#page/2/mode/2up.
17. Shirley Abbott ,*The Bookmaker's Daughter* (Fayetteville: University of Arkansas Press, 2006), xvi-xvii.
18. Lawrence Goodwyn, *The Populist Movement* (Oxford: Oxford University Press, 1978), 20; Theresa Hefner-Babb, "Interstate Commerce Act of 1887," *The Social History of Crime and Punishment in America: An Encyclopedia*, ed. Wilbur Miller (Thousand Oaks, CA: Sage Publications, 2012), 856; Cooper and Terrill, *American South*, 2:495.
19. "Historical Highlights of the IRS," last reviewed or updated July 6, 2016, https://www.irs.gov/uac/Historical-Highlights-of-the-IRS.
20. Hacker and Kendrick, *United States Since 1865*, 73, 89; Cooper and Terrill, *American South*, 496; Jack Beatty, *Age of Betrayal* (New York: Alfred A. Knopf, 2007), 196.
21. H. W. Brands, *American Colossus* (New York: Anchor Books, 2010), 466; Infoplease, "Past U.S. Supreme Court Members," www.infoplease.com/ipa/ A0101281.html.
22. Randall and Donald, *Civil War and Reconstruction*, 580.
23. Matthew Josephson, *The Politicos* (New York: Harcourt, Brace, 1958), 13-14.
24. Randall and Donald, *Civil War and Reconstruction*, 580; Wikipedia, "38th United States Congress," page last modified Dec. 29, 2016, https://en.wikipedia.org/wiki/38th_United_States_Congress.
25. Cooper and Terrill, *American South*, 2:426.
26. Arthur Schlesinger, *The Age of Jackson* (Boston: Little, Brown, 1953), 507.
27. Josephson, *Robber Barons*, 294.
28. Ron Hayduk, "The History of Immigrant Voting Rights in California," Immigrant Voting Project and New York University Law Students for Human Rights, http://ronhayduk.com/immigrant-voting/around-the-us/state-histories/california-history/; Yuning Wu, "Chinese Exclusion Act," *Encyclopedia Britannica*, www.britannica.com/topic/Chinese-Exclusion-Act.
29. Foner, Reconstruction, 207.
30. US Census Bureau, *Historical Statistics of the United States, Colonial Times to 1970, Part 2* (Washington, DC: Government Printing Office, 1975), 1146; Francis Simkins and Charles Roland, *A History of the South* (New York: Alfred A. Knopf, 1973), 310-11; Claudia Goldin and Frank Lewis, "Economic Costs of the American Civil War," *Journal of Economic History* 35, no. 2 (June, 1975): 304.
31. Hacker and Kendrick, *United States Since 1865*, 88; Stampp, *Era of Reconstruction*, 111; Edward Royce, *The Origins of Southern Sharecropping* (Philadelphia: Temple University Press, 2010), 93-94; Foner, *Reconstruction*, 207; Beatty, *Age of Betrayal*, 196; John Ezell, *The South Since 1865*, 2nd ed. (New York: Macmillan, 1975), 51.

CHAPTER ONE: FOUNDATIONS OF CHANGE

1. "Confiscation Acts," *Mr. Lincoln and Freedom*, Lehrman Institute, www.mrlincolnandfreedom.org/inside.asp?ID=38&subjectID=3; Sean Wilentz, "Congress Confiscates Confederates' Slaves," *Opinionator: Disunion* (blog), *New York Times*, July

16, 2012, http://opinionator.blogs.nytimes.com/2012/07/16/congress-confiscates-confederatesslaves/?_r=0.
2. "Confiscation Acts."
3. Ibid.; Wilentz, "Congress Confiscates Confederate Slaves."
4. Randall and Donald, *Civil War and Reconstruction*, 284; "Confiscation Acts."
5. Stampp, *Era of Reconstruction*, 42; Ludwell Johnson, *Division and Reunion* (New York: John Wiley & Sons, 1978), 116; John Franklin, *Reconstruction* (Chicago: University of Chicago Press, 1961), 16; Manuel Gottlieb, "The Battle for Democracy by James S. Allen," book review in *Science & Society* 2, no. 4 (Feb. 1938): 543; David Donald, *Lincoln* (London: Jonathan Cape, 1995), 560.
6. Donald, *Lincoln*, 367; Ezell, *South Since 1865*, 52.
7. Ezell, *South Since 1865*, 52.
8.Gavin Wright, *Slavery and American Economic Development* (Baton Rouge: LSU Press, 2013), 60; National Park Service, "Industry and Economy During the Civil War," https://www.nps.gov/articles/industry-and-economy-during-the-civil-war.htm.
9. Donald, *Lincoln*, 363.
10. James McPherson, *Battle Cry of Freedom* (New York: Oxford University Press, 1988), 504; Donald, *Lincoln*, 364.
11. Donald, *Lincoln*, 362; Paul Finkelman, "The Coming of the Emancipation Proclamation," *Opinionator: Disunion* (blog), *New York Times*, July 13, 2012, http://opinionator.blogs.nytimes.com/2012/07/13/the-coming-of-the-emancipationproclamation/.
12. Donald, *Lincoln*, 365; Abraham Lincoln, "Abraham Lincoln's Draft of the Emancipation Proclamation" (July 22, 1862), Civil War Trust, www.civilwar.org/education/history/primarysources/abraham-lincolns-draft-of.html.
13. Donald, *Lincoln*, 365-66; Ethan Rafuse, *McClellan's War* (Bloomington: Indiana University Press, 2005), 243.
14. Abraham Lincoln, *The Collected Works of Abraham Lincoln, Vol. 5*, ed. Roy Basler (New Brunswick, NJ: Rutgers University Press, 1953), 421.
15. Michael Burlingame, *Abraham Lincoln: A Life* (Baltimore: Johns Hopkins University Press, 2008), 417; John Franklin, *The Emancipation Proclamation* (Wheeling, IL: Harlan Davidson, 1963), 43.
16. Burlingame, *Lincoln*, 417; Louis Masur, *Lincoln's Hundred Days* (Cambridge, MA: Belknap Press, 2012), 123–24.
17. Masur, *Lincoln's Hundred Days*, 123–25; Burlingame, *Lincoln*, 417; Allen Guelzo, *Lincoln's Emancipation Proclamation* (New York: Simon & Schuster, 2006), 178.
18. Jones, *Blue and Gray Diplomacy* (Chapel Hill: University of North Carolina Press, 2010), 230; Matthew Andrews, *Virginia: The Old Dominion* (Garden City, NY: Doubleday, Doran, 1937), 632n; McPherson, *Battle Cry*, 771, 773, 805.
19. Jones, *Blue and Gray*, 120.
20. Abraham Lincoln, "Second Presidential Inaugural Address," Mar. 4, 1865, Avalon Project, Yale Law School, http://avalon.law.yale.edu/19th_century/lincoln2.asp.
21. Walter R. Borneman, *Rival Rails* (New York: Random House: 2010), Kindle location 734.
22. Ibid., 358, 507.
23. Stephen Ambrose, *Nothing Like It in the World* (New York: Touchstone, 2000), 94.
24. Brands, *American Colossus*, 46-47, 58.

25. Philip Leigh, *Trading with the Enemy* (Yardley, PA: Westholme, 2013), 142; Ambrose, *Nothing Like It*, 80, 86.
26. Ambrose, *Nothing Like It*, 80-81; Robert S. Henry, "The Railroad Land Grant Legend in American History Texts," *Mississippi Valley Historical Review* 32, no. 2 (Sept. 1945), 182-83; "Railroads, Federal Land Grants," *Gale Encyclopedia of U.S. Economic History* (2000), Encyclopedia.com, Jan. 19, 2016, www.encyclopedia.com/doc/1G2-3406400787.html.
27. Ambrose, *Nothing Like It*, 95-96; Borneman, *Rival Rails*, 913; Hacker and Kendrick, *United States Since 1865*, 113.
28. Ambrose, *Nothing Like It*, 78; Stampp, *Era of Reconstruction*, 106; Johnson *Division and Reunion*, 110.
29. Samuel Morison and Henry Commager, *The Growth of the American Republic*, vol. 2, 4th ed. (New York: Oxford University Press, 1950), 112.
30. Borneman, *Rival Rails*, 913; "Railroads, Federal Land Grants," *Gale Encyclopedia.*
31. McPherson, *Battle Cry*, 450.
32. Johnson, *Division and Reunion*, 110-11; H. W. Brands, *The Reckless Decade* (New York: St. Martin's Press, 1995), 181; "Railroads, Federal Land Grants," *Gale Encyclopedia.*
33. Henry, "Railroad Land Grant Legend," 182.
34. Peter Zavoknyki, *The Rise of the Federal Colossus* (Santa Barbara, CA: ABC-CLIO, 2001), 148.
35. Percy Ashley, *Modern Tariff History* (New York: Howard Fertig, 1970), 179-80; Mark Thornton and Robert Ekelund, *Tariffs, Blockades, and Inflation* (Wilmington, DE: SR Books, 2004), 25; Census Bureau, *Historical Statistics of the United States*, 888; Marc-William Palen, "The Civil War's Forgotten Transatlantic Trade Debate," *Journal of the Civil War Era* 3, no. 1 (Mar. 2013): 35, 47.
36. Jay Sexton, *Debtor Diplomacy: Finance and Foreign Relations in the Civil War* (Oxford: Clarendon, 2005), 92.
37. Palen, "Forgotten Transatlantic Trade Debate," 35, 47; Jones, *Blue and Gray*, 14.
38. Gallagher, *American Civil War*, 22-23; Gene Dattel, *Cotton and Race in the Making of America* (Lanham, MD: Ivan R. Dee, 2009), 82.
39. Census Bureau, *Historical Statistics of the United States*, 1106; John and Charles Lockwood, "First South Carolina, Then New York?" *Opinionator: Disunion* (blog), *New York Times*, Jan. 6, 2001, http://opinionator.blogs.nytimes.com/2011/01/06/first-south-carolina-then-newyork/?_r=0.
40. Census Bureau, *Historical Statistics of the United States*, 1106.
41. Ida Tarbell, *The Tariff in Our Times* (New York: Macmillan, 1911), 1-2.
42. Murray N. Rothbard, *A History of Money and Banking in the United States* (Auburn, AL: Ludwig von Mises Institute, 2002), 57.
43. Randall and Donald, *Civil War and Reconstruction*, 340; Paul Studenski and Herman Krooss, *Financial History of the United States* (New York: McGraw-Hill, 1952), 119–20.
44. Studenski and Krooss, *Financial History*, 137–38.
45. Leigh, *Trading with the Enemy*, 142.
46. Carl Sandburg, *Abraham Lincoln*, vol. 4 (New York: Charles Scribner's Sons, 1940), 194; Irwin Unger, *The Greenback Era* (Princeton, NJ: Princeton University Press, 1964), 15.

47. H. W. Brands, *Greenback Planet* (Austin: University of Texas Press, 2011), 13-14; Unger *Greenback Era*, 152; Walter Nugent, *Money and American Society: 1865-1880* (New York: Free Press, 1968), 168.
48. Rothbard, *History of Money and Banking*, 127-29.
49. Unger, *Greenback Era,* 18-19; Michael Holt, *By One Vote: The Disputed Presidential Election of 1876* (Lawrence: University Press of Kansas, 2008), 15.
50. Holt, *By One Vote*, 15.
51. Studenski and Krooss, *Financial History*, 154-56; Nugent, *Money and American Society*, 10.
52. Studenski and Krooss, *Financial History,* 154-56; Unger, *Greenback Era*, 19; Bureau of Engraving and Printing, *Currency Notes*, 5, https://www.moneyfactory.gov/images/Currency_notes_508.pdf.
53. Theda Skocpol, "America's First Social Security System: The Expansion of Benefits for Civil War Veterans," *Political Science Quarterly* 108, no. 1 (Spring 1993): 95; Hacker and Kendrick, *United States Since 1865*, 88; Census Bureau, *Historical Statistics of the United States*, 1146; Curt Mills, "U. S. Still Paying a Civil War Pension," *U. S. News and World Report*, Aug. 8, 2016, www.usnews.com/news/articles/2016-08-08/civil-war-vets-pension-still-remains-ongovernments-payroll-151-years-after-last-shot-fired.

CHAPTER TWO: WARTIME RECONSTRUCTION

1. Randall and Donald, *Civil War and Reconstruction*, 552; Letter from Union Major General Gillmore to Union General-in-Chief Henry Halleck on January 31, 1864, *Official Records of the Union and Confederate Armies*, vol. 35, pt. 1, 279; Ludwell Johnson, *Red River Campaign* (Kent, OH: Kent State University Press, 1993), 46.
2. Abraham Lincoln, *Proclamation 108—Amnesty and Reconstruction*, Dec. 8, 1863, www.presidency.ucsb.edu/ws/index.php?pid=69987.
3. Johnson, *Red River Campaign*, 85; John Waugh, *Reelecting Lincoln* (New York: Crown, 1997), 191; Rick Beard, "Louisiana's Stillborn Constitution," *Opinionator: Disunion* (blog), *New York Times,* Sept. 11, 2014, http://opinionator.blogs.nytimes.com/2014/09/11/louisianas-stillbornconstitution/?_r=0.
4. Foner, *Reconstruction*, 43-44, Randall and Donald, *Civil War and Reconstruction*, 554.
5. McPherson, *Battle Cry*, 297-99.
6. Louis P. Masur, "The Battle over Reconstruction," *Opinionator: Disunion* (blog), *New York Times*, July 7, 2014, http://opinionator.blogs.nytimes.com/2014/07/07/the-battle-overreconstruction/.
7. Waugh, *Reelecting Lincoln*, 259, 261-62.
8. Ibid., 260.
9. Randall and Donald, *Civil War and Reconstruction*, 524.
10. Donald, *Lincoln*, 560.
11. Ibid., 558, 559.
12. J. G. Randall and Richard Current, *Lincoln the President* (Urbana: University of Illinois Press, 1999), 335.
13. Donald, *Lincoln*, 560-61.
14. Lincoln, "Second Inaugural Address."
15. Abraham Lincoln, "Last Public Address," Washington, DC, Apr. 11, 1865, Abraham Lincoln Online, www.abrahamlincolnonline.org/lincoln/speeches/last.htm.

16. Donald, *Lincoln*, 574.
17. Ibid., 580, 591, 592.
18. Myrta Avary, *Dixie After the War* (New York: Doubleday, Page, 1906), 91.
19. Abraham Lincoln, *Political Debates between Abraham Lincoln and Stephen A. Douglas* (Cleveland: Burrows Brothers, 1897), 358; Abraham Lincoln, *Speech on the Dred Scott Decision*, June 26, 1857, www.virginia.edu/woodson/courses/aas-hius366a/lincoln.html.
20. Donald, *Lincoln*, 367; Rick Beard, "Lincoln's Panama Plan," *Opinionator: Disunion* (blog), *New York Times*, Aug. 12, 2012, http://opinionator.blogs.nytimes.com/2012/08/16/lincolnspanama-plan/?_r=0; Sebastian Page, "Lincoln, Colonization and the Sound of Silence," *Opinionator: Disunion* (blog), *New York Times*, Dec. 4, 2012, http://opinionator.blogs.nytimes.com/2012/12/04/lincoln-colonization-and-the-sound-of-silence/.
21. Stampp, *Era of Reconstruction*, 35, 38; William J. Cooper, *We Have the War upon Us* (New York: Alfred A. Knopf, 2012), 75-76; Charles Sellers Jr., "Who Were the Southern Whigs?," *American Historical Review* 59, no. 2 (Jan. 1954): 341.

CHAPTER THREE: RUINATION

1. Johnson, *Division and Reunion*, 186-88.
2. Robert Selph Henry, *The Story of Reconstruction* (Indianapolis: Bobbs-Merrill, 1938), 18, 20; Johnson, *Division and Reunion*, 190.
3. Johnson, *Division and Reunion*, 189-90; Cohn, *King Cotton*, 142; E. Merton Coulter, *The South During Reconstruction* (Baton Rouge: LSU Press, 1947), 3-4; Simkins and Roland, *History of the South*, 243; National Park Service, "The Civil War: Facts," www.nps.gov/civilwar/facts.htm; Infoplease, "Population by Age, Race, and Nativity: 1860–2010," www.infoplease.com/ipa/A0110384.html; Walter Fleming, *Documentary History of Reconstruction*, vol. 1 (Cleveland: Arthur H. Clark, 1906), 19.
4. Johnson, *Division and Reunion*, 190; Henry, *Story of Reconstruction*, 21, 61; Simkins and Roland, *History of the South*, 242.
5. Cohn, *King Cotton*, 145-46.
6. Johnson, *Division and Reunion*, 189-90; Coulter, *South During Reconstruction*, 155-56.
7. Matthew Hammond, *The Cotton Industry: An Essay in American Economic History* (New York: American Economic Association by MacMillan, 1897), 325; James L. Watkins, *King Cotton: A Historical and Statistical Review* (New York: J. L. Watkins & Sons, 1908), 30.
8. Coulter, *South During Reconstruction*, 8, 10; Jeffrey Hummel, *Emancipating Slaves, Enslaving Free Men* (Peru, IL: Open Court, 1996), 293.
9. Henry, *Story of Reconstruction*, 64-65.
10. Coulter, *South During Reconstruction*, 13.
11. Myrta Avary, *Dixie After the War*, 158; Henry, *Story of Reconstruction*, 22.
12. Hodding Carter, *The Angry Scar* (New York: Doubleday, 1959), 33.
13. Cohn, *King Cotton*, 144-5.
14. Avary, *Dixie After the War*, 160.
15. Ibid., 155-56, 162.
16. Abraham Lincoln, *Recollected Words of Abraham Lincoln*, ed. Don and Virginia Fehrenbacher (Palo Alto, CA: Stanford University Press, 1996), 89.

CHAPTER FOUR: "JOSHUA" JOHNSON

1. Gene Smith, *High Crimes and Misdemeanors* (New York: William Morrow, 1977), 89-90.
2. Smith, *High Crimes*, 88.
3. Ibid., 91, 103-4.
4. Craven, *Reconstruction*, 93.
5. Smith, *High Crimes*, 31-34, 40.
6. Ibid., 42-45; Stampp, *Era of Reconstruction*, 58.
7. Smith, *High Crimes*, 39, 304.
8. Ibid., 49-52.
9. Waugh, *Reelecting Lincoln*, 197, 200; Stampp, *Era of Reconstruction*, 110-11.
10. Craven, *Reconstruction*, 84; Stampp, *Era of Reconstruction*, 52.
11. Randall and Donald, *Civil War and Reconstruction*, 561-62; Craven, *Reconstruction*, 80.
12. Craven, *Reconstruction*, 88-89; Randall and Donald, *Civil War and Reconstruction*, 560-61.
13. Randall and Donald, *Civil War and Reconstruction*, 562-63.
14. Ezell, *South Since 1865*, 66.
15. Smith, *High Crimes*, 135-36.
16. Johnson, *Division and Reunion*, 250.
17. Randall and Donald, *Civil War and Reconstruction*, 111; Hummel, *Emancipating Slaves*, 306.
18. Simkins and Roland, *History of the South*, 242-43.
19. Randall and Donald, *Civil War and Reconstruction*, 576-77, 595.
20. Simkins and Roland, *History of the South*, 262.
21. Herman Belz, *A New Birth of Freedom* (New York: Fordham University Press, 2000), 42; Lincoln, *Collected Works*, 6:48-49.
22. Simkins and Roland, *History of the South*, 262; Ezell, *South Since 1865*, 47-48.
23. Dattel, *Cotton and Race*, 211-12.
24. Davis, *High Crimes*, 110; Johnson, *Division and Reunion*, 214; Ezell, *South Since 1865*, 69; Henry, *Story of Reconstruction*, 45, 210-11.
25. Randall and Donald, *Civil War and Reconstruction*, 580.
26. Randall and Donald, *Civil War and Reconstruction*, 580-81; Johnson, *Division and Reunion*, 200–1, 206.
27. Randall and Donald, *Civil War and Reconstruction*, 577-78; Johnson, *Division and Reunion*, 209-10.
28. Johnson, *Division and Reunion*, 211-13.
29. Ibid.; Davis, *High Crimes*, 162-64; Civil Rights Act of 1866, TeachingAmericanHistory.org, http://teachingamericanhistory.org/library/document/the-civil-rights-act-of-1866/.
30. Johnson, *Division and Reunion*, 214.
31. Randall and Donald, *Civil War and Reconstruction*, 581-84.
32. Henry, *Story of Reconstruction*, 79.
33. Randall and Donald, *Civil War and Reconstruction*, 634.
34. Brooks Simpson, *The Reconstruction Presidents* (Lawrence: University Press of Kansas, 2009), 104-5.
35. Davis, *High Crimes*, 176-83.
36. Johnson, *Division and Reunion*, 223-24; Ezell, *South Since 1865*, 79.

37. Coulter, *South During Reconstruction*, 132-33.
38. Coulter, *South During Reconstruction,* 118-120, 133, 136; Johnson, *Division and Reunion*, 226-27.
39. Johnson, *Division and Reunion*, 228.
40. Andrew Johnson, "Veto Message," Mar. 2, 1867, American Presidency Project, www.presidency.ucsb.edu/ws/?pid=72072.
41. Davis, *High Crimes*, 211-12.
42. Ibid., 221-23.
43. Ibid., 237, 243-44, 258, 268.
44. Curt Anders, *Powerlust: Radicalism in the Civil War Era 1850–1875* (Garrison, NY: Highlands Press, 2010), 494; Davis, *High Crimes*, 244, 265; Henry, *Story of Reconstruction*, 304.
45. Davis, *High Crimes*, 243, 279.
46. Ibid., 263.
47. Henry, *Story of Reconstruction*, 308.
48. Chester G. Hearn, *The Impeachment of Andrew Johnson* (Jefferson, NC: McFarland, 2007), 202; Craven, *Reconstruction*, 221; John W. Johnson, *Historic U. S. Court Cases* (Abingdon, UK: Routledge, 2003), 320.
49. Hearn, *Impeachment of Andrew Johnson*, 292.
50. Anders, *Powerlust*, 533.
51. Randall and Donald, *Civil War and Reconstruction*, 640-41.
52. Henry, *Story of Reconstruction*, 206-7.
53. Ibid., 310-12.
54. Ezell, *South Since 1865*, 52, 87.

CHAPTER FIVE: CARPETBAGGED

1. Ezell, *South Since 1865*, 82.
2. Johnson, *Division and Reunion*, 226-27, 245; Ezell, *South Since 1865*, 82-83.
3. Randall and Donald, *Civil War and Reconstruction*, 620-22; Johnson, *Division and Reunion*, 226-27.
4. Johnson, *Division and Reunion*, 226-27, 246; Ezell, *South Since 1868*, 93; Coulter, *South During Reconstruction*, 141.
5. Coulter, *South During Reconstruction*, 155-56; Hummel, *Emancipating Slaves*, 316; Johnson, *Division and Reunion*, 248.
6. Stephen Yafa, *Cotton* (New York: Penguin, 2005), 175-76.
7. South Carolina General Assembly, 1878, *Report of the Joint Investigating Committee on Public Frauds Part 7* (Columbia, SC: Calvo & Patton, 1878), 32.
8. Ezell, *South Since 1865*, 85-86.
9. Ezell, *South Since 1865*, 85-87; Randall and Donald, *Civil War and Reconstruction*, 630.
10. Randall and Donald, *Civil War and Reconstruction*, 630-32.
11. Ezell, *South Since 1865*, 88.
12. Ibid., 88-90.
13. Carter, *Angry Scar*, 163; Allan Nevins, *The Emergence of Modern America* (New York: Macmillan, 1927), 355; Carl H. Moneyhon, "Brooks-Baxter War," *Encyclopedia of Arkansas History & Culture*, www.encyclopediaofarkansas.net/encyclopedia/entry-detail.aspx?entryID=2276.
14. Ezell, *South Since 1865*, 91; Carter, *Angry Scar*, 279-87.

CHAPTER SIX: RAILROADED

1. Gabriel Kolko, *Railroads and Regulation: 1877-1916* (Princeton, NJ: Princeton University Press, 1965), 1.
2. Morison and Commager, *Growth of the American Republic*, 2:3.
3. Webb, *Divided We Stand*, 11.
4. Josephson, *Robber Barons*, 145, 315.
5. Beatty, *Age of Betrayal*, 67; Hacker and Kendrick, *United States Since 1865*, 125.
6. Morison and Commager, *Growth of the American Republic*, 2:112.
7. Walter Borneman, *Iron Horse* (Boston: Little, Brown, 2014), 98; Josephson, *Robber Barons*, 87.
8. Josephson, *Robber Barons*, 92-93.
9. Beatty, *Age of Betrayal*, 230.
10. Morison and Commager, *Growth of the American Republic*, 2:112.
11. Borneman, *Rival Rails*, 17-32; Edward Martin, *Behind the Scenes in Washington*, ch. 8, "A Complete and Graphic Account of the Credit Mobilier Investigation" (Continental Publishing and National Publishing, 1873), http://cprr.org/Museum/Credit_Mobilier_1873.html.
12. Josephson, *Robber Barons*, 125-33.
13. Ibid., 284-85.
14. Borneman, *Rival Rails*, 453-69.
15. Josephson, *Robber Barons*, 95-97; Nevins, *Emergence of Modern America*, 294-99.
16. Beatty, *Age of Betrayal*, 232-33; Josephson, *Robber Barons*, 169-70.
17. Beatty, *Age of Betrayal*, 233-34; Josephson, *Robber Barons*, 168; Brands, *American Colossus*, 89; Josephson, *Politicos*, 235; Nevins, *Emergence of Modern America*, 294-99; TreasuryDirect.gov, "Historical Debt Outstanding—Annual 1850–1899," www.treasurydirect.gov/govt/reports/pd/histdebt/histdebt_histo2.htm.
18. Cooper and Terrill, *American South*, 2:462.
19. Beatty, *Age of Betrayal*, 233-34.
20. Brands, *American Colossus*, 121-32; Josephson, *Politicos*, 236-38; Cashman, *America in the Gilded Age*, 111; Hacker and Kendrick, *United States Since 1865*, 190.
21. McFeely, *Grant*, 397.
22. Cashman, *America in the Gilded Age*, 316; Brands, *American Colossus*, 483, 488; Paul Dempsey, "The Rise and Fall of the Interstate Commerce Commission," *Marquette Law Review* 5, no. 4 (Summer 2012): 1155.
23. Kolko, *Railroads and Regulation*, 16-7.
24. Josephson, *Robber Barons*, 307-13.
25. Beatty, *Age of Betrayal*, 219; Hacker and Kendrick, *United States Since 1865*, 230, 234-36; Cashman, *America in the Gilded Age*, 359-60; Josephson, *Politicos*, 491; Dempsey, "Rise and Fall," 1160.
26. Marc Scribner, "The Sad Early History of Railroad Regulation," Competitive Enterprise Institute, Sept. 17, 2012, https://cei.org/blog/sad-early-history-railroad-regulation-subsidiesnationalization; Dempsey, "Rise and Fall," 1165.
27. Foner, *Reconstruction*, 535-36.
28. Ezell, *South Since 1865*, 151-52.
29. Dempsey, "Rise and Fall," 1165.
30. C. Vann Woodward, *Origins of the New South* (Baton Rouge: LSU Press, 1971), 312-15, 318.

31. National Emergency Council, *Report on Economic Conditions,* 59, https://archive.org/stream/reportoneconomic00nati#page/2/mode/2up.
32. Woodward, *Origins of the New South*, 315-16; "Southern Steel Mills Profiting," *Tuscaloosa News,* June 26, 1939.
33. Woodward, *Origins of the New South*, 314.
34. Harold Henderson, *The Politics of Change in Georgia* (Athens: University of Georgia Press, 1991), 118-25, 130.

CHAPTER SEVEN: CORRUPTED

1. Hacker and Kendrick, *United States Since 1865*, 44.
2. Smith, *Grant*, 493; Josephson, *Robber Barons*, 95, 144; McFeely, *Grant*, 343; Brands, *American Colossus*, 362-63.
3. McFeely, *Grant*, 290-3, 298, 343.
4. Elizabeth Purdy and Lawrence Salinger, eds., "Grant, Ulysses S.," *Encyclopedia of White Collar and Corporate Crime*, vol. 1 (Los Angeles: Sage, 2005), 374-75.
5. McFeely, *Grant*, 322-28.
6. Ibid., 337-44.
7. Foner, *Reconstruction*, 565-6; McFeely, *Grant*, 347-48.
8. Raleigh DeGeer Amyx, "Scandals of Ulysses S. Grant—General & President," American Heritage Blog, Raleigh DeGeer Amyx Collection, posted Apr. 10, 2014, http://blog.americanheritage1.com/blog/bid/109596/Scandals-of-Ulysses-S-Grant-GENERALPRESIDENT.
9. J. Martin Klotsche, "The Star Route Cases," *Mississippi Valley Historical Review* 22, no. 3 (Dec. 1935): 410, https://www.jstor.org/stable/1892626?seq=1#page_scan_tab_contents.
10. Cashman, *America in the Gilded Age*, 228.
11. McFeely, *Grant*, 397; Josephson, *Politicos*, 183-84; Hacker and Kendrick, *United States Since 1865*, 48.
12. McFeely, *Grant*, 376.
13. Ibid., 404-15; Allan Nevins, *Dictionary of American Biography* (New York: Charles Scribner's Sons, 1929), 55-56; Hacker and Kendrick, *United States Since 1865*, 49.
14. McFeely, *Grant*, 414.
15. Purdy and Salinger, "Grant," 374-75; McFeely, *Grant*, 430-31.
16. McFeely, *Grant*, 432-33, 435, 437.
17. Ibid., 432.
18. Roy Morris Jr., *Fraud of the Century* (New York: Simon & Schuster, 2003), 51, 53-4, 78-81, 99, 104, 119, 135.
19. Ibid., 176, 194-96.
20. Ibid., 188-89.
21. Ibid., 178-79, 180-82.
22. Ibid., 218-33; Carter, *Angry Scar*, 321.
23. Morris, *Fraud of the Century*, 245-46; Foner *Reconstruction*, 543, 604-5.
24. Morris, *Fraud of the Century*, 245-46; Foner, *Reconstruction*, 543, 604-5.
25. The following discussion of Radical Republican Reconstruction is based on Daniel H. Chamberlain, "Reconstruction in South Carolina," *Atlantic Monthly* 87, no. 522 (Apr. 1901): 473-83, http://ebooks.library.cornell.edu/cgi/t/text/pageviewer-

idx?c=atla;cc=atla;rgn=full percent20text;idno=atla0087-4;didno=atla0087-4;view=image;seq=00481;node=atla0087-4 percent3A1.
26. The following discussion of the transformation of the Republican Party is based on Woodward, *Origins of the New South*, 26-47.

CHAPTER EIGHT: SOUTHERN REPARATIONS

1. Cohn, *King Cotton*, 148-49.
2. Nugent, *Money and American Society*, 11-12, 168.
3. USgovernmentspending.com; Randall and Donald, *Civil War and Reconstruction*, 584; Studenski and Krooss, *Financial History*, 143-44.
4. US Department of Commerce, *Historical Statistics of the United States: 1789-1945* (Washington, DC: Department of Commerce, 1949), 247-48; Hummel, *Emancipating Slaves*, 322-23, 330.
5. Thaddeus Stevens, address to the US House of Representatives, Dec. 18, 1865, Thaddeus Stevens Papers Online, Furman University, http://history.furman.edu/benson/hst41/blue/stevens1.htm.
6. Coulter, *South During Reconstruction*, 10-13; Cooper and Terrill, *American South*, 2:447; US Department of Agriculture, *Report of the Commissioner of Agriculture* (Washington, DC: Government Printing Office, 1868), xii.
7. Hacker and Kendrick, *United States Since 1865*, 88; Claudia Goldin and Frank Lewis, "Economic Costs of the American Civil War," *Journal of Economic History* 35, no. 2 (June 1975), 304; Census Bureau, *Historical Statistics of the United States*, 1146; Morison and Commager, *Growth of the American Republic*, 2:4.
8. Skocpol, "America's First Social Security System," 92-93.
9. Ibid., 90, 102.
10. Ibid., 95; Census Bureau, *Historical Statistics of the United States*, 1106.
11. Skocpol, "America's First Social Security System," 95; Hacker and Kendrick, *United States Since 1865*, 88; Census Bureau, *Historical Statistics of the United States*, 1146; Claudia Goldin and Frank Lewis, "Economic Costs of the American Civil War," *Journal of Economic History* 35, no. 2 (June 1975): 304.
12. Jill Quadagno, *The Transformation of Old Age Security* (Chicago: University of Chicago Press, 1988), 36.
13. Ibid., 37, 42.
14. Skocpol, "America's First Social Security System," 100, 102.
15. Ibid., 104; Quadagno, *Transformation of Old Age Security*, 46.
16. Carter, *Angry Scar*, 190-91.
17. Ibid., 96; Quadagno, *Transformation of Old Age Security*, 45.
18. Beth Linker, *War's Waste: Rehabilitation in World War I America* (Chicago: University of Chicago Press, 2011), 21; Hacker and Kendrick, *United States Since 1865*, 89-90; Webb, *Divided We Stand*, 12-13.
19. Byron W. Holt, "The Relation of the Protective Tariff to the Trusts," *Publications of the American Economic Association*, 3rd ser., vol. 8, no.1 (Feb. 1907): 213.
20. Ibid., 217-18, 220.
21. Webb, *Divided We Stand*, 12.
22. Richard Sylla, "Federal Policy, Banking Market Structure, and Capital Mobilization in the United States, 1863–1913," *Journal of Economic History* 29, no. 4 (Dec. 1969): 659, 664.
23. Ibid., 663, 664.

24. Ibid., 664.
25. John Hicks, *Populist Revolt* (Minneapolis: University of Minnesota Press, 1931), 39-40.
26. Studenski and Krooss, *Financial History,* 154–155.
27. Ibid., 178; Cooper and Terrill, *American South*, 2:457–58, 460; Sylla, "Federal Policy," 663-64.
28. Sylla, "Federal Policy," 657-59, 661-62.
29. Cashman, *America in the Gilded Age*, 318.
30. Unger, *Greenback Era*, 42-43.
31. Brands, *Greenback Planet*, 17-18; Cashman, *America in the Gilded Age*, 250; William Hesseltine, "Economic Factors in the Abandonment of Reconstruction," *Mississippi Valley Historical Review* 22, no. 2 (Sept. 1935): 196.
32. Cashman, *America in the Gilded Age*, 318.
33. Hacker and Kendrick, *United States Since 1865*, 256-57.
34. Cohn, *King Cotton*, 149-50.
35. Amanda Foreman, *A World on Fire* (New York: Random House, 2010), 24; Sanchez Manning, "Britain's Colonial Shame: Slave-Owners Given Huge Payouts After Abolition," *Independent*, Feb. 23, 2013, www.independent.co.uk/news/uk/home-news/britains-colonial-shameslave-owners-given-huge-payouts-after-abolition-8508358.html.

CHAPTER NINE: SHARECROPPED

1. Robert Futrell, "Federal Trade with the Confederate States: 1861-1865" (PhD diss., Vanderbilt University, 1950), 155; Willie Lee Rose, *Rehearsal for Reconstruction* (New York: Vintage Books, 1964), 82-83, 204.
2. Akiko Ochiai, "The Port Royal Experiment Revisited," *New England Quarterly* 74, no. 1 (Mar. 2001): 104-5.
3. Foner, *Reconstruction*, 54-56; Lawrence N. Powell, *New Masters* (New York: Fordham University Press, 1998), 84.
4. Dattel, *Cotton and Race*, 212-14, 224.
5. Ibid., 212-14.
6. Robert Somers, *The Southern States Since the War* (London: R. Clay & Sons, 1871), 153.
7. Craven, *Reconstruction*, 119-22.
8. Stampp, *Era of Reconstruction*, 127-28.
9. Cohn, *King Cotton*, 160.
10. Henry, *Story of Reconstruction*, 101.
11. Stampp, *Era of Reconstruction*, 42, 127; Randall and Donald, *Civil War and Reconstruction*, 284-85; Donald, *Lincoln*, 560; Manuel Gottlieb, review of *Reconstruction: The Battle for Democracy*, by James S. Allen, *Science & Society* 2, no. 4 (Fall 1938): 543.
12. Cohn, *King Cotton*, 158-59.
13. Morison and Commager, *Growth of the American Republic*, 2:22.
14. James Webb, *Born Fighting* (New York: Broadway Books, 2004), 269; National Emergency Council, *Report on Economic Conditions*, 46; Thomas D. Clark and Albert D. Kirwan, *The South Since Appomattox* (New York: Oxford University Press, 1967), 92.

15. Dattel, *Cotton and Race*, 341-44; "Salsbury Makes Full Confession," *Chicago Daily Tribune*, Mar. 5, 1902, 1.
16. Dattel, *Cotton and Race*, 344-45.
17. Ibid., 345-46.
18. Dattel, *Cotton and Race*, 346.
19. Yafa, *Cotton*, 281-82.
20. Hummel, *Emancipating Slaves*, 324; Clark and Kirwan, *South Since Appomattox*, 85, 104.
21. Ezell, *South Since 1865*, 124-25.
22. Clark and Kirwan, *South Since Appomattox*, 90.
23. Ibid., 90-91.
24. Morison and Commager, *Growth of the American Republic*, 2:25.
25. Fleming, *Documentary History*, 1:89-90.
26. Yafa, *Cotton*, 179.
27. Booker T. Washington, *Up from Slavery* (New York: A. L. Burt, 1900), 21-22.
28. Cohn, *King Cotton*, 245; Ezell, *South Since 1865*, 135.
29. Cohn, *King Cotton*, 239; Yafa, *Cotton*, 174.

CHAPTER TEN: REDEEMED

1. Johnson, *Division and Reunion*, 189; Craven, *Reconstruction*, 256; US Census Bureau, "Merchandise Imports, Exports, and Trade Balance: 1790-2006," *Historical Statistics of the United States from Colonial Times to 1970*, pt. 2 (Washington, DC: Government Printing Office, 1975), 865, www.econdataus.com/tradeall.html.
2. Stampp, *Era of Reconstruction*, 206-7.
3. Hesseltine, "Economic Factors," 206; Henry, *Story of Reconstruction*, 522-23; Foner, *Reconstruction*, 533; Simkins and Roland, *History of the South*, 282; Mark David Richards, "Alexander R. Shepherd and the Race Issue in Washington," *Washington History* (Spring/Summer 2004): 59, 70; Mark David Richards, "Touring Hidden Washington: Living in the Shadow of Congress," DCWatch, June 2001, www.dcwatch.com/richards/0106.htm.
4. Stampp, *Era of Reconstruction*, 207; Randall and Donald, *Civil War and Reconstruction*, 658; Foner, *Reconstruction*, 484-85.
5. Stampp, *Era of Reconstruction*, 191; Randall and Donald, *Civil War and Reconstruction*, 659.
6. Hesseltine, "Economic Factors," 203–4.
7. Craven, *Reconstruction*, 294.
8. Foner, *Reconstruction*, 508; Randall and Donald, *Civil War and Reconstruction*, 659.
9. Randall and Donald, *Civil War and Reconstruction*, 684.
10. Foner, *Reconstruction*, 509; Randall and Donald, *Civil War and Reconstruction*, 660; Morris, *Fraud of the Century*, 36.
11. Randall and Donald, *Civil War and Reconstruction*, 660.
12. Randall and Donald, *Civil War and Reconstruction*, 685; Craven, *Reconstruction*, 296; Simkins and Roland, *History of the South*, 284.
13. Foner, *Reconstruction*, 528, 588; Brent Tarter, "Conservative Party of Virginia," *Encyclopedia of Virginia*, www.encyclopediavirginia.org/Conservative_Party_of_Virginia.
14. Foner, *Reconstruction*, 588-89.

15. Ezell, *South Since 1865*, 175-77.
16. Ibid., 174-75.
17. Foner, *Reconstruction*, 588-89; Stampp, *Era of Reconstruction*, 197; Woodward, *Origins of the New South*, 58-59; Ezell, *South Since 1865*, 107.
18. Foner, *Reconstruction*, 588; Simkins and Roland, *History of the South*, 313; J. G. de Roulhac Hamilton, "Those Southern Repudiated Bonds," *Virginia Quarterly Review* 3, no. 4 (Autumn 1927), www.vqronline.org/essay/those-southern-repudiated-bonds.
19. Henry, *Story of Reconstruction*, 444.
20. Foner, *Reconstruction*, 541; Simkins and Roland, *History of the South*, 315; Hamilton, "Those Southern Repudiated Bonds."
21. Simkins and Roland, *History of the South*, 316-17; Woodward, *Origins of the New South*, 67-69.
22. Woodward, *Origins of the New South*, 61-63.
23. Foner, *Reconstruction*, 589; Woodward, *Origins of the New South*, 215.
24. Woodward, *Origins of the New South*, 60.
25. Ezell, *South Since 1865*, 102-5, 111-12; Webb, *Born Fighting*, 244.
26. Woodward, *Origins of the New South*, 61, 65.
27. Cooper and Terrill, *American South*, 2:493-94.

CHAPTER ELEVEN: DIVORCED

1. Brands, *Reckless Decade*, 177, 178.
2. Ibid., 178-79; Hicks, *Populist Revolt*, 104.
3. Brands, *Reckless Decade*, 183-84.
4. Ibid., 186, 190.
5. Ibid., 191-93.
6. Ibid., 195.
7. Ibid.
8. Webb, *Born Fighting*, 249.
9. Brands, *Reckless Decade*, 190-91.
10. Ibid., 191; Webb, *Born Fighting*, 249.
11. Wilbur Cash, *The Mind of the South* (New York: Vintage Books, 1969), 251.
12. Alicia Knight, *Pauline Hopkins and the American Dream* (Knoxville: University of Tennessee Press, 2012), 29; Woodward, *Origins of the New South*, 321-23, 326; Brands, *Reckless Decade*, 240; Paul H. Buck, *The Road to Reunion* (New York: Vintage Books, 1959), 291.
13. Hacker and Kendrick, *United States Since 1865*, 262; Ezell, *South Since 1865*, 175-76; Edward Wells, *Hampton and Reconstruction* (Columbia, SC: State Company, 1907), 90, 94.
14. Woodward, *Origins of the New South*, 324-25.
15. Ibid., 321; Ezell, *South Since 1865*, 178.
16. Brands, *American Colossus*, 549.
17. US Constitution, US National Archives and Records Administration, www.archives.gov/exhibits/charters/constitution_transcript.html.
18. Webb, *Divided We Stand*, 117.
19. Brands, *American Colossus*, 611; Hacker and Kendrick, *United States Since 1865*, 391-93, 395; Robert Higgs, *The Transformation of the American Economy* (New York: John Wiley, 1971), 21.

20. Ezell, *South Since 1865*, 138, 142-43, 214.
21. Henry, *Story of Reconstruction*, 564; Stephen Kantrowitz, *Ben Tillman and the Reconstruction of White Supremacy* (Chapel Hill: University of North Carolina Press, 2000), 65-68.
22. Ezell, *South Since 1865*, 93.
23. Henry, *Story of Reconstruction*, 314, 416, 444; Foner, *Reconstruction*, 386, 439, 605; Brands, *Reckless Decade*, 189; Ezell, *South Since 1865*, 93.
24. Brands, *Reckless Decade*, 190; Ezell, *South Since 1865*, 164; Kantrowitz, *Ben Tillman*, 513.
25. Kantrowitz, *Ben Tillmany*, 166.
26. Ezell, *South Since 1865*, 165.
27. Ezell, *South Since 1865*, 167; Kantrowitz, *Ben Tillman*, 167; Clark and Kirwan, *South Since Appomattox*, 323.
28. Brands, *Reckless Decade*, 257; Ezell, *South Since 1865*, 166.
29. Ezell, *South Since 1865*, 183-84.
30. Herbert Agar, *The Price of Union* (Boston: Houghton Mifflin, 1950), 466-67.
31. Ezell, *South Since 1865*, 183; Abbott, *Bookmaker's Daughter*, xvii.

CHAPTER TWELVE: RACIAL ADJUSTMENT

1. Brands, *Reckless Decade*, 215-16.
2. Stampp, *Era of Reconstruction*, 93-94; Beatty *Age of Betrayal*, 145-46; Ezell, *South Since 1865*, 72.
3. Morison and Commager, *Growth of the American Republic*, 2:38.
4. Henry, *Story of Reconstruction*, 212-15 Bowdoin College, *Data Analysis: African Americans on the Eve of the Civil War*, www.bowdoin.edu/~prael/lesson/tables.htm.
5. Johnson, *Division and Reunion*, 232; Henry, *Story of Reconstruction* 45, 210; Dattel, *Cotton and Race*, 235.
6. Johnson, *Division and Reunion*, 232; Henry, *Story of Reconstruction*, 45, 210-11.
7. Gene Dattel, "King Cotton," *New Criterion* 33, no. 2 (Oct. 2014), https://www.newcriterion.com/articles.cfm/King-cotton-7964.
8. Kevin McGruder, "Black New York and the Draft Riots," *Opinionator: Disunion* (blog), *New York Times*, July 26, 2013, http://opinionator.blogs.nytimes.com/2013/07/26/black-new-yorkand-the-draft-riots/?_r=0.
9. Stampp, *Era of Reconstruction*, 194.
10. Benjamin C. Truman, "Report Relative to the Conditions of the Southern People and the States in Which the Rebellion Existed," Senate Executive Documents, 39th Cong., 1st sess., Ex. Doc. No. 43, May 7, 1866, 7, https://books.google.com/.
11. Ibid., 2, 5.
12. Ibid., 2, 6.
13. Ibid., 8.
14. Ibid., 10.
15. Alexander H. Stephens, *Alexander H. Stephens in Public and Private* (National Publishing, 1866), 131.
16. Truman, "Report," 11-12.
17. Washington, *Up from Slavery*, 84.
18. Foner, *Reconstruction*, 545-47.
19. Ezell, *South Since 1865*, 97-98.
20. Cash, *Mind of the South*, 116.

21. Robert E. Lee, *White Sulphur Manifesto*, Aug. 26, 1868, http://rosecransheadquarters.org/Rosecrans/WhiteSulphurManifesto/Lee.htm.
22. Henry, *Story of Reconstruction*, 468.
23. Harriet Beecher Stowe, *Life of Harriet Beecher Stowe*, ed. Charles Stowe (London: S. Low, Marston, Searle & Rivington, 1889), 396-97.
24. James Ford Rhodes, *The History of the United States from the Compromise of 1850 to the McKinley-Bryan Election of 1896* (New York: Macmillan, 1906), 10.
25. Simpson, *Reconstruction Presidents*, 105; Johnson, *Division and Reunion*, 220; Stephen Ash, *A Massacre in Memphis* (New York: Farrar, Straus and Giroux, 2013), 69; Jack Hurst, *Nathan Bedford Forrest* (New York: Random House, 1994), 276.
26. Smith, *High Crimes*, 171.
27. Henry, *Story of Reconstruction*, 185-88; Michael Holt, *By One Vote*, 195-96.
28. Morris, *Fraud of the Century*, 245-46.
29. Johnson, *Division and Reunion*, 220.
30. Randall and Donald, *Civil War and Reconstruction*, 645.
31. Simkins and Roland, *History of the South*, 267; Ezell, *South Since 1865*, 81, 248; Carter, *Angry Scar*, 189.
32. Ezell, *South Since 1865*, 81-82; Dattel, *Cotton and Race*, 235.
33. Coulter, *Reconstruction*, 128; Michael Fitzgerald, *The Union League Movement in the Deep South* (Baton Rouge: LSU Press, 1989), 43, 216.
34. Christopher Phillips, "The Rise of the Union Leagues," *Opinionator: Disunion* (blog), *New York Times*, Nov. 15, 2013, http://opinionator.blogs.nytimes.com/2013/11/15/the-rise-of-theunion-leagues/?_r=0.
35. Coulter, *Reconstruction*, 127, 132-33.
36. Simkins and Roland, *History of the South*, 266.
37. Carter, *Angry Scar*, 60-62; Walter Fleming, *The Sequel of Appomattox* (New Haven, CT: Yale University Press, 1919), 175, 190; Walter Fleming, *Documentary History of Reconstruction*, vol. 2 (Cleveland: Arthur H. Clark, 1907), 4, 20, 22; Coulter, *Reconstruction*, 156.
38. John Chodes, *Washington's KKK: The Union League During Southern Reconstruction* (Columbia, SC: Shotwell, 2016), Kindle locations 314-20, 320-26.
39. Otis Singletary, *Negro Militia and Reconstruction* (Austin: University of Texas Press, 1957), 54-55, 61-64.
40. Fleming, *Sequel to Appomattox*, 225.
41. Ezell, *South Since 1865*, 91-92.
42. Henry, *Story of Reconstruction,* 491-92.
43. Jeffry Wert, *General James Longstreet* (New York: Simon & Schuster, 1993), 416.
44. Coulter, *South During Reconstruction*, 165.
45. Henry, *Story of Reconstruction*, 236; Hurst, *Nathan Bedford Forrest*, 290; Bob Duncan, "The Most Hated Man in Tennessee History," *Columbia (TN) Daily Herald*, May 7, 2016, http://columbiadailyherald.com/opinion/columns/most-hated-man-tennessee-history.
46. Johnson, *Division and Reunion*, 226; Hurst, *Nathan Bedford Forrest*, 289.
47. Ezell, *South Since 1865*, 85; Hurst, *Nathan Bedford Forrest*, 290; Fitzgerald, *Union League Movement*, 216.
48. Hurst, *Nathan Bedford Forrest*, 277-78.
49. Ibid., 296.
50. Ibid., 293, 305, 307, 311-12, 314-15.

51. Henry, *Story of Reconstruction*, 379-80, Philip Langsdon, *Tennessee: A Political History* (Franklin, TN: Hillsboro Press, 2000), 190-93.
52. Hurst, *Nathan Bedford Forrest*, 327-29, 344; Bowers, *Tragic Era*, 311.
53. Johnson, *Division and Reunion*, 254; Foner, *Reconstruction*, 454.
54. Foner, *Reconstruction*, 455-59.
55. Ezell, *South Since 1865*, 104-6.
56. Brands, *Reckless Decade*, 218; Woodward, *Origins of the New South*, 210-12.
57. Woodward, *Origins of the New South*, 211.
58. Brands, *Reckless Decade*, 218.
59. Foner, *Reconstruction*, 529-31.
60. Agar, *Price of Union*, 499; Cashman, *America in the Gilded Age*, 223-34; Supreme Court of the United States, "Members of the Supreme Court of the United States," https://www.supremecourt.gov/about/members.aspx.
61. Hacker and Kendrick, *United States Since 1865*, 58-59.
62. Cooper and Terrill, *American South*, 2:571, 573, 578-79.
63. Ibid., 2:575.
64. The following discussion of Booker T. Washington is based on Brands, *Reckless Decade*, 241-50.

CHAPTER THIRTEEN: PROTRACTED CONSEQUENCES

1. National Emergency Council, *Report on Economic Conditions,* 32-34, 38-39.
2. Ibid., 21-23, 44, 46.
3. Ibid., 23; Webb, *Divided We Stand*, 18.
4. National Emergency Council, *Report on Economic Conditions*, 26-28, 40, 42.
5. Ibid., 53-55.
6. C. Clayton Brown, *King Cotton in Modern America* (Oxford: University Press of Mississippi, 2010), 106-111.
7. National Emergency Council, *Report on Economic Conditions*, 17-18.
8. Thomas Woods, *The Politically Incorrect Guide to American History* (Washington, DC: Regnery, 2004), 151.

CONCLUSION

1. Tim Lacey, "Removing Confederate Monuments: History Cleansing or Correction?" Society for U.S. Intellectual History, July 30, 2015, http://s-usih.org/2015/07/removing-confederatemonuments-history-cleansing-or-correction.html.
2. Vanderbilt University, "History of Vanderbilt University," www.vanderbilt.edu/about/history/; Lyle Lankford, "Women to the Rescue," *Vanderbilt Magazine*, Aug. 6, 2009, http://news.vanderbilt.edu/vanderbiltmagazine/ women-to-the-rescue/; T. J. Stiles, "The Commodore's Civil War," *Vanderbilt Magazine*, Apr. 11, 2011, http://news.vanderbilt.edu/vanderbiltmagazine/the-commodores-civil-war/.
3. Tom Fremantle, *The Moonshine Mule* (London: Robinson, 2003), 293.
4. "Black Mayors," BlackDemographics.com, http://blackdemographics.com/culture/blackpolitics/black-mayors/.
5. Tim Kane, "Who Bears the Burden?," Center for Data Analysis on National Security and Defense, Report 05-08, Nov. 7, 2005, www.heritage.org/research/reports/2005/11/whobears-the-burden-demographic-characteristics-of-us-military-recruits-before-and-after-9-11; Seth McKee, *Republican Ascendancy in the Southern U.S. House Elections* (Boulder, CO: Westview Press, 2009), 193.

6. Webb, Born *Fighting*, 237.

APPENDIX

1. Richard Sylla, "Federal Policy, Banking Market Structure, and Capital Mobilization in the United States, 1863–1913," *Journal of Economic History* 29, no. 4 (Dec. 1969): 663.
2. Cooper and Terrill, *American South*, 2:458.
3. Nugent, *Money and American Society*, 132.

Bibliography

MEMOIRS, DIARIES, PERSONAL PAPERS

Grant, Ulysses. *The Papers of Ulysses S. Grant.* Vol. 22. Edited by John Y. Simon. Carbondale: Southern Illinois University Press, 1967.

Lee, Robert E. *White Sulphur Manifesto.* August 26, 1868. http://rosecransheadquarters.org/Rosecrans/WhiteSulphurManifesto/Lee.htm.

Lincoln, Abraham. *The Collected Works of Abraham Lincoln.* Vols 5 and 6. Edited by Roy Basler. New Brunswick, NJ: Rutgers University Press, 1953.

———. *Recollected Words of Abraham Lincoln.* Edited by Don Fehrenbacher and Virginia Fehrenbacher. Palo Alto, CA: Stanford University Press, 1996.

Stephens, Alexander H. *Alexander H. Stephens in Public and Private.* National Publishing, 1866.

Stevens, Thaddeus. "Address to U.S. House of Representatives." Dec. 18, 1865. Thaddeus Stevens Papers Online, Furman University. http://history.furman.edu/benson/hst41/blue/stevens1.htm.

Washington, Booker T. *Up from Slavery.* New York: A. L. Burt, 1900.

HISTORICAL DOCUMENTS

Civil Rights Act of 1866. TeachingAmericanHistory.org. http://teachingamericanhistory.org/library/document/the-civil-rights-act-of-1866/.

Johnson, Andrew. "Veto Message." Mar. 2, 1867. American Presidency Project. http://www.presidency.ucsb.edu/ws/?pid=72072.

Letter from Union Major General Gillmore to Union General-in-Chief Henry Halleck, January 31, 1864. *Official Records of the Union and Confederate Armies.* Ser. 1, vol. 35, pt. 1.

Lincoln, Abraham. "Abraham Lincoln's Draft of the Emancipation Proclamation." July 22, 1862. Civil War Trust. http://www.civil war.org/education/history/primarysources/abraham-lincolns-draft-of.html.

———. "Last Public Address." Washington, DC. Apr. 11, 1865. Abraham Lincoln Online. http://www.abrahamlincolnonline.org/lincoln/speeches/last.htm.

———. *Political Debates between Abraham Lincoln and Stephen A. Douglas.* Cleveland: Burrows Brothers, 1897.

———. *Proclamation 108—Amnesty and Reconstruction.* December 8, 1863. http://www.presidency.ucsb.edu/ws/index.php?pid=69987.

———. "Second Presidential Inaugural Address." Mar. 4, 1865. Avalon Project, Yale Law School. http://avalon.law.yale.edu/19th_century/lincoln2.asp.

———. Speech on the Dred Scott Decision. June 26, 1857. http://www.virginia.edu/woodson/courses/aas-hius366a/lincoln.html.

National Emergency Council. *Report on Economic Conditions of the South.* July 25, 1938. https://archive.org/stream/reportoneconomic00nati#page/2/mode/2up.

South Carolina General Assembly, 1878. *Report of the Joint Investigating Committee on Public Frauds Part 7.* Columbia, SC: Calvo & Patton, 1878.

Truman, Benjamin C. "Report Relative to the Conditions of the Southern People and the States in Which the Rebellion Existed." Senate Executive Documents. 39th Cong., 1st sess. Ex. Doc. No. 43, May 7, 1866. https://books.google.com/books.

US Census Bureau. *Historical Statistics of the United States, Colonial Times to 1970.* Pt. 2. Washington, DC: Government Printing Office, 1975.

———. *Statistical Abstract of the United States.* Washington, DC: Government Printing Office, 2003.

US Constitution. US National Archives and Records Administration. http://www.archives.gov/exhibits/charters/constitution_transcript.html.

US Department of Agriculture. *Report of the Commissioner of Agriculture.* Washington, DC: Government Printing Office, 1868.

BOOKS AND COMPILATIONS

Abbott, Shirley. *The Bookmaker's Daughter.* Fayetteville: University of Arkansas Press, 2006.

Agar, Herbert. *The Price of Union.* Boston: Houghton Mifflin, 1950.

Ambrose, Stephen. *Nothing Like It in the World.* New York: Touchstone, 2000.

Anders, Curt. *Powerlust: Radicalism in the Civil War Era 1850-1875.* Garrison, NY: Highlands Press, 2010.

Ash, Stephen. *A Massacre in Memphis.* New York: Farrar, Straus and Giroux, 2013.

Ashley, Percy. *Modern Tariff History.* New York: Howard Fertig, 1970.

Avary, Myrta. *Dixie After the War.* New York: Doubleday, Page, 1906.

Beatty, Jack. *Age of Betrayal.* New York: Alfred A. Knopf, 2007.

Belz, Herman. *A New Birth of Freedom.* New York: Fordham University Press, 2000.
Borneman, Walter. *Iron Horse.* Boston: Little, Brown, 2014.
———. *Rival Rails.* New York: Random House, 2010. Kindle edition.
Bowers, Claude. *The Tragic Era.* Cambridge, MA: Riverside Press, 1929.
Brands, H. W. *American Colossus.* New York: Anchor Books, 2010.
———. *Greenback Planet.* Austin: University of Texas Press, 2011.
———. *The Reckless Decade.* New York: St. Martin's Press, 1995.
Brown, C. Clayton. *King Cotton in Modern America.* Oxford: University Press of Mississippi, 2010.
Buck, Paul H. *The Road to Reunion.* New York: Vintage Books, 1959.
Burlingame, Michael. *Abraham Lincoln: A Life.* Baltimore: Johns Hopkins University Press, 2008.
Carter, Hodding. *The Angry Scar.* New York, Doubleday, 1959.
Cash, Wilbur. *The Mind of the South.* New York: Vintage Books, 1969.
Cashman, Sean. *America in the Gilded Age.* 3rd ed. New York: New York University Press, 1993.
Chodes, John. *Washington's KKK: The Union League During Southern Reconstruction.* Columbia, SC: Shotwell, 2016. Kindle edition.
Clark, Thomas D., and Albert D. Kirwan. *The South Since Appomattox.* New York: Oxford University Press, 1967.
Cohn, David L. *The Life and Times of King Cotton.* New York: Oxford University Press, 1956.
Cooper, William J. *We Have the War Upon Us.* New York: Alfred A. Knopf, 2012.
Cooper, William J., and Thomas Terrill. *The American South: A History.* Vol. 2. 4th ed. Lanham, MD: Rowman & Littlefield, 2009.
Coulter, E. Merton. *The South During Reconstruction.* Baton Rouge: LSU Press, 1947.
Craven, Avery. *Reconstruction.* New York: Holt, Rinehart & Winston, 1969.
Dattel, Gene. *Cotton and Race in the Making of America.* Lanham, MD: Ivan R. Dee, 2009.
Donald, David. *Lincoln.* London: Jonathan Cape, 1995.
Ezell, John. *The South Since 1865.* 2nd ed. New York: Macmillan, 1975.
Fitzgerald, Michael. *The Union League Movement in the Deep South.* Baton Rouge: LSU Press, 1989.
Fleming, Walter. *Documentary History of Reconstruction.* Vols. 1 and 2. Cleveland: Arthur H. Clark, 1906-7.
———. *The Sequel of Appomattox.* New Haven, CT: Yale University Press, 1919.
Foner, Eric. *Reconstruction: America's Unfinished Revolution.* New York: Harper & Row, 1988.
Foreman, Amanda. *A World on Fire.* New York: Random House, 2010.

Franklin, John. *The Emancipation Proclamation.* Wheeling, IL: Harlan Davidson, 1963.
———. *Reconstruction.* Chicago: University of Chicago Press, 1961.
Fremantle, Tom. *The Moonshine Mule.* London: Robinson, 2003.
Gallagher, Gary. *The American Civil War: The War in the East 1861–May 1863.* Oxford: Osprey Books, 2001.
Goodwyn, Lawrence. *The Populist Movement.* Oxford: Oxford University Press, 1978.
Guelzo, Allen. *Lincoln's Emancipation Proclamation.* New York: Simon & Schuster, 2006.
Gutzman, Kevin R. C. *The Politically Incorrect Guide to the Constitution.* Washington, DC: Regnery, 2007.
Hacker, Louis, and Benjamin Kendrick. *The United States Since 1865.* 4th ed. New York: Appleton-Century-Crofts, 1949.
Hammond, Matthew. *The Cotton Industry: An Essay in American Economic History.* New York: American Economic Association by Macmillan, 1897.
Hearn, Chester G. *The Impeachment of Andrew Johnson.* Jefferson, NC: McFarland, 2007.
Henderson, Harold. *The Politics of Change in Georgia.* Athens: University of Georgia Press, 1991.
Henry, Robert Selph. *The Story of Reconstruction.* Indianapolis: Bobbs-Merrill, 1938.
Hicks, John. *Populist Revolt.* Minneapolis: University of Minnesota Press, 1931.
Higgs, Robert. *The Transformation of the American Economy.* New York: John Wiley, 1971.
Holt, Michael. *By One Vote.* Lawrence: University Press of Kansas, 2008.
Hummel, Jeffrey. *Emancipating Slaves, Enslaving Free Men.* Peru, IL: Open Court, 1996.
Hurst, Jack. *Nathan Bedford Forrest.* New York: Random House, 1994.
Johnson, John W. *Historic U. S. Court Cases.* Abingdon, UK: Routledge, 2003.
Johnson, Ludwell. *Division and Reunion.* New York: John Wiley & Sons, 1978.
———. *Red River Campaign.* Kent, OH: Kent State University Press, 1993.
Jones, Howard. *Blue and Gray Diplomacy.* Chapel Hill: University of North Carolina Press, 2012.
Josephson, Matthew. *The Politicos.* New York: Harcourt, Brace, 1958.
———. *The Robber Barons.* New York: Harcourt, Brace, 1934.
Kantrowitz, Stephen. *Ben Tillman and the Reconstruction of White Supremacy.* Chapel Hill: University of North Carolina Press, 2000.
Kibler, James. *Our Fathers Fields.* Columbia: University of South Carolina Press, 1998.

Knight, Alicia. *Pauline Hopkins and the American Dream*. Knoxville: University of Tennessee Press, 2012.

Kolko, Gabriel. *Railroads and Regulation: 1877-1916*. Princeton, NJ: Princeton University Press, 1965.

Langsdon, Philip. *Tennessee: A Political History*. Franklin, TN: Hillsboro Press, 2000.

Leigh, Philip. *Trading with the Enemy*. Yardley, PA: Westholme, 2013.

Linker, Beth. *War's Waste: Rehabilitation in World War I America*. Chicago: University of Chicago Press, 2011.

Martin, Edward. *A Complete and Graphic Account of the Credit Mobilier Investigation*. Continental and National Publishing, 1873. http://cprr.org/Museum/Credit_Mobilier_1873.html.

Masur, Louis. *Lincoln's Hundred Days*. Cambridge, MA: Belknap Press, 2012.

McFeely, William. *Grant: A Biography*. New York: W. W. Norton, 1981.

McKee, Seth. *Republican Ascendancy in the Southern U.S. House Elections*. Boulder, CO: Westview Press, 2009.

McPherson, James. *Battle Cry of Freedom*. New York: Oxford University Press, 1988.

Miller, Wilbur, ed. *The Social History of Crime and Punishment in America: An Encyclopedia*. Thousand Oaks, CA: Sage Publications, 2012.

Morgan, Kathleen, and Scott Morgan, eds. *State Rankings in 2014: A Statistical View of America*. Thousand Oaks, CA: CQ Press, 2014.

Morison, Samuel Eliot, and Henry Steele Commager. *The Growth of the American Republic*. Vol. 2. 4th ed. New York: Oxford University Press, 1950.

Morris, Roy Jr. *Fraud of the Century*. New York: Simon & Schuster, 2003.

Nevins, Allan. *Dictionary of American Biography*. New York: Charles Scribner's Sons, 1929.

———. *The Emergence of Modern America*. New York: Macmillan, 1927.

Nugent, Walter. *Money and American Society: 1865-1880*. New York: Free Press, 1968.

Powell, Lawrence N. *New Masters*. New York: Fordham University Press, 1998.

Purdy, Elizabeth, and Lawrence Salinger, eds. *Encyclopedia of White Collar Crime and Corporate Crime*. Vol. 1. Los Angeles: Sage Publications, 2005.

Quadagno, Jill. *The Transformation of Old Age Security*. Chicago: University of Chicago Press, 1988.

Rafuse, Ethan. *McClellan's War*. Bloomington: Indiana University Press, 2005.

Randall, James, and David Donald. *The Civil War and Reconstruction*. Boston: D. C. Heath, 1961.

Randall, J. G., and Richard Current. *Lincoln the President*. Urbana: University of Illinois Press, 1999.

Rhodes, James Ford. *The History of the United States from the Compromise of 1850 to the McKinley-Bryan Election of 1896.* New York: Macmillan, 1906.

Rose, Willie Lee. *Rehearsal for Reconstruction.* New York: Vintage Books, 1964.

Rothbard, Murray N. *A History of Money and Banking in the United States.* Auburn, AL: Ludwig von Mises Institute, 2002.

Royce, Edward. *The Origins of Southern Sharecropping.* Philadelphia: Temple University Press, 2010.

Sandburg, Carl. *Abraham Lincoln.* Vol. 4. New York: Charles Scribner's Sons, 1940.

Schlesinger, Arthur. *The Age of Jackson.* Boston: Little, Brown, 1953.

Sexton, Jay. *Debtor Diplomacy: Finance and Foreign Relations in the Civil War.* Oxford: Clarendon, 2005.

Simkins, Francis, and Charles Roland. *A History of the South.* New York: Alfred A. Knopf, 1973.

Simpson, Brooks. *The Reconstruction Presidents.* Lawrence: University Press of Kansas, 2009.

Smith, Gene. *High Crimes and Misdemeanors: The Impeachment and Trial of Andrew Johnson.* New York: William Morrow, 1977.

Smith, Jean Edward. *Grant.* New York: Touchstone, 2001.

Singletary, Otis. *Negro Militia and Reconstruction.* Austin: University of Texas Press, 1957.

Somers, Robert. *The Southern States Since the War.* London: R. Clay & Sons, 1871.

Stampp, Kenneth. *The Era of Reconstruction.* New York: Alfred A. Knopf, 1965.

Stowe, Harriet Beecher. *Life of Harriet Beecher Stowe.* Edited by Charles Stowe. London: S. Low, Marston, Searle & Rivington, 1889.

Studenski, Paul, and Herman Krooss. *Financial History of the United States.* New York: McGraw-Hill, 1952.

Tarbell, Ida. *The Tariff in Our Times.* New York: Macmillan, 1911.

Thornton, Mark, and Robert Ekelund. *Tariffs, Blockades, and Inflation.* Wilmington, DE: SR Books, 2004.

Unger, Irwin. *The Greenback Era.* Princeton, NJ: Princeton University Press, 1964.

Watkins, James L. *King Cotton: A Historical and Statistical Review.* New York: J. L. Watkins & Sons, 1908.

Waugh, John. *Reelecting Lincoln.* New York: Crown, 1997.

Webb, James. *Born Fighting.* New York: Broadway Books, 2004.

Webb, Walter. *Divided We Stand.* Austin, TX: Acorn Press, 1944.

Wells, Edward. *Hampton and Reconstruction.* Columbia, SC: State Company, 1907.

Wert, Jeffry. *General James Longstreet.* New York: Simon & Schuster, 1993.

Woods, Thomas. *The Politically Incorrect Guide to American History.* Washington, DC: Regnery, 2004.

Woodward, C. Vann. *Origins of the New South.* Baton Rouge: LSU Press, 1971.

Wright, Gavin. *Slavery and American Economic Development.* Baton Rouge: LSU Press, 2013.

Yafa, Stephen. *Cotton.* New York: Penguin, 2005.

Zavoknyki, Peter. *The Rise of the Federal Colossus.* Santa Barbara, CA: ABC-CLIO, 2001.

ARTICLES

Amyx, Raleigh. "Scandals of Ulysses S. Grant—General & President." American Heritage Blog. Raleigh DeGeer Amyx Collection. Posted Apr. 10, 2014. http://blog.americanheritage1.com/blog/bid/109596/Scandals-of-Ulysses-S-Grant-GENERAL-PRESIDENT.

Beard, Rick. "Louisiana's Stillborn Constitution." *Opinionator: Disunion* (blog). *New York Times,* Sept. 11, 2014. http://opinionator.blogs.nytimes.com/2014/09/11/louisianas-stillborn-constitution/?_r=0.

Chamberlain, Daniel H. "Reconstruction in South Carolina." *Atlantic Monthly* 87, no. 522 (April, 1901). http://ebooks.library.cornell.edu/cgi/t/text/pageviewer-idx?c=atla;cc=atla;rgn=full%20text;idno=atla0087-4;didno=atla0087-4;view=image;seq=00481;node=atla0087-4%3A1.

Chicago Daily Tribune. "Salsbury Makes Full Confession." Mar. 5, 1902.

Dattel, Gene. "King Cotton." *New Criterion* 33, no. 2 (Oct. 2014). https://www.newcriterion.com/articles.cfm/King-cotton-7964.

Dempsey, Paul. "The Rise and Fall of the Interstate Commerce Commission." *Marquette Law Review* 5, no. 4 (Summer 2012): 1151-1189.

Duncan, Bob. "The Most Hated Man in Tennessee History." *Columbia (TN) Daily Herald,* May 7, 2016. http://columbiadailyherald.com/opinion/columns/most-hated-man-tennessee-history.

Finkelman, Paul. "The Coming of the Emancipation Proclamation." *Opinionator: Disunion* (blog). *New York Times,* July 13, 2012. http://opinionator.blogs.nytimes.com/2012/07/13/the-coming-of-the-emancipation-proclamation/.

Goldin, Claudia, and Frank Lewis. "Economic Costs of the American Civil War." *Journal of Economic History* 35, no. 2 (June 1975): 299-326.

Gottlieb, Manuel. "The Battle for Democracy by James S. Allen." Book review. *Science & Society* 2, no.4 (Feb. 1938): 543.

Hamilton, J. G. de Roulhac. "Those Southern Repudiated Bonds." *Virginia Quarterly Review* 3, no.4 (Autumn 1927). http://www.vqronline.org/essay/those-southern-repudiated-bonds.

Hayduk, Ron. "The History of Immigrant Voting Rights in California." Immigrant Voting Project and New York University Law Students for Human

Rights. http://ronhayduk.com/immigrant-voting/around-the-us/state-histories/california-history/.

Henry, Robert Selph. "The Railroad Land Grant Legend in American History Texts." *Mississippi Valley Historical Review* 32, no. 2 (Sept. 1945): 171-194.

Hesseltine, William B. "Economic Factors in the Abandonment of Reconstruction." *Mississippi Valley Historical Review* 22, no. 2 (Sept. 1935): 191-210.

Holt, Byron W. "The Relation of the Protective Tariff to the Trusts." *Publications of the American Economic Association.* 3rd ser., vol. 8, no.1 (Feb. 1907): 212-228.

Kane, Tim. "Who Bears the Burden?" Center for Data Analysis on National Security and Defense. Report 05-08, Nov. 7, 2005. http://www.heritage.org/research/reports/2005/11/who-bears-the-burden-demographic-characteristics-of-us-military-recruits-before-and-after-9-11.

Klotsche, J. Martin. "The Star Route Cases." *Mississippi Valley Historical Review* 22, no. 3 (Dec. 1935): 407-418.

Lacey, Tim. "Removing Confederate Monuments: History Cleansing or Correction?" Society for U.S. Intellectual History. July 30, 2015. http://s-usih.org/2015/07/removing-confederate-monuments-history-cleansing-or-correction.html.

Lankford, Lyle. "Women to the Rescue." *Vanderbilt Magazine*, August 6, 2009. http://news.vanderbilt.edu/vanderbiltmagazine/women-to-the-rescue/.

Lockwood, John, and Charles Lockwood. "First South Carolina, Then New York?" *Opinionator: Disunion* (blog). *New York Times*, Jan. 6, 2001. http://opinionator.blogs.nytimes.com/2011/01/06/first-south-carolina-then-new-york/?_r=0.

Manning, Sanchez. "Britain's Colonial Shame: Slaveholders Given Huge Payouts After Abolition." *Independent*, February 23, 2013. http://www.independent.co.uk/news/uk/home-news/britains-colonial-shame-slave-owners-given-huge-payouts-after-abolition-8508358.html.

Masur, Louis P. "The Battle over Reconstruction." *Opinionator: Disunion* (blog). *New York Times*, July 7, 2014. http://opinionator.blogs.nytimes.com/2014/07/07/the-battle-over-reconstruction/.

McGruder, Kevin. "Black New York and the Draft Riots." *Opinionator: Disunion* (blog), *New York Times*, July 26, 2013. http://opinionator.blogs.nytimes.com/2013/07/26/black-new-york-and-the-draft-riots/?_r=0.

Mills, Curt. "U. S. Still Paying Civil War Pension." *U.S. News and World Report*, Aug, 8, 2016. http://www.usnews.com/news/articles/2016-08-08/civil-war-vets-pension-still-remains-on-governments-payroll-151-years-after-last-shot-fired.

Moneyhon, Carl H. "The Brooks-Baxter War." *Encyclopedia of Arkansas History & Culture.* http://www.encyclopediaofarkansas.net/encyclopedia/entry-detail.aspx?entryID=2276.

Ochiai, Akiko. "The Port Royal Experiment Revisited." *New England Quarterly* 74, no. 1 (March 2001): 94-117.

Page, Sebastian. "Lincoln, Colonization and the Sound of Silence." *Opinionator: Disunion* (blog), *New York Times*, Dec. 4, 2012. http://opinionator.blogs.nytimes.com/2012/12/04/lincoln-colonization-and-the-sound-of-silence/.

Palen, Marc-William. "The Civil War's Forgotten Transatlantic Trade Debate." *Journal of the Civil War Era* 3, no. 1 (March 2013): 35-61.

Phillips, Christopher. "The Rise of the Union Leagues." *Opinionator: Disunion* (blog), *New York Times*, Nov. 15, 2013. http://opinionator.blogs.nytimes.com/2013/11/15/the-rise-of-the-union-leagues/?_r=0.

"Railroads, Federal Land Grants." *Gale Encyclopedia of U.S. Economic History* (2000). Encyclopedia.com, Jan. 19, 2016. http://www.encyclopedia.com/doc/1G2-3406400787.html.

Richards, Mark David. "Alexander R. Shepherd and the Race Issue in Washington." *Washington History* (Spring/Summer 2004): 55-82.

———. "Touring Hidden Washington: Living in the Shadow of Congress." DCWatch, June 2001. http://www.dcwatch.com/richards/0106.htm.

Scribner, Marc. "The Sad Early History of Railroad Regulation." Competitive Enterprise Institute, Sept. 17, 2012. https://cei.org/blog/sad-early-history-railroad-regulation-subsidies-nationalization.

Sellers, Charles, Jr. "Who Were the Southern Whigs?" *American Historical Review* 59, no. 2 (Jan. 1954): 335-346.

Skocpol, Theda. "America's First Social Security System: The Expansion of Benefits for Civil War Veterans." *Political Science Quarterly* 108, no. 1 (Spring 1993): 85-116.

Stiles, T. J. "The Commodore's Civil War." *Vanderbilt Magazine*, April 11, 2011. http://news.vanderbilt.edu/vanderbiltmagazine/the-commodores-civil-war/.

Sylla, Richard. "Federal Policy, Banking Market Structure, and Capital Mobilization in the United States, 1863–1913." *Journal of Economic History* 29, no. 4 (Dec. 1969): 657-686.

Tarter, Brent. "Conservative Party of Virginia," *Encyclopedia of Virginia.* http://www.encyclopediavirginia.org/Conservative_Party_of_Virginia.

Tuscaloosa News. "Southern Steel Mills Profiting." June 26, 1939.

Wilentz, Sean. "Congress Confiscates Confederate Slaves." *Opinionator: Disunion* (blog). *New York Times*, July 16, 2012. http://opinionator.blogs.nytimes.com/2012/07/16/congress-confiscates-confederates-slaves/?_r=0.

Wu, Yuning. "Chinese Exclusion Act." *Encyclopedia Britannica.* www.britannica.com/topic/Chinese-Exclusion-Act.

DISSERTATION

Futrell, Robert. "Federal Trade with the Confederate States: 1861–1865." PhD diss., Vanderbilt University, 1950.

MISCELLANEOUS

BlackDemographics.com. "Black Mayors." http://blackdemographics.com/culture/black-politics/black-mayors/.

Bowdoin College. *Data Analysis: African Americans on the Eve of the Civil War*. http://www.bowdoin.edu/~prael/lesson/tables.htm.

Bureau of Engraving and Printing. *Currency Notes*. www.moneyfactory.gov/images/Currency_notes_508.pdf.

"Confiscation Acts." *Mr. Lincoln and Freedom*. Lehrman Institute. www.mrlincolnandfreedom.org/inside.asp?ID=38&subjectID=3.

Federal Reserve Bank of St. Louis. "Per Capita Personal Income in Illinois." https://fred.stlouisfed.org/series/ILOPCI.

———. "Per Capita Personal Income in Mississippi." https://fred.stlouisfed.org/series/MSOPCI/.

Infoplease. "Past U.S. Supreme Court Members." www.infoplease.com/ipa/A0101281.html.

———. "Population by Age, Race, and Nativity: 1860–2010." www.infoplease.com/ipa/A0110384.html.

Internal Revenue Service. "Historical Highlights of the IRS." www.irs.gov/uac/Historical-Highlights-of-the-IRS.

National Park Service. "The Civil War: Facts." www.nps.gov/civilwar/facts.htm.

———. "Industry and Economy During the Civil War." www.nps.gov/resources/story.htm?id=251.

US Census Bureau. "Merchandise Imports, Exports, and Trade Balances: 1790-2006." Pt. 2. Washington, DC: Government Printing Office, 1975. www.econdataus.com/tradeall.html.

Usgovernmentspending.com.

US Supreme Court. "Members of the Supreme Court of the United States." www.supremecourt.gov/about/members.aspx.

US Treasury. "Historical Debt Outstanding—Annual 1850–1899." www.treasurydirect.gov/govt/reports/pd/histdebt/histdebt_histo2.htm.

Vanderbilt University. "History of Vanderbilt University." www.vanderbilt.edu/about/history/.

Wikipedia. "38th United States Congress." https://en.wikipedia.org/wiki/38th_United_States_Congress.

Index

Page numbers followed by *ph* indicate illustrations and their captions.